Encyclopedia of
Fictional and Fantastic Languages

Encyclopedia of

Fictional and Fantastic Languages

Tim Conley and Stephen Cain

Foreword by Ursula K. Le Guin

GREENWOOD PRESS
Westport, Connecticut • London

Library of Congress Cataloging-in-Publication Data

Conley, Tim, 1972–
    Encyclopedia of fictional and fantastic languages / Tim Conley and Stephen Cain ; foreword by Ursula K. Le Guin.
      p. cm.
    Includes bibliographical references and index.
    ISBN 0–313–33188–X (alk. paper)
    1. Imaginary languages—Encyclopedias.   I. Cain, Stephen, 1970–   II. Title.
    P120.I53C66   2006
    809'.9334—dc22   2006009757

British Library Cataloguing in Publication Data is available.

Library of Congress Catalog Card Number: 2006009757
ISBN: 0–313–33188–X

First published in 2006

Greenwood Press, 88 Post Road West, Westport, CT 06881
An imprint of Greenwood Publishing Group, Inc.
www.greenwood.com

Printed in the United States of America

The paper used in this book complies with the
Permanent Paper Standard issued by the National
Information Standards Organization (Z39.48–1984).

10 9 8 7 6 5 4 3 2 1

to

Garnett & Cyan

and

Bradley & Ryan

future readers

✑ Contents ✑

List of Entries

Guide to Related Topics

The following categories represent loose groupings of popular "kinds" of fictional languages and are presented here for the reader's interest and assistance. Individual titles may be listed under more than one category.

ANIMAL LANGUAGES

"The Author of the Acacia Seeds"
Gulliver's Travels
The Princess Hoppy
Sylvie and Bruno

Tarzan of the Apes
Watership Down
The White Bone
The Wind on the Moon

DINOSAUR LANGUAGES

Dinotopia
Foreigner (Robert J. Sawyer)

West of Eden

EXTRATERRESTRIAL LANGUAGES

Acorna, The Unicorn Girl
Across the Zodiac
After Long Silence
An Alien Heat
Alien Nation
Alien Tongue
"And Some Were Savages"
Babel-17
Battlefield Earth
Carson of Venus
Cathouse
Chanur's Legacy
Close Encounters of the Third Kind
The Color of Distance

The Comical History of the States and
    Empires of the Moon and the Sun
"Confluence"
Dark Skies
"Day of Burning"
The Day of the Klesh
The Day the Earth Stood Still
"Decoding of the Martian Language"
The Dispossessed
A Door Into Ocean
Downward to the Earth
The Dramaturges of Yan
Dune
Earth: Final Conflict

GENDER-BASED LANGUAGES

GESTURAL LANGUAGES

Haroun and the Sea of Stories
I Never Promised You a Rose Garden
Icosameron
The Maze Game
Noise

Stars in My Pocket Like Grains of Sand
The Uplift War
Venus on the Half-Shell
West of Eden

MARTIAN LANGUAGES

Across the Zodiac
"Decoding of the Martian Language"
Memoirs of a Spacewoman
"No Jokes on Mars"

Out of the Silent Planet
Stranger in a Strange Land
Two Planets

MUSICAL LANGUAGES

After Long Silence
Close Encounters of the Third Kind
*The Comical History of the States and Empires of
    the Moon and the Sun*
"Decoding of the Martian Language"

Icosameron
The Jupiter Theft
The Man in the Moon
Voyage to Faremido and *Capillaria*

SYNCRETIC/POLYLINGUAL LANGUAGES

Las adventures des inspector Cabillot
All's Well That Ends Well
Ambient
Blade Runner
Code 46
The Confidential Agent
Gargantua and Pantagruel

Hellflower
The Name of the Rose
"New Arcadia"
Noise
"The Rats in the Walls"
"We Have Always Spoken Panglish"

TERRESTRIAL LANGUAGES (INCLUDING FICTIONAL NATIONS)

Baudolino
Bend Sinister
Devil of a State
A Dweller on Two Planets
Erewhon
Gargantua and Pantagruel
Gulliver's Travels
*An Historical and Geographical Description of
    Formosa, An Island Subject to the Emperor of
    Japan*
The History of the Sevarites or Severambi
The Interpreter
Islandia
Mardi, and A Voyage Thither
Mistress Masham's Repose
Molvanîa: A Land Untouched by Modern Dentistry

*The Narrative of Arthur Gordon Pym of
    Nantucket*
Pale Fire
Riallaro: The Archipelago of Exiles
Scoop
"Solus Rex"
The Southern Land, Known
*A Strange Manuscript Found in a Copper
    Cylinder*
*The Surprising Travels and Adventures of Baron
    Munchausen*
Tarzan the Terrible
Tarzan Triumphant
The Travels and Adventures of James Massey
A Voyage to Cacklogallinia
Voyage to Faremido and *Capillaria*

The Voyages, Travels, and Wonderful Discoveries of   *When the World Shook*
   Captain John Holmesby   *The Wind on the Moon*

UR-LANGUAGES

Atlantis: The Lost Empire   "Remarks of the Scholar Graduate"
One Million Years B.C.   *West of Eden*
Quest for Fire   *The Winds of Time*

UTOPIAN/DYSTOPIAN LANGUAGES

Across the Zodiac   *Mad Max: Beyond Thunderdome*
Always Coming Home   *Native Tongue*
Ambient   *Neutopia*
Baudolino   *Nineteen Eighty-Four*
A Clockwork Orange   *The Player of Games*
The Coming Race   *Riddley Walker*
The Dispossessed   *The Southern Land, Known*
A Dweller on Two Planets   *Utopia*
Erewhon   *Voyage to Faremido* and *Capillaria*

❧ *Foreword* ❧

It begins with naming. Those who write fiction with an entirely imaginary setting—fantasy or far-future or alien-world science fiction—play Adam: they must make up names for the characters and creatures of their fictive world.

Invented names are a quite good index of writers' interest in their instrument, language, and their ability to play it. In a crude stage of such naming, back in the pulp days of science fiction, invention was largely by convention. Heroes resisted it entirely: whizzing through distant galaxies in the thirtieth century, they were still Bob, and Buck, and Jack. Aliens were Xbfgg and Psglqkxxk, unless they were princesses, in which case they were Laweena or Zu-Zolla.

If you're creating a world out of words, and there are speaking creatures in it, you suggest a great deal—whether you mean to or not—by naming them. The old pulp-science-fiction naming conventions implied the permanent hegemony of manly, English-speaking men, the risible grotesqueness of non-English languages, and the inviolable rule that pretty women have musical names ending in "a." And so it still drags on in movie sci-fi, with a hero named Luke, an alien named Chewbacca, and a princess named Leia.

A more thoughtful and inventive approach to naming may offer less naively unexamined social and moral implications. Take Swift's horses in *Gulliver's Travels*, the Houyhnhnms. The best guide to how to say the name is provided by the Professor and Maria in T. H. White's *Mistress Masham's Repose*; according to them it involves not moving your tongue while squealing through the back of your nose. I find that tossing your head and shaking it at the same time helps. It isn't easy. But Houyhnhnm isn't a contemptuously meaningless and unpronounceable clump of letters: on the contrary, it's a conscious attempt to spell how a horse might say who it is and a deliberate challenge to the English speaker. If you're willing to learn to say that one word of the horses' language, you may be that much more able to think like a horse. Swift is not dismissing the nonhuman but inviting us into to it.

Many, many children draw maps of strange countries and name them: Islandia, Angria. . . . With the name comes a hint of the color of the hills, the weather, the temper of the people there. Some children explore these lands, returning to them in imagination, sometimes all their lives. To make up a name of a person or a place is to open the way to the world of the language the name belongs to. It's a gate to Elsewhere. How do they talk in Elsewhere? How do we find out how they talk?

The best thing ever written on the subject is J.R.R. Tolkien's essay "A Secret Vice." It is a splendid and often very funny description, explanation, and defense of the creation of fictive languages. It discusses how such languages, when carried through to any extent, are mythopoeic: they bear in them an intrinsic mythology, a view of the world—even, as with Swift's horses, a new morality. Tolkien discusses the aesthetic motivation of such creations with characteristic vigor and insight. He says:

> The instinct for "linguistic invention"—the fitting of notion to oral symbol, and *pleasure in contemplating the new relation established*, is rational, and not perverted. . . . Certainly it is the contemplation of the relation between sound and notion which is the main source of pleasure. We see it in an alloyed form in the peculiar keenness of the delight scholars have in poetry or fine prose in a foreign language, almost before they have mastered that language. (206)

What such scholars (and I would add poets, and any readers of a certain bent) find in reading a language new to them, he says, is the pleasure roused by "a great freshness of perception of the word-form" (206).

Many critics and teachers of fiction are so deaf or indifferent to the sound of prose that they, and their students, may find this statement puzzling or trivial, or fail to see how it applies to one's own language. I can only say that, to me, it holds an invaluable suggestion of how I come at my invention of fictions as a writer, and my appreciation of fiction as a reader. I seek the appropriateness of sound to sense.

I first discovered the particular pleasure of a "new relation established" between the two when I was eight or so. The kindly Swiss lady who was trying to teach me French picked up a little china whale from my desk and said smiling, "Ah! Le Moby-Dick!" Lemobeedeek? Slowly, the mysterious, senseless, charming noise revealed the whale: a revelation. Leviathan! Leviathan made new!

A few years later, when I first read Lord Dunsany's fantasies, the fine, playful relation of sound and sense in his made-up names—the evil gnoles, for instance, or the doomed city Perdóndaris, through which flows the great river Yann—gave me joy. But as strong was the magic of half-guessed meaning in a language whose mystery was merely that I didn't know it.

> Muy más clara que la luna
> sola una
> en el mundo tu nacistes . . .

That song in Hudson's *Green Mansions* held all romance in it for me at thirteen, all the moon, all love and yearning—more than it could possibly have held if I had known Spanish. This, says Tolkien, is the advantage of seeing things at a distance. It is the great gift of hearing words as music.

Language is "for" communicating, but when we come to such phenomena as poetry and made-up names and languages, the function of communication and the construction of meaning become as impenetrable to intellect alone as the tune of a song. The writer has to listen. The reader has to hear. "Pleasure in articulate sound, and in the symbolic use of it" (208), is what moves the maker of a poem, and also the maker of a fictional language, even if her tongue is the only one that will ever speak it and her ear alone is tuned to it.

The undertaking of this book is, as its makers confess, ambitious: to gather all the imaginary languages into one tower of Babel. So widespread and so public is the Secret Vice these days that the authors have had to omit from detailed consideration not only such languages as Esperanto, which though utopian are not fictional, but also the "constructed languages" that fill whole Web sites and the "alien languages" presented in comics and video and role-playing games. A lot of people are busy making up new ways to speak. This encyclopedia comes in the nick of time to guide us into the myriad worlds thus suggested. Rightly, it concentrates on languages that belong to an imagined race of speakers, a society, a world—genuinely fictive languages, not exclusive codes and not games, even though some of them are immensely playful.

In the beginning is the word: one may imagine a language before imagining who speaks it. This is how it was, evidently, with Tolkien. A linguist playing with language for the joy of it, he found his invented languages bringing to life the mythology of a people and thence an anthropology, a history, a topography. It can also happen the other way round: the development of an imagined world beyond a certain point demands the development of a language to suit it. This was the case with my *Always Coming Home*. I thought a few dozen words of the language of the Kesh people would suffice to suggest their key concepts and had already blithely written that "the difficulty of translation from a language that doesn't yet exist is considerable, but there's no need to exaggerate it." But when Todd Barton began to write the music of the Valley for a recording to accompany the first edition of the book, he needed the Kesh text for the songs. I had to be an honest woman, sit down, and invent Kesh—at least enough of the grammar and syntax and vocabulary to get me through writing the poems that I had pretended to translate into English before they existed in Kesh. The difficulty of that process needs no exaggeration.

Usually it's not so convoluted. To give the impression of a language, the flavor of it, a few mysterious words in it—which is all most novels need to do—all the inventor has to do is find a couple of rules and obey them. Whether there is an actual Universal Grammar I don't know, but an incoherent language is a contradiction in terms. A language is, in a sense, its rules. It is a symbolic pact, a convention, a social contract. Whether it's the limited choice of sounds used (the phoneme pool), the combination of those sounds to make words, or the combination of those words in syntax, every aspect of any language is largely arbitrary, intensely regular, and perfectly characteristic. In English you never pronounce "u" the way the French do, and in French you never say "th" the way the English do. Mandarin would perish rather than agglutinate. The rules are so pervasive that you can identify a language by a single word—"Achtung!"

This self-consistence is convenient to the novelist. If she only needs a few words or names for local color, all she has to do is make up some that don't sound like the language in which she's writing (her inventions may have a strong lurking flavor of her native tongue, but probably only readers who come to it from other languages will taste it). Then she merely needs to ask herself: is it humanly sayable? (this is where Xbfgg and Psglqkxxk fail the test, though Houyhnhmn passes it)—and do all the words and names seem to come from the same language? For if one character is named Krzgokhbazthwokh and another Lia-lua-liuli, readers will reasonably assume that the two come from different parts of Elsewhere.

I see no languages in this encyclopedia that are constructed "to violate universal grammar," which Noam Chomsky, as quoted in the Preface, seems to assume is the purpose of language invention. Possibly Borges, with his perverse and marvelous daring, gave us one sentence in such a genuinely revolutionary tongue. As far as I can see, most of us just follow the rules we made up as variations on the rules of the languages we know. Any appearance of linguistic terrorism turns out to be inept rule making or mere ignorance that there are rules. Professor Chomsky may sleep soundly in his bed.

But the mad variety of the rules in this book, their proliferation into jungles of exuberant glossolalia—the laborious delight with which sane people translate utter, deliberate nonsense into English, and vice versa—the touching spectacle of poets blissfully writing poems in languages nobody ever heard or heard of—this is a side of humanity I like very much. These are people doing what only people can do, a peculiarly human and peculiar thing. They do it without malice and without any gain or profit in sight, except the increase of pleasure. If the pleasure can be shared—as it is, liberally, here—so much the better; but the thing is done, like most good things, and all art, for the doing of it.

Ursula K. Le Guin

NOTE

Quotes from "A Secret Vice" taken from J.R.R. Tolkien, *The Monsters and the Critics, and Other Essays*, ed. C. Tolkien (Boston: Houghton Mifflin, 1984). The italics are in the original.

✑ *Preface* ✑

It could be argued that every fiction has a language of its own, as distinct as the universe a given fiction itself creates and embodies. Indeed, the pressing question *what is the value of inventing an artificial language?* is strikingly correlative to the question *what is the value of fiction?* To create, to invent, is, as the bewildered Houyhnhnms express it to Gulliver, to say "the thing which is not"[1]: it is a curious pursuit, but one that may be psychologically, even cognitively necessary. The human attribute of language, with which we can uniquely articulate possibilities, conjectures, and falsehoods, constitutes, as George Steiner has repeatedly observed, a powerful means to our "refusal to accept the world as it is."[2] Imaginary languages thus represent the most extreme attempt to envision a different reality.

To make this assertion, one need not affirm the deterministic Sapir–Whorf hypothesis, sometimes called the linguistic relativity hypothesis, according to which a given language's limits of expression circumscribe its speakers' thoughts. (Certainly, though, there are many among the languages collected here whose foundations borrow or even depend upon such conceptions and, in some cases, on rather wilder theories.) Nor is the claim simply humanist agitprop. Asked whether the failure of artificial languages is generally comparable to the failure of utopian societies, linguist Noam Chomsky is equivocal but says:

> One cannot learn an artificial language constructed to violate universal grammar as readily as one learns a natural language, simply by being immersed in it. At most, one might conceive of such a language as a game, a puzzle. . . . In the same way we can imagine a society in which no one would survive as a social being because it does not correspond to biologically determined perceptions and social needs.[3]

Whether or not one subscribes to the notion of "universal grammar" (or the tantalizingly unexamined questions of whether a human-made language *could* "violate" it and what that potential may portend), it must be admitted that, for better or worse, there are limitations to being human. These limits are most palpable within society. In our own thoughts—*in our own words*—we are hardened voyagers to far-flung places, cunning sorcerers commanding the elements, laughing and ocean-diving creatures, or simply slightly better versions of ourselves. In the company of other people—*in the words of others*—such hopes and fantasies have no currency.

This is where fiction came in, of course: "we can imagine" societies and places and languages with which to speak of and to them. The *Encyclopedia of Fictional and Fantastic Languages* represents an attempt to document the ingenuity brought to the problem of artificial languages by fabulists of many different nations and eras. It is an ambitious attempt, it should be said, and we have tried to approach an abundance of material with careful distinctions and guidelines.

Languages meant to change the world directly, by means of their adoption and everyday and/or real-world use, to activate or communicate with any forces or beings unknown to rational observation and the world at large, or merely to amuse their inventors—these lie beyond the purview of this book. Interesting though they are, Basic English, Volapük, and Esperanto and its progenies are not included here; nor are any other private codes,[4] incantations, technical jargon, and computer programming languages. The World Wide Web is laden with many sites devoted to various fanciful idiolects, as many culled from favorite novels, films, comic books, and role-playing games as there are those seeded and fastidiously cultivated by the site's own designers. (Many is the scholar of medieval literature who, either inspired or fortified by the example of J.R.R. Tolkien, is a closet architect of altogether baroque syntactic mansions, usually uninhabited.) These "conlangs"—short for "constructed languages," just as their proprietors sometimes title themselves "conlangers"—make for a fascinating sociological subject and deserve study, but their private fictions cannot be accommodated here.[5]

In making this decision of editorial focus we neither denigrate the creative and social experiments and efforts these artificial languages represent nor explicitly agree or endorse the view expressed by Chomsky above. This encyclopedia exclusively surveys languages that originate within fictional realms (specifically, prose literature, film, and television).[6] Certainly one may find, say, large numbers of *Star Trek* devotees who converse in Klingonese—indeed, it is sometimes erroneously suggested there are many more speakers of Klingonese than of Esperanto in the world—and who perhaps entertain notions of political revolution in their doing so, but the genesis and the greatest currency of the language lie within Gene Roddenberry's multimedia fantasy (at least, *pace* the devotees, for now).

Likewise omitted are approximations of exotic speech or "dialect writing," where the purpose is simply to reproduce—with whatever degree of realism or fancy—linguistic difference as it is experienced in the real world. Mark Twain's rendering of southern black American speech, for example, might be called an invention or even a fiction, but such a claim constitutes a value judgment of Twain's performance, the kind of judgment that we have tried to avoid or at least restrain here. The language of Jim in *Huckleberry Finn* is presented to the reader of the novel as a recognizable feature of the South, not something to be thought remarkable in itself or wondered at.

A similar though somewhat more cautious logic is applied when it comes to speaking animals. Mere transcriptions of animal sounds and other noises are not included: again, they are primarily representations or renderings rather than complete inventions.

(The caution, of course, lies in the fact that a talking kangaroo is already a proposition deep in fiction.)

The languages gathered here are living languages in that each has at least one reasonably fluent user—not necessarily human, and often not—or palpable source (a document, for example, or a recording) within a given fictional sphere, regardless of what degree of "realism" the sphere itself may have in its presentation. A very simple way of contemplating the languages noted in this book is to think of them as having been recorded by "real" researchers who have traveled into and through the territories of "fiction."

This last word poses its own difficulties for definition. There are myriad works of literature that investigate the origins, contradictions, and boundaries of expression, but many would evade the label of fiction. James Joyce's *Finnegans Wake* (1939), certainly the twentieth century's most infamous of these ventures, resounds with incomprehension: daunted readers may ironically take comfort in the recognition that no one speaks "Wakese," not even the book's own "characters"—a term that here simultaneously denotes personages, places, and typographical imprints.

> Scuse us, chorley guy! You tollerday donsk? N. You tolkatiff scowegian?
> Nn. You spigotty anglease? Nnn. You phonio saxo? Nnnn. Clear all so!
> 'Tis a Jute. Let us swop hats and excheck a few strong verbs weak oach
> eather yapyazzard abast the blooty creeks.[7]

The polyglot mash is not an operative language but a poetics embodied, just as Esperanto is an allegory of a political vision. Thus, the aesthetic extremes posed by artists in the modernist experiment—Joyce, Ezra Pound, and Gertrude Stein, among many others—and the various contingents of subsequent "LANGUAGE poetry" are also excluded from this book's attentions. Likewise omitted are those languages that, although primarily aesthetic in purpose, also have communicative value, such as Armand Schwerner's pictographs, Khlebnikov's and Kruchenykh's *zaum*, Hugo Ball's *lautgedichte*, and various other practitioners of *poésie sonore*. For the purposes of this encyclopedia, "fiction" refers to a narrative of imaginary events in which an artificial language is represented as a natural (however strange or aberrant) one. Thus, tales of fantastic travels and accounts of this or that utopia are included despite whatever pretensions of nonfiction they might wear.

Science fiction, whose presence of course looms large here, includes two default conventions in plots involving interaction between, typically, human beings and aliens of a different speech. Both represent ways of getting around the challenge of portraying linguistic difference directly or with specificity, and both are worth noting here in further elaboration of what our working definition of fictional language allows. The first, telepathy, usually involves the two-part assumption that while sentient creatures do think in words rather than, say, images, or some more complex semiotic pattern, the words of thought are above the differences of spoken and written language. The second is the so-called universal translator, a device made both to speed the plot and to spare the writer and whose workings and schematics, unsurprisingly, tend to be almost entirely unexplored. In cases where such conventions are used, where the fictional language is exhibited as distinct we afford here attention commensurate to the degree of the distinction made and detail given.

Naturally, there is a certain amount of guesswork employed in some instances: where, for example, a fictional character communicates in a recognizable language with another character, whose responses are altogether alien, we have had to judge whether the latter character's answer is indeed supposed to represent a working but untranslated language (this we take to be the case, for example, of Chewbacca in the *Star Wars* films) or is simply a nonlinguistic gesture (like a cat purring in response to being stroked). It has also been our concern that we not impose with undue force given linguistic fiats, for maintaining a prescriptive or otherwise needlessly rigid definition of language might mean neglecting or missing potentially important challenges to such definitions that the realm of imaginative writing may very well (and, in our view, not infrequently does) provide.

We have endeavored to be comprehensive but, as we have already observed, human beings have definite limits, though their inspirations may not. "What makes language possible," the writer and critic Maurice Blanchot has memorably aphorized, "is that it strives for the impossible."[8] By its example, this encyclopedia is meant to underscore and celebrate this principle.

HOW TO USE THIS BOOK

This volume offers no complete dictionary, grammar, or usage guidelines for any of the languages within it (though it does refer interested readers to such resources where they are available). Instead, it is a collection of over 200 critical summaries of instances of fictional languages as they appear, in various degrees of detail and sophistication, in novels, short stories, films, television shows, and children's books. We have relied upon English translations of works originally written in other languages, where they have been available, for the sake of consistency.

A complete list of the book's entries appears at the front of the book, followed by a Guide to Related Topics. Each entry in the encylopedia is headed by a title of the work or series in focus (e.g., *Cat's Cradle* or *Star Trek*), and entries appear in alphabetical order. Where fictional languages have proper names (e.g., **Formosan** or **Orkish**), the name appears in boldface in the text of those entries. References prefaced by an asterisk (*) point to other entries within the encyclopedia. All sources (texts, films, television shows, and Web sites) are listed at the end of each entry.

A Selected Bibliography at the back of the book provides a brief list of sources which the interested reader may wish to consult for further study. Beyond it are two different indices: the first allows searches by names of languages and a second allows searches by authors' names, subjects, and all other general information.

We hope that readers will find this searchable structure useful.

NOTES

1. Jonathan Swift, *Gulliver's Travels and Other Writings*, ed. Louis A. Landa (Boston: Houghton Mifflin, 1960), 199.

2. George Steiner, *After Babel: Aspects of Language and Translation*, 3rd ed. (Oxford: Oxford University Press, 1998), 228.

3. Noam Chomsky, *Language and Responsibility* (New York: Pantheon, 1979), 70.

4. Fictional languages whose design is itself a codification system are distinguished from fictional codes. That is, instances where characters in a fiction contrive to communicate in a code or system of signals are not considered in this encyclopedia, while fictions by authors who therein present a functional language whose basis in the "real world" is an encryption (see, for example, James Blish's "Writing of the Rat") are.

5. A mere handful of conlang examples includes Sally Caves's "Teonacht," Robert Ben Madison's "Talossan," Matt Pearson's "Tokana," and Tony Skaggs's "Alphistian," all of which have extensive Web sites sometimes about their elaborate histories, always about their punctilious usage, and often with details (of varying clarity) of their raisons d'être. Jeffrey Henning's online newsletter LangMaker.com is a valuable resource for those interested in conlang web culture, as is The Scattered Tongues webring: http://www.ifi.ntnu.no/~hannemo/sc/index.html.

6. We do wish to recognize comic books as another obvious fertile field for this inquiry, but we cannot do justice to that field here. The number of, for example, alien languages in comic books published in the last twenty years would themselves alone consume the resources of this book and its authors. More recently, role-playing games and video games have become thickened with ornate languages and alphabets that, again, we acknowledge as of interest but are beyond the scope of this book.

7. James Joyce, *Finnegans Wake* (New York: Penguin, 1976), 16.

8. Maurice Blanchot, *The Sirens' Song: Selected Essays*, ed. Gabriel Josipovici, trans. Sacha Rabinovitch (Brighton, United Kingdom: Harvester Press, 1982), 38.

✍ *Acknowledgments* ✍

To imagine a language means to imagine a form of life.
—Ludwig Wittgenstein, *Philosophical Investigations*

Putting together a volume like this one has involved many consultations and conversations, often verging on the surreal. Its publication may give relief to some, who may hope never to be asked about extraterrestrial accents and talking animals again.

For their various and often recherché tips and suggestions, as well as their enthusiasm and support, we wish to thank Bakka Books (Toronto), Chris Churchill, Walter Cipin and Wayfarer Books (Kingston), Peter Clandfield, James Griffith, Steven Heighton, Shelley King, Fred Lock, Laura Murray, Elisabeth Oliver, Jennifer Panek, Jed Rasula, Gail and Alexander Scala, Justine Scala, Diana Reed Slattery, and Adam Tolkien.

We give thanks in every conceivable language to Ursula K. Le Guin, whose generosity is equaled only by her patience. We hope that her advice to "stay sane" while completing this project has carried the day.

Tim thanks the following people: Anthony N. Chandler, friend and occasional cryptologist; colleagues at Brock University for their longanimity; the Social Sciences and Humanities Research Council of Canada, which funded another project, in some ways the obverse of this one, but whose support became crucial for both; and Clelia Scala, without whom nothing.

Stephen thanks the following people: Scott Ries, "Ivan," and other members of the Ubuweb who attempted to solve Roubaud's Superior Dog; Matt Pearson for his essential information on Hivespeak, as well as his enthusiasm for the project in general; a fellow struggler, poet, academic, and ingenious creator of artificial languages, Christian Bök, for great conversations and suggestions; and, most of all, Sharon Harris for scanning many of the alphabets and scripts of these languages, for her patience, and for her sympathetic and astounding heart.

A

Acharnians

Written and set during the Peloponnesian War, Aristophanes's play *Acharnians* (425 B.C.) is a satire on war and its proponents. Pseudartabas, one of the minor characters, is (supposedly) a Persian ambassador, grandly called "The King's Eye." He has one line of dialogue in the play, allegedly a message from his king: "Iartaman exarxas apisona satra" (49; in the original, ίαρταμαν ἐξαρξς ἀπισονα σατρα [48]). The prefix "pseud" in the speaker's name suggests his phoniness as much as his pseudo-Persian language does. Translator Alan H. Sommerstein detects "traces of the names Artaxerxes and Xerxes and the title 'satrap'" (162n100), but there is little doubt that Aristophanes intended a comic effect, a recognition that this was a nonsensical utterance.

Reference: Aristophanes. *Acharnians.* Edited and translated by Alan H. Sommerstein. *The Comedies of Aristophanes*, Vol. 1. Warminster, United Kingdom: Aris and Phillips, 1980.

Acorna, The Unicorn Girl

Acorna is the heroine of a series of eight science fiction/fantasy novels. A horn protruding from her forehead gives her the ability to purify air and water and to heal the sick, and this powerful horn attracts various enemies. Acorna's people and their language are called **Linyaari** (the word means "civilized"; *Ka*-Linyaari is its antonym, "something against all Linyaari beliefs" [McCaffrey and Scarborough 282]). Novels such as *Acorna, The Unicorn Girl* (1997) and *Acorna's Search* (2001) include smatterings of vocabulary and names, but very little grammar can be deduced from the texts. Some of the novels (*Acorna's Search*, for instance) include a glossary of terms and proper names, among them *fiinyefalaran* ("mourning, mourned"), *mitanyaakhi* (a "large number [slang—like our 'zillions']"), and *thiilel* ("destruction" [291–292]).

In an afterword-like note appended to the later *Acorna* books, Margaret Ball, Ann McCaffrey's "collaborator in transcribing the first two tales of Acorna" (Ball 289), explains that she used her graduate training in linguistics to help shape the Linyaari language. She also provides some notes on pronunciation, plurals, and adjective, verb, and participle formations, none of which are particularly complicated (noun plurals, for example, "are formed by adding a final vowel, usually -i: one Liinyar, two Linyaari" [291]). Ball suggests that a "truly definitive dictionary and grammar" do not yet exist, and that such "an undertaking will surely be of inestimable value" (290).

References: Ball, Margaret. "Brief Notes on the Linyaari Language." McCaffrey and Scarborough, 289–292; McCaffrey, Anne, and Margaret Ball. *Acorna, The Unicorn Girl.* New York: HarperCollins, 1997; McCaffrey, Anne, and Elizabeth Ann Scarborough. *Acorna's Search: The Further Adventures of the Unicorn Girl.* New York: HarperCollins, 2001.

Across the Zodiac

A Victorian science fiction novel, Percy Greg's *Across the Zodiac* (1880) is more remarkable for its "science" than its fiction. It is one of the earliest novels to use a scientifically sound space ship to get to another planet and features numerous chemical, geographic, geologic, and economic digressions. Its narrative recounts the translation of a manuscript from an unnamed scientist (also without a given national identity) who has visited Mars and brought back a record of his discoveries and encounters. Orientalists will find a rich vein to mine in examining Martian (or, as Greg writes, Martial) culture, as it features numerous women in veils, harems, and suzerains.

The **Martial** language is developed in detail and follows a strict logical order. A utopian language, it has been constructed deliberately, rather than arising from natural expression. It has, therefore, no irregular forms or exceptions. In phonology, the alphabet consists of twelve vowel sounds and forty consonants. In conjugation, a verb has six tenses and six persons; as illustrated by Greg, the verb "to be" is rendered:

Singular	*Masc.*	*Fem.*	*Plural*	*Masc.*	*Fem.*
I am	avâ	ava	*We are*	avau	avaa
Thou art	avo	avoo	*You are*	avou	avu
He or she is	avy	ave	*They are*	avoi	avee

The author also uses this case to illustrate tense, with the past being indicated by the addition of an "n," the future with an "m," the imperative with an "s," and the conditional with an "r"—thus, *avnâ* ("I have been"), *avmâ* ("I will be"), *avsâ* ("I *will* be"), and *avrâ* ("I should have been").

Nouns also follow a similar logic, with a root word offering similar declensions. Taking the word for the animal servants of the Martials, the *ambau,* as an example, Greg writes:

	Singular	*Plural*
Nominative	ambâs	ambaus
Accusative	ambâl	ambaul
Dative, *to* or *in*	ambân	ambaun
Ablative, *by* or *from*	ambâm	ambaum

The relation between nouns and verbs is also clear and follows set rules from a common morpheme. For example, *dâc* (to strike) is connected to *dâcâ* (a weapon), *dâco* (a stroke), *dâca* (an anvil), *dâcoo* (a blow), and *dâke* (a thing beaten). Greg provides several additional examples of these grammatical connections over a number of pages.

Less detail is given of Martial syntax, but several phrases are offered, usually in the form of a maxim or proverb, such as *Gavart dax Zveltâ gavart gedex Zinta* ("Never let the member strike, never let the Order spare") and *Zefoo zevleel, zave marneel, clafte cratheneel* ("A child cries for the stars, a maiden for the matron's dress, a woman for her shroud"), which clearly illustrate the Martial sense of order and balance (approaching chiasmus) in sentence structure.

The Martial writing system follows a similar pattern of exactitude. One form of transcription involves speaking into a recording device, which then generates a print text (a phonogram) of that sound: "Here then was the alphabet of the Martial tongue—an alphabet not arbitrary, but actually produced by the vocal sounds it represented. . . . Each character is a true physical type, a visual image, of the spoken sound; the voice, temper, accent, sex, of a speaker affect the phonograph, and are recognizable in the record" (101). The second system (stylographic) is more conventional, featuring "arbitrary" letters but employing numerous contractions and abbreviations so that it is close to a form of verbal shorthand.

Originally published in two volumes, *Across the Zodiac* was reprinted in 1974 as a single text with an introduction by Sam Moskowitz.

Reference: Greg, Percy. *Across the Zodiac: The Story of a Wrecked Record.* Westport, CT: Hyperion Press, 1974.

Las adventures des inspector Cabillot

The stories of Diego Marani's hapless detective from the European Agency of Strange Matters ("Service des Bizarre Affairs" [31]) are told in **Europanto**, an altogether haphazard blend of Italian, English, French, Spanish, German, and Flemish. The language's compound name, which mates "European" with "Esperanto," reflects the social setting for these satirical stories, an amalgamated Europe whose harmony and peace "sich extended undisturbada from Portugilla tot Slovakkia, from Finlandia tot Cypro" (45). Marani's 1999 book opens with eight brief lessons in Europanto, to allow the reader to get accustomed to the eccentricities of the language: these include scenes in a restaurant, a bank, a disco, and so on, all of them gentle parodies of the Berlitz-style language guidebooks. Then follow seven tales of Inspector Cabillot, in which the hero (a combination of James Bond, Maigret, and Clouseau) foils schemes to disrupt, discredit, or destroy the European Union. The villains, who have such names as Finnko Brutaalo and Frictos Kalamaros (Finnish and Greek, respectively), are nationalist stereotypes whose plots and sinister dialogue lean to the ridiculous, while Inspector Cabillot himself is most vexed by his difficulties with a "crossverba" (crossword [120]). After the Cabillot stories are several brief pieces, vignettes, and bagatelles in Europanto: political satires in the forms of recipes and how-to guides, a telephone call between Jacques Chirac and Bill Clinton, and a proposed solution to the Israeli–Palestinian crisis (by merging religions and creating "Jehovallah" [184–186]). The comedy of the narratives and the language itself focus on misunderstandings and discrepancies between recognizable cultures.

A reader knowledgeable in at least two European languages will read *Las adventures* slowly but with comprehension and amusement. Marani seldom if ever allows two words from the same language to stand beside each other in a sentence, as phrases like *tu esse nicht por slapen bezaled* ("*you are not being paid to sleep*" [112]) and *you jonge vaquas van todag esse mucho more intelligente dann nostra generatio* ("*you young cows of today are much more intelligent than our generation*" [78]) illustrate. At his funniest, Marani remixes words themselves (somewhat like Joyce does in *Finnegans Wake*). For example, "nevertheless" is transformed into *neverdermoins*, and *tenfinally* manages to combine "enfin" and "finally." A few times, however, Marani's jokes seem to contravene the conceptual framework of Europanto. When, for instance, he employs the word "mobidick" for "whale" (97), he is inexplicably using an American, rather than a European, literary reference, whereas in the adventure in the "Eurodisney" theme park, "Sleeping Beauty" is sensibly rechristened "Belle Sleepante" (110). One could argue, however, that rather than contradictions, these nods to American culture might be interpreted as pointed comments on the American influence on the new collective "Euro" culture.

Marani, an Italian translator, writes columns in Europanto for the newspapers *Le Soir Illustré* of Brussels and *Le Temps* of Geneva. Europanto is comparable to the language **Entrenationo** in Graham Greene's * *The Confidential Agent.*

Reference: Marani, Diego. *Las adventures des inspector Cabillot.* Paris: Mazarine, 1999.

After Long Silence

Sheri Tepper's 1987 novel is set on the planet Jubal, where human beings have an uncertain and sometimes dangerous relationship with crystalline structures known as the Presences. Travelers on the planet must be accompanied by Tripsingers, carefully trained musicians who sing "Passwords" to communicate with or at least palliate these Presences, which otherwise can and often do violently erupt. The plot of *After Long Silence* (the title echoes that of a poem by William Butler Yeats) pursues the question of whether the Presences are sentient, the political implications of which pit those who study and those who revere these crystals against the planet's exploitive rulers and industries, who would be legally forced to abandon the planet if the answer comes in the affirmative. Although it turns out that the Tripsingers' hunch about the answer is correct (the Presences are indeed sentient), their notions about the music they use and about other life forms on Jubal are really misguided.

It is not clear what language the humans speak in the novel, but it seems to be a future variation of English, since one character misquotes an expression "rets are deserting the sinking ship" even though she is without "any clear idea what rets were" (227), and other characters make occasional reference to **Urthish** (surely to be read as Earthish) words and phrases, which the reader may reasonably infer are somehow archaic. It is important to ascertain some idea of the humans' language here because most of the novel's characterization of the language of the Presences is comparative.

Tripsinger doctrine states that the Passwords have no linguistic value (or "meaning"): "the sounds, when properly sung and backed up with appropriate orchestration, merely damped the vibration in the crystalline Presences" (8). Some Tripsingers, including the hero of the novel, believe or at least suspect that the Password scores do constitute a language, that pronouncements like *Arndaff duh-roomavah* are intelligible, possibly translatable utterances. Although the first general part of this theory is entirely correct, the second represents a feeble understanding of the language itself. The years of study prior to the climax to the events of the novel represent amount, as one senior Tripsinger bitterly observes, to "singing lullabies" to the Presences, who were sleeping and oblivious to human efforts at opening dialogue (299); the previously recorded "squeaks, howls, snores, gurgles" (108) from the Presences were just that.

The communication divide is crossed not by human ingenuity but via intervention by another species. Wild furry creatures called viggies, never seriously considered sentient by humans, sing in their own language and can converse with the Presences. The **viggy** language seems to be a combination of words and sounds, though next to none of the lexical vocabulary is given in the novel (*An-dar-ououm* means something like "Let the edges sleep" [234]), and vague descriptions of tonality and melody vary from accounts of chirping, humming, and gurgling to phrases like "one great harmonic chord" (257). Where the text seeks to represent the spoken dialogue of characters using the language shared by the viggies and the Presences, it regularly includes parenthetical groups of synonyms to suggest and perhaps effectively dramatize the process of translation. For instance, one Presence asks the human protagonists why "you have not proclaimed (sung, announced) our sentience before—if you have known it (contained a concept for) as you say you have known it" (252).

As the phrase "contained a concept for" signals, the legacy of the Sapir–Whorf hypothesis lingers in *After Long Silence*. The viggies pride themselves on their strict codes of ethics and honor and that their songs are "true"; neither they nor the Presences fully understand the concept of a lie—or, for that matter, terms such as "love" and "hope" and "fear" (258). One viggy character, who finds the foreign properties of sarcasm and irony attractive, remarks that the human language is, like humans themselves, "bumpy," while one of the Presences admires how "it is a good language for puzzles, because it can mean many things" (260–261).

Reference: Tepper, Sheri S. *After Long Silence*. Toronto: Bantam, 1987.

Afterlands

Steven Heighton's historical novel is a recounting of the 1871 *Polaris* expedition to the North Pole during which an international group of explorers are cast adrift upon an ice floe for six months before rescue.

In the second part of the novel, Heighton explores the aftereffects of this ordeal on several survivors. Kruger, the German nonconformist character, seeks solace in Mexico where he develops a close relationship to the Sina, an indigenous people of the Chihuahua State.

Heighton's rendering of the Sina is exceptionally realistic—so much so that most readers of *Afterlands* will not realize that the Sina are a fictional creation. In keeping with this verisimilitude, Heighton creates a **Sina** language, based on the Uto-Aztecan language family, and includes such phrases as *sehamic, timaquis* ("water, please") as well as the culturally specific nouns *tauhmec* (a type of freshwater fish) and *halcumah* (a red-pepper paste).

Reference: Heighton, Steven. *Afterlands*. New York: Knopf, 2005.

An Alien Heat

Set several billion years in the future, Michael Moorcock's first novel of the "Dancers at the End of Time" trilogy describes a true fin de siècle where the visions of the Decadent and Symbolist writers are materially realized by the advanced technology of a small society. In *An Alien Heat* (1972), the protagonist Jherek Carnelian (the final incarnation of the Eternal Champion who has previously been manifested as Elric of Melniboné and Jerry Cornelius) falls in love with, and pursues, Mrs. Amelia Underwood, a time traveler from the nineteenth century.

As the characters in this novel exist in a state where every desire can be fulfilled instantaneously, they have no concept of such words as "virtue," "evil," or "modesty" and often seek to understand these expressions from earlier millennia. Language has also evolved so radically that even acknowledged experts on different time periods have difficulty conversing in the dialect of these eras. For example, when Jherek first attempts to converse with Amelia in nineteenth-century English, he says: "*Good evening, fräulein. I parle the yazhak. Nây m-sdi pâ. . . . The fräulein this . . . is pense que t'a make love to elle*" (37).

The principal means other characters use to speak with beings from other planets and time periods is by way of translation pills (which do not, however, give the user the ability to read other languages), although other translation machines also exist. The extraterrestrial figure Yusharisp from Pweeli, for example, uses such a tool. When the communication device malfunctions, readers are given snippets of the language of Pweeli, which remain untranslated, such as *srrti oowo* and *ryof chio lar, oof*. Yusharisp's speech is also frequently punctuated by the phrases "skree" and "roar," but whether these are untranslatable words, phatic ejaculations, or the sound of a malfunctioning translator is not evident from the text.

Reference: Moorcock, Michael. *An Alien Heat.* In *The Dancers at the End of Time*. London: Orion, 1993. 1–179.

Alien Nation

Alien Nation began as a film directed by Graham Baker and later spawned a television series and several spin-off novels. The premise of each is the same: alien beings biologically engineered for difficult labor (i.e., industrial slavery) are uneasily welcomed into human society. Eventually the species is identified as the Tenctonese, but in the original 1988 film they are politely euphemized "Newcomers" or else denigrated as "slags." Prejudice in naming extends to individuals, too, for Newcomers are apparently assigned new "English" names (at least in the United States) as part of their integration, but the process yields absurd names as a kind of belittling joke. For example, the film's Newcomer hero is called San Francisco, while a Newcomer gangster is introduced as Rudyard Kipling.

Tenctonese, the language, has altered and evolved in the course of the different *Alien Nation* incarnations, but it is nonetheless unsophisticated and largely nebulous: the grammar, for instance, is basically that of American English. Van Ling, credited as "linguistic consultant" for the film, borrowed sounds from various languages (including Samoan and Chinese) for actors to use in speaking, and a written form of Tenctonese appears on various signs and posters in the film. The writers of the television series and spin-off novels solidified the language somewhat, constructing an alphabet for both printed and cursive writing as well as offering a definite if notably limited vocabulary (for instance, *jovan* is "hello" and *nok e vot* is "thank you").

References: Alien Nation. Directed by Graham Baker. Screenplay by Rockne S. O'Bannon, 1988; *Alien Nation.* FOX Network, 1989–1990.

Alien Tongue

The birdlike aliens in Stephen Leigh's novel *Alien Tongue* (1991) speak a language called **Avian** by the human astronaut Kaitlin Turek, who encounters them after traveling through a wormhole discovered at the edge of the solar system. Their speech is described as "a burst of high-pitched syllables that sounded half song and half warble" (62), and verbs like "chirped" and "trill" characterize their utterances. The pronunciation of one Avian name, *G•Ren•Bei••ui*, is described by a human observer as having "intricate half whistles at the beginning of each syllable" and "guttural swallows halfway through" (92). *Bei* signifies this character's family name, an important factor in an essentially dynastic culture. Suffixes appended to names indicate status or caste (*••ai* for high status, *••ui* for the lowest status, and *••yi* for average or relative status; the very young and unnamed are *••ii* ["thing"]), and except for periods when a family's EggMother is in estrus, there is no gender to pronouns (i.e., no "he" and "she"; only the all-purpose *•ee*). Unlike English, which Avians call "the Flat Tongue," the Avian vocabulary is very small: one Avian, admitting that *•ee* comprehends familial duty but not love and friendship, identifies the problem as "too many words." Leigh prefaces the novel with a succinct glossary. Some words are direct compounds (e.g., *LongDark* [winter] and *ShortDark* [summer]), but more often the dot-punctuation—which is never explained—harnesses together letters and groups of letters: for example, *n•ai•r*, a word which "sounded like a strangling man's whistle," is the noun for "debt, obligation." Syntax and grammar as they are represented in the novel are those of simple English, even in those instances where an Avian serves as narrator.

Probably the most significant Avian word in the novel is *ma•ii•ii* ("literally, 'mistaken observation'" [xix]), as the concept of lying or intentional untruth (including the idea of fiction) is apparently unknown to the species prior to their encounter with human beings and is the pivot for both the book's plot and theme. "One can refuse to answer," attests an Avian, "but one cannot say that something is not when it is" (141; compare this with the language of the Houyhnhnms in **Gulliver's Travels*). Collective, quasi-eidetic memory is the basis of Avian society, and though they do not possess any kind of writing, they do have a process by which they distill into a liquid a dying individual's memories. This liquid, called *To•cha••ii* (meaning "history" [xix]), is then ingested by the dominant EggMother, and the memories are thus preserved within the clan. When a badly wounded Turek (called *Kai•t•lin Tu••rek*) is discovered by the Avia, they extract *To•cha••ii*, and the EggMother *Hr•Tyi•Bei••k•ai* learns—or is infected by—the capacity to make intentional *ma•ii•ii*, and so in turn are her brood and minions. This development plagues human–Avia relations and threatens the stability and welfare of Avian society itself.

Reference: Leigh, Stephen. *Alien Tongue.* New York: Bantam Books, 1991.

All's Well That Ends Well

In order to fool and expose the braggart Parolles in this late Shakespearean comedy (ca. 1602–1603), a French lord and group of soldiers pretend to converse in a language that is actually invented on the spot: "He must think us some band of strangers . . . he hath a smack of all neighboring languages; therefore we must every one be a man of his own fancy, not to know what we speak one to another . . . choughs' language, gabble enough, and good enough" (IV.i.14–20).

The name *chough*, a type of Cornish crow, suggests that this language is mere chatter or babble, but the fact that Parolles claims to recognize it as a form of Russian suggests that the lines were intended to be recited with a Slavic inflection. Here, Parolles first encounters **choughs' language**:

> [2.] *Lord. Troca movousus, cargo, cargo, cargo.*
> *All. Cargo, cargo, cargo, villianda par corbo, cargo.*
> . . . .
> [1. *Sold. as*] *Interpreter. Boskos thromuldo boskos.*
> *Par.* I know you are the Muskos' regiment,
> And I shall lose my life for want of language.
> . . . .
> *Interp.* O, pray, pray, pray! *Manka revania dulche.*
> [2.] *Lord. Oscorbidulchos volivorco* (IV.i.65–79)

Despite its fanciful composition and nonsensical intention, choughs' language does have consistency. The repetition of *boskos* above suggests a set signifier, and this is enhanced by its use in a subsequent scene:

> *Interp. Bosko chimurcho.*
> [*1. Lord.*] *Boblibindo chicurmurco.* (IV.iii.124–125)

Beyond Parolles's misinterpretation of this language as Russian, chough's language, judging from its terminals, appears to be based on Latin. However, there are also smatterings of French (*par*) and English (cargo, villain) and suggestions of Italian (e.g., *cargo = caro*; *dulche = dolce*), making choughs' language one of the earliest examples of syncretic language.

Reference: Shakespeare, William. *All's Well That Ends Well.* Riverside edition. Edited by G. B. Evans. Boston: Houghton Mifflin, 1974. 504–541.

"Alpha Ralpha Boulevard"

Cordwainer Smith (the pseudonym of Paul Myron Anthony Linebarger) first published the story "Alpha Ralpha Boulevard" in *The Magazine of Fantasy and Science Fiction* in 1961. Paul and Virginia live and love in a brave new world designed by the Instrumentality, an unseen force that is part secret government, part God. This era is "the Rediscovery of Man, when the Instrumentality dug deep in the treasury, reconstructing the old cultures, the old languages, and even the old troubles" (49). Thus the "ancient" French language and culture that Paul and Virginia enjoy are constructs—to the point of being crude caricatures—and novelties. So too, however, are their passions and freedoms: "Alpha Ralpha Boulevard" is a perverse rewriting of the Genesis story, with an Adam and Eve tempted to know whether their lives are entirely predetermined and themselves preprogrammed. Paul recalls the **Old Common Tongue**—though he is not always capable of using it in speech in his new "French" incarnation—a language that seems to have no means for expressing emotion. Faced with an interruption, Paul demands "who asked you to interfere?" and immediately reflects that such an utterance "was not the kind of language that we had ever used when speaking the Old Common Tongue—when they had given us a new language they had built in temperament as well" (57). Use of the Old Common Tongue also seems to have a certain cache of authority, too, since Paul uses it in the story (telepathically) to try to pull rank on what he views as inferior beings. The Old Common Tongue might best be understood, then, in a dialectical allegory sense: on the one hand, it is like a machine code or programmer's language, and on the other, it is comparable to an ur-language, possibly divine in nature.

Reference: Smith, Cordwainer. "Alpha Ralpha Boulevard." *The Norton Book of Science Fiction: North American Science Fiction 1960–1990*. Edited by Ursula K. Le Guin and Brian Attebery. New York: Norton, 1993. 49–73.

Always Coming Home

The opening sentence of Ursula K. Le Guin's 1985 book reads, "The people in this book might be going to have lived a long, long time from now in Northern California" (xi). This sentence is itself the best introduction to this unique work of fiction—not despite the strangeness of the sentence, but precisely because of it. *Always Coming Home* is a compendium, an anthropological anatomy of the culture of the Kesh, a future people (who are also, in a sense, a people of the past, clearly modeled as they are on Native Americans), as astonishing in its variety of materials as in its thoroughness. The book is made up of many stories and accounts and has maps as well as illustrations (by Margaret Chodos). Collectors should be sure to obtain the edition that includes the audiocassette, which has recordings of Kesh songs, dances, and poems (composer Todd Barton set Le Guin's ideas and words to music).

The strangeness of that first sentence lies in the grammar, where one tense is seemingly set against another and the conditional blinks unexpectedly before them. Moreover, there is an intriguing disruption of causality in the sentence, since the book seems to be both the cause and the result of its subject. If the sentence sounds a little like a translation, that is perhaps the best way to understand it, since Le Guin's conception of the Kesh, their culture, and their language depends upon a rejection of what she calls "binary" thinking. The Kesh make no cut-and-dried distinction between fact and fiction or history and myth: "the kind of narrative that tells 'what happened' is never clearly defined by genre, style, or valuation from the kind that tells a story 'like what happened' " (500).

In a talk given in 1982, "A Non-Euclidean View of California as a Very Cold Place to Be," Le Guin contemplated her birthplace, California, and the meaning of utopia. She presented as her own "motto" (80) a phrase from Cree, *Usà puyew usu wapiw*: "He

The Kesh Alphabet

KESH ALPHABET	ENGLISH ALPHABET	INTERNATIONAL PHONETIC ALPHABET
(Kesh glyph)	k	[k]
(Kesh glyph)	g	[g]
(Kesh glyph)	sh	[ʃ]
(Kesh glyph)	ch	[tʃ]
(Kesh glyph)	l	[l], [ɫ] (The two kinds of l in 'little')
(Kesh glyph)	n	[n]
(Kesh glyph)	s	[s]
(Kesh glyph)	d	[d], [ḍ], [ð]
(Kesh glyph)	t	[t]
(Kesh glyph)	r	[ř], [ɾ], [dr], [ð] (See note below)
(Kesh glyph)	f	[f]
(Kesh glyph)	v	[v]
(Kesh glyph)	m	[m]
(Kesh glyph)	b	[b]
(Kesh glyph)	p	[p]
(Kesh glyph)	w	[w], [ʷ]
(Kesh glyph)	hw	[hw] (As in English "what")
(Kesh glyph)	y	[y], [ʸ]
(Kesh glyph)	h	[h], sometimes [x]
(Kesh glyph)	o	[ɔ] (As in English "off")
(Kesh glyph)	ó	[o] (As in "oat" without glide)
(Kesh glyph)	ou	[ow] (As in "go")
(Kesh glyph)	ú	[u] (As in "toot")
(Kesh glyph)	u	[ə]; [ʌ] (As in "the"; as in "but," "dumb")
(Kesh glyph)	e	[ɛ] (As in "yet")
(Kesh glyph)	a	[a] (As in "father")
(Kesh glyph)	ai	[aʸ] (as in "tie")
(Kesh glyph)	i	[ɪ] (As in "pit")
(Kesh glyph)	í	[i] (As in "meet")
(Kesh glyph)		Five-House sign, pronounced [z] (a suffix to words in the Five House mode, which is not used in most kinds of writing)
(Kesh glyph)		Four-House sign (there is no spoken sign)
(Kesh glyph)		Doubled letter sign, written over the letter.

Note concerning the Kesh *r*: depending on context it may be a trill, a flap (as in English "steady" or "Betty"), the fricative [ð] as in "then," or a stop [dr]; and as a final sound it is often very like American English "hard *r*" in "her."

The complete Kesh alphabet, from *Always Coming Home.* Reprinted by permission of Ursula K. Le Guin.

goes backward, looks forward" (84). This expression as well as the poetics of English poet and painter William Blake (1757–1827), whom Le Guin is fond of quoting, are sources for the characterization of the Kesh. The Kesh have a close spiritual relationship with their environment, and their stories often involve Coyote (called *yówayo* by the Kesh), the trickster of native American myth, rather than an oppressive god of reason like Blake's Urizen. In "A Non-Euclidean View of California as a Very Cold Place to Be," Le Guin points to Austin Tappan Wright's *Islandia* as a valuable but often overlooked example of where utopia may be seen to exist and suggests that utopia lies not "forward"—the choice between going forward or falling behind is simply a symptom of "the binary computer mentality"—but can be arrived at "only roundabout or sideways" (98). In the same way that Blake rejects the linear thinking and unimaginative, or even anti-imaginative, constraints of common grammar, the quasi-mystical, utopian mode of going backward while looking forward informs the philosophy, structure, and vocabulary of the **Kesh** language.

One of the most essential words for the Kesh is *heyiya*, a compounding of *hey-* or *heya* ("the untranslatable statement of praise/greeting/holiness/being sacred") and *iya* (a hinge, but metaphorically "a source of change, as well as a connection"), a word related to *iye*, "energy" (489). Translating *heyiya* entails listing possible definitions rather than yielding a single, definitive one: it can mean, among other things, "sacred, holy, or important thing" or "to move in a spiral, to gyre" or "to become" or "to praise" (515). The expression *weyiya heyiya*, "everything hinges [is connected], is holy" (491), epitomizes the holistic worldview of the Kesh. Nouns and verbs are thus not always strictly demarcated. Yet Kesh, the language, is also made of finely made distinctions, usually in relation to specific life experience. There are half a dozen Kesh words for "love," though they are not at all interchangeable. For instance, *unne*, both a noun and a verb, suggests tenderness and affection, as in the expression, "I love her like a sister," while *iyakwun*, also noun and verb, has a deeper level of affection implied, "the love that moves the sun and the other stars" (493). Certain socially and morally repulsive ideas are markedly outside expression:

PUNCTUATION

In inscriptions and mural writing little punctuation was used except for a slanting stroke to divide sentences. In ordinary and literary writing, punctuation was careful and complex, including indications of expression and tempo which we use only for music. The principal signs were:

— Equivalent to our period

⌐ A "double period," roughly equivalent to a paragraph break

ꞏ Equivalent to our comma, indicating a phrase within a continuing sentence

? Equivalent to our semicolon, indicating a self-contained phrase within a continuing sentence

These four signs, like our punctuation, were syntactically meaningful and aided clarity. The next five concern dynamics and tempo:

/ Equivalent to our dash, signifying a pause. Repeated, a long pause: repeated more than once, a longer pause

word Kesh underlining, just like ours, denotes emphasis or stress

w̶o̶r̶d̶ The opposite of underlining: de-emphasis, a soft or even tone

⌢ Written over a word, a fermata: prolong the word. Written in the margin: rallentando: read this line or these lines slowly

A Written in the margin: speed up, or resume normal reading pace

A primer on Kesh punctuation and written usage, from *Always Coming Home*. Reprinted by permission of Ursula K. Le Guin.

for example, "Kesh grammar makes no provision for a relation of ownership between living beings" (42).

Always Coming Home ends with a lengthy glossary, which includes several more words besides those found in the preceding text, including a list of Kesh numbers (*dai, hú, íde, kle, chem* run the numerals one through five). Here, too, Le Guin makes a deferential nod to "an illustrious predecessor" who named this habit of language building a "Secret Vice" (509): J.R.R. Tolkien (see *The Lord of the Rings*). This glossary is not, however, external to the narrative frame, nor is it an appendix: although it is found within a section of over 100 pages called "The Back of the Book" and admittedly "consists largely of information," it is inseparable from the continuum of the enterprise (i.e., "informational" as it may be, it is no more or less "fictional" than the other documents about the Kesh, and the whole of *Always Coming Home* can and perhaps should be read nonsequentially, dipping into the glossary as often or as randomly as any of the stories, poems, etc.). The following brief sample from the glossary is illustrative:

rahem souls (the various souls of one being, or the souls of many beings).

rava speech, language, tongue. To speak, with or without words, to talk (see *arra* [word, or speech involving words]).

recha hunt, hunting. To hunt.
rechudé, rechúdiv hedom: Hunters Lodge.

reysh line; anything very long, thin, and straight.
húreysh: the Line, tracks of the train.

rip rib, spoke, bar.

ro (reflexive pronoun) self.

rón   care. To care; to take care, be careful.
                uvrón: careful. (519)

Interestingly, the Kesh do not "consider speaking and writing as one activity taking different forms" (494). Their twenty-nine-character alphabet is "pretty nearly phonetic" (495) and replaced an older, larger, and more ornate "fesu" alphabet centuries before the ethnographer-narrators of *Always Coming Home* made their visit. This alphabet is known as the *aihu* ("new") alphabet. Punctuation includes "indications of expression and tempo which we use only for music" (498). "The Back of the Book" contains many further notes on pronunciation, usage, and rhetoric.

> *References:* Le Guin, Ursula K. *Always Coming Home.* New York: Harper and Row, 1985. This edition includes the audiocassette; Le Guin, Ursula K. "A Non-Euclidean View of California as a Very Cold Place to Be." *Dancing at the Edge of the World: Thoughts on Words, Women, Places.* New York: Grove Press, 1989. 80–99.

Ambient

The twenty-first-century New Yorkers of Jack Womack's novel *Ambient* (1987) speak a slang-filled English inflected with various degrees of patois (Rasta and Spanish mostly). As a rule its speakers use a considerable amount of abbreviation and anthimeria. "In a mo" (42) and "who behinded it?" (26), for example, are faster ways of saying "in a moment" and "who was behind it?"

Slightly more complex is the language used by Ambients, a religious sect of deformed, wounded, and self-mutilating people. Their speech has lyrical tendencies, peppered as it is with quasi-biblical phrasings and archaic vocabulary, and is not readily understood by other New Yorkers unaccustomed to its inventiveness and perversity. Consider the following typical utterance by an Ambient: "I spec he was all agog to let swive her unshelled motherspearl. . . . Much maidenhead *he'll* answer for at trumpet-time" (164). "Trumpet-time" refers to the Book of Revelations and thus the time of apocalypse, "spec" is probably a condensed blend of "expect" and "speculate," and "swive" comes from Middle English and last had currency in some bawdy eighteenth-century verse.

Publisher's copy compares the novel (the first of a series called the Dryco quintet) to *A Clockwork Orange*—an appropriate comparison as regards the unusual "dystopian" language, since Womack's future English, and particularly the speech of the Ambients, owes much to the **nadsat** of Burgess's novel; it also bears comparison to *Riddley Walker*, although the narrative of *Ambient* is not itself told in an English much different than that of the modern reader.

> *Reference:* Womack, Jack. *Ambient.* New York: Weidenfeld & Nicolson, 1987.

"And Some Were Savages"

Human space travelers visit the planet Savannah in an effort to curtail a plague among the nonhuman residents that a previous visit started, but, as the title of James Blish's story suggests, the benevolence and assumptions of the helpful, more "advanced" species are called into question. Medication itself is a simple enough procedure, but communicating with the patients turns out to be a problem, despite the existence of a technical process ("an ordeal to the student and absolutely unendurable to the by-stander" [95]) by which someone can learn a language "in about eight hours." (This device of heuristics is a favorite of Blish's: he uses it again, for instance, in the story "A Dusk of Idols," also included in the collection *Anywhen*.) **Savannahan** is a "highly inflected language" (98), and although it first appears to the human observers that the "savages" detained for study refuse to do other than give their names "in a rapid rattle which went right around the circle, always in the same direction" (97), the connection between their names turns out to be grammatical, and as a sequence the names form a significantly intelligent statement. The eight names *Ukimfaa, Mwenzio, Kwa, Jua, Naye, Atakufaa, Kwa, Mvua* are bound by the word *Kwa*, which means "if-then" (97). This sequence is translated as "RAINYSEASON / SOMEONE / HELP / HIM / IF-THEN / DRY SEASON / MAYBE / YOU"; it is in turn recognized as a pragmatic paraphrase of the "Golden Rule" of the complex games theory (98). The appointed student of the language notes how the "only grammatically unique word" in the sequence is the word for "help," *Mwenzio*; "the others are duplicates, either in meaning or function" (98). Dialogue begins, it seems, when the humans understand how to address the "savages": a cry for *Mwenzio* promptly brings the answer from one of the clan, *Mpo kuseya* ("I cannot fail" [98]). The only other vocabulary given in the story is the word *Mbote* ("life") and the phrase *Lokuta te*: "This is no lie" (99).

Reference: Blish, James. "And Some Were Savages." *Anywhen*. New York: Doubleday, 1970. 75–103.

Angel

Angel, the eponymous hero of the television show spin-off of *Buffy the Vampire Slayer*, is a private investigator and a vampire who wants to be a mortal human again. In the course of his adventures he often encounters demons who speak a number of different demon languages: each language seems to be particular to its speakers' specific type or genus of demon. When they are used in shows, they are accompanied by English subtitles. Among these demon languages are **Aratuscan** and **Kungai**.

In addition, the overall plot of the series concerns scrolls known as the prophecies of Aberjian. According to these prophecies, the vampire with a soul (possibly Angel) may *shanshu* (achieve mortality) after several arcane conditions are met, including a sufficient number of good deeds done by the vampire. The prophecies are said to be written "in a dozen different languages, some of which aren't even human," and occasional plot twists derive from errors in translating the prophecies.

Reference: Angel. Warner Bros. Network (WB), 1999–2004.

Artemis Fowl

Artemis Fowl is the protagonist of Eoin Colfer's popular series of novels about the young criminal mastermind who often finds himself at odds with the underground fairy authorities (aka the Lower Elements Police, or LEPrecon). In the first novel of the series, *Artemis Fowl* (2001), Artemis connives to get fairy gold by obtaining a copy of *The Booke of the People*, a secret volume of fairy magic's rules and regulations "written in the old tongue" (14), a script called **Gnommish**. The alphabet may well be the forerunner of and inspiration for ancient Egyptian hieroglyphs. The text below represents the opening lines of the *Booke*:

> Carry me always, carry me well.
> I am thy teacher of herb and spell.
> I am thy link to power arcane.
> Forget me and thy magic shall wane. (27)

As readers will quickly observe, the Gnommish alphabet is—at least as the text of the novel (including the continuous scroll of Gnommish along the bottom of each page) presents it—just a glyphic cipher for English, easily decoded once each character is identified. Yet *Artemis Fowl* does suggest that the fairies do have a unique language. The only palpable trace of it, however, is the expletive *D'arvit*, uttered by angered elves, and the narrator assures us that "there is no point translating that word as it would have to be censored" (110).

Reference: Colfer, Eoin. *Artemis Fowl*. London: Puffin, 2002.

Atlantis: The Lost Empire

Designed by University of California linguist Marc Okrand (also responsible for the development of *Star Trek's* Klingon language) for a Walt Disney animated film, **Atlantean** belongs to the category of Adamic or **pre-Babel** languages. As an ur-civilization, the architecture, clothing, and visual arts of Atlantis are amalgams of various ancient cultures, from Egyptian to Native American; similarly, the language shares roots and sound structures common to many linguistic groups. Indeed, Okrand's goal in inventing Atlantean was to recreate Indo-European, and it thus borrows from several languages yet contains no recognizable words from these linguistic systems. For example, the number two is *doot* in Atlantean, which suggests an English sound as well as the French (*deux*), as does the Atlantean number nine, *niht*. In the course of the film, several dialogues take place entirely in Atlantean, and the language appears to have an extensive invented lexicon. Some other common words are *supak* (hello), *kwam* (no), and *tig* (yes).

Little detail regarding the grammatical structure of Atlantean is provided in the film, although Okrand has indicated elsewhere that Atlantean verbs fall at the end of phrases. Atlantean also appears to be a fairly mutable language—during one moment of the film, when a multilingual group of explorers encounters several Atlanteans, the natives are able to converse with the Europeans and Americans in their respective tongues. Like Esperanto was intended to be, Atlantean appears to function as a universal system, as all modern languages are outgrowths of this primal discourse.

The script of written Atlantean was created by animator John Emerson and has several interesting qualities. Each unit corresponds to a sound value—adding three characters not found in the English alphabet for "sh," "th," and "ch"—but the script also appears to be pictographic. For example, the Atlantean "a" is designed to resemble the city of Atlantis, featuring a central point, surrounded by a swirl that may suggest walls or a shell—an appropriate image (suggesting the foundations and beginnings of a civilization) for the beginning of the Atlantean alphabet and the first letter of the

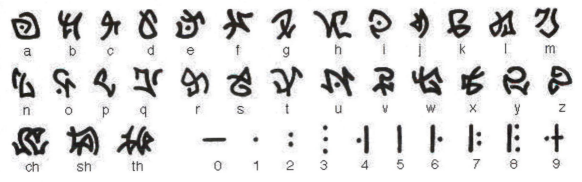

The Atlantean alphabet created by John Emerson for Disney's animated film *Atlantis: The Lost Empire*. It appears to be a somewhat pictographic script; for example, the letter representing "a" suggests the lost city surrounded by walls or a protective shell.

culture's name. Atlantean is also a boustrophedonic script, to be read left to right, with the following line read right to left, alternating down the page in a zigzag fashion. Okrand has noted that this was intended to create the effect of waves, again fitting for an aquatic culture.

Atlantean is thus a relatively sophisticated language for an animated feature that has not (thus far) garnered a wide audience of followers. The DVD edition of *Atlantis: The Lost Empire* also contains a short feature, "How to Speak Atlantean," in which Okrand provides instruction on the use of common Atlantean phrases in a parody of 1950s educational films.

References: Atlantis: The Lost Empire. Directed by Gary Trousdale and Kirk Wise. Screenplay by Tab Murphy, 2001; see also the following Web sites: LangMaker: www.langmaker.com/atlantean.htm and Omniglot: A Guide to Written Language: www.omniglot.com/writing/atlantean.htm.

"The Author of the Acacia Seeds"

Subtitled "And Other Extracts from the *Journal of the Association of Therolinguistics*," Ursula K. Le Guin's 1974 short story is at once a parody of academic histrionics and a contribution to 'pataphysics (after Alfred Jarry's "science of imaginary solutions"). "Therolinguistics" is the study of animal languages. The three-part text is composed of a detailed article on ant writings and their ambiguities, an announcement of an expedition to Antarctica to study the balletic language of Emperor penguins ("the most difficult, the most remote, of all the dialects of Penguin" [9]), and a provocative editorial that warns therolinguists against complacency by pointing to the "the almost terrifying challenge of the Plant" (12) and the related question, if language can be noncommunicative, whether noncommunication logically determines the absence of language in a species. Although Le Guin's story is comic—witness phrases like "the delicate, transient lyrics of the lichen" (14)—the final question about the nature of language is piercing and serves as a drive for the present volume.

Reference: Le Guin, Ursula K. "The Author of the Acacia Seeds." *The Compass Rose*. New York: HarperCollins, 2005. 3–14.

B

"Babel II"

In Damon Knight's 1953 short story "Babel II," a comic-book artist named Cavanaugh meets a strange being nicknamed by the narrator "the Hooligan" after its physical resemblance to the title character of Frederick Burr Opper's cartoon strip, *Happy Hooligan* (begun in 1900). After some friendly trade is established between them, the hero misguidedly pours the Hooligan a glass of wine, who happily reciprocates by activating "a smallish green and white doodad" which causes Cavanaugh to have "the odd sensation that someone was stirring his brains with a swizzle stick" (134–135). After the Hooligan leaves, Cavanaugh discovers what the "doodad" has wrought: all human language has become scattered idiolects, and no one person can understand the utterances of another. For example, a cab driver says to Cavanaugh, "Zawss . . . owuh kelg trace wooj'l, fook. Bnog nood ig ye nolik?" (136; this and many other lines of dialogue in the story are untranslated). Letters and phonemes have apparently been randomly interchanged for every speaker of every language, but even this is not the fullest extent of the phenomenon. All written words have also been scrambled: every book, every newspaper, every sign or bill or label with letters or numbers is no longer intelligible. Images are not affected, and Cavanaugh manages to communicate a little to others by drawing hieroglyph cartoons. Despairing of ever understanding or being understood by another person again and yet also glad for the newfound end to previously unchecked human blather, Cavanaugh reencounters the Hooligan and asks, "Could you fix just the writing—not the speech?" (151). The Hooligan complies; the story ends with Cavanaugh smiling at the thought that "the human race was now permanently a little tipsy" (152).

The Hooligan does speak a language of his own in the story, not dissimilar to the drunken-seeming babble the affected humans do. Its occasional lines of dialogue—ejaculations like "Khoi-ptoo!" (132) and "Hakdaz!" (150) are fair examples—are not translated. The Hooligan communicates with Cavanaugh both with gesture and with a small disk that expresses ideas in silent moving pictures. Where the Hooligan is from, or exactly what he is, is never revealed.

"Babel II" includes winking references to *Finnegans Wake* as well as to fictional journeys with fictional languages in them, such as Jonathan Swift's **Gulliver's Travels* and H. G. Wells's **The First Men on the Moon.*

> *Reference:* Knight, Damon. "Babel II." *The Worlds of Science Fiction.* Edited by Robert P. Mills. New York: Paperback Library, 1965. 129–152.

Babel-17

Samuel R. Delany's 1966 novel *Babel-17* is set in a future intergalactic war between factions known as the Alliance and the Invaders. Intercepted messages in **Babel-17** are linked with otherwise inexplicable incidents of sabotage and attacks on the Alliance, and an investigation led by poet and linguist Rydra Wong traces the signal to one speaker, an unknowing agent of the Invaders. Wong discovers a dizzying analytical language capable of expressing a large amount of technical data with great concision but that precludes the recognition and use of the pronouns "I" and "you" and is vulnerable to logical paradox. It is structurally comparable to computer programming languages like Onoff and Fortran, where metonymic concepts appear in combinations of strict binaries. "Thinking in Babel-17," in Wong's experience, is "like suddenly seeing all the way down through water to the bottom of a well that a moment ago you'd thought was only a few feet deep" (113). The language is essentially a weapon: it programs its user to perform a given function "and then blot out the fact with self-hypnosis so you won't discover what you're doing and try and stop yourself " (215). No samples of vocabulary are given, though it is revealed that "the word for Alliance in Babel-17 translates literally into English as: one-who-has-invaded" (215).

At the end of the novel, Wong generates a "corrected" version of Babel-17, which she calls **Babel-18**. A note left for the Alliance war planners promises that a "possibility will be semantically imprinted in their minds" (218), a possibility embodied by the statement "This war will end within six months" (219). Just as Babel-17 programmed its users to negate their self-reflective and critical capabilities to commit sabotage, Babel-18 operates as hypnotic suggestion.

Wong also mentions in passing the **Çiribian** language. Çiribians are an extra-terrestrial species whose "whole culture is based on heat and changes in temperature" (153). They have three forms of the first-person pronoun, whose distinctions correspond to the speaker's temperature and its effect on the reproductive process: "I-below-a-temperature-of-six-degrees-centigrade [meaning sterile], I-between-six-and-ninety-three-degrees-centigrade [able to conceive], and I-above-ninety-three [able to give birth]" (152). Çiribians have no word for "house" or "home" or "dwelling."

In *Aliens and Linguists*, Walter E. Meyers offers some significant criticisms of a number of linguistic misconceptions in Delany's novel (179–181), though he does commend Delany as "the most adventurous and thoughtful writer now concerning himself with human communication" (182).

> *References:* Delany, Samuel R. *Babel-17.* New York: Vintage, 2001; Meyers, Walter E. *Aliens and Linguists: Language Study and Science Fiction.* Athens: University of Georgia Press, 1980.

Battlefield Earth

Set in the year A.D. 3000, the 2000 film *Battlefield Earth* (based on a book by Scientology founder L. Ron Hubbard) concerns a human insurrection against alien slavers from the planet Psychlo. In an attempt to increase mining production, the Psychlos—who are inexplicably greedy for gold—decide to train the lowly "man animals" to work complex machinery, abilities they have lost and forgotten over the past thousand years of subjection. One human, the film's hero, is first given accelerated lessons in the **Psychlo** language by a machine that fires some sort of energy beam directly into his brain. This tutorial is accompanied by an apologetic tutor, a "language slave" whose prerecorded message suggests that he may no longer exist at the time of the lesson.

The Psychlo language is largely a matter of grunts and growls; there is little evidence that any effort at a plausible syntax or even morphemes was made in this production. The film does include many shots of Psychlo writing, on both computer projections and screens as well as on sheets of metal with raised inscriptions (the favored form of documentation, apparently, among Psychlos).

Reference: Battlefield Earth. Directed by Roger Christian. Screenplay by Corey Mandell and J. D. Shapiro, 2000.

Baudolino

Allegedly "a lingua no Kristian ever heard," the language of the thirteenth-century Frescheta people has its only extant example in the writings of Baudolino, adventurer, simonist, prophet, and the narrator of Umberto Eco's novel *Baudolino* (2002). In his palimpsest, Baudolino admits that there is uncertainty as to whether his people's way of speaking, which confuses outsiders, really is a "langwadge" and also that "noboddy knows to write it down" (2). Only via orthographic irregularities such as these (indicative of an approximating translation in mediation) do we have any sense of the strangeness of the **Freschetan** tongue, and of the tongue itself we only know that it is strange.

In seeking out the mythical land of Prester John, Baudolino and his traveling companions discover instead the land of Pndapetzim and its fantastic inhabitants: the skiapods, the blemmyae, the panotians, the giants, the nubians, the eunuchs, and others. Eco's novel includes some cursory and largely untranslated examples of the speech of these different cultures, though Eco has appropriated and adapted for his purposes the linguistic schemas of conceptual and analytical languages—so-called universal languages—constructed by writers such as John Wilkins (1614–1672). Skiapods, swift-moving, child-sized beings with one large foot, "prayed saying *Hai coba*, which for them meant Pater Noster, and they called fire *deba*, rainbow *deta*, and dog *zita*" (394). Wilkins subdivided and classified the universe by elements and species: according to Jorge Luis Borges (whose strong influence on his own work Eco has acknowledged), Wilkins "assigned a monosyllable of two letters; to each difference, a consonant; to each species, a vowel. For example, *de* means element; *deb*, the first of the elements, fire; *deba*, a portion of the element of fire, a flame" ("John Wilkins'

Analytical Language" 230). The amiable skiapod known as Gavagai offers a Hebrew-like welcome with *Aleichem sabi', Iani kala' bensor* while a blemmy greets Baudolino with "something like: *Ouiii, ouioioioi, aueua!*" (366). In the nubians' language, a horse is a *nek*, while the headless, squat blemmyae (the plural term) use the term *houyhmhmm* (reminiscent, of course, of Swift's Houyhnhnms in **Gulliver's Travels*). Perhaps the strangest of the languages of the region—for even Baudolino, a gifted linguist and quick study, "never managed to decipher their language" (415)—is that of the "ponces" or eunuchs. The one sample given in the novel ("*Prug frest frinss sorgdmand strochdt drhds pag brlelang gravot chavygny rusth pkalhdrcg*" [415]) identifies it, word for word, as Panurge's "Lantern-language" from Rabelais's **Gargantua and Pantagruel*. Pndapetzim's status as a utopia of sorts is affirmed by the currency such fabled languages have within it.

References: Borges, Jorge Luis. "John Wilkins' Analytical Language." Translated by Eliot Weinberger. In *Selected Non-Fictions*. Edited by Eliot Weinberger. New York: Viking, 1999. 229–232; Eco, Umberto. *Baudolino*. Translated by William Weaver. New York: Harcourt, 2002; Eco, Umberto. *The Search for the Perfect Language*. Translated by James Fentress. Oxford: Blackwell, 1995.

Bend Sinister

Bend Sinister (1947), the first novel Vladimir Nabokov wrote in the United States, is set in a fictional country, Sinisterbad, a socialist police state. The ruling party, the Ekwilists (i.e., illiterate "equalists"), bear a marked similarity to the pomp and brutality of the Stalin regime, and the Ekwilist virtues of interchangeability and facelessness can be detected in the way the names of so many characters are anagrams of those of other characters. The country's unfortunate population speaks, according to Nabokov's 1964 introduction to the novel, "a mongrel blend of Slavic and Germanic with a strong strain of ancient Kuranian [presumably a blend of Kurlandian and Ukrainian] running through it (and especially prominent in ejaculations of woe); but colloquial Russian and German are also used by representatives of all groups, from the vulgar Ekwilist soldier to the discriminating intellectual" (xvi). The novel is peppered with exemplary words and expressions, many of them comic sounding, all of them followed by brief and sometimes amusing translations. Phrases such as "*vsemi tzvetami radugi* [with all the hues of the rainbow]" (167), "*togliwn ochnat divodiv* [the daily surprise of awakening]" (30), and—a unique national proverb—"*domusta barbarn kapusta* [the ugliest wives are the truest]" (37) demonstrate that this language is as evocative, expressive, and often ludicrous as that of Zembla in Nabokov's later book, **Pale Fire*.

Nabokov's penchant for linguistic games cannot be overlooked here. A character named Ember is engaged in a translation of *Hamlet*, a task complicated by the state's rigid interpretation of the play, according to which Fortinbras is the hero come to reform decadent Denmark, whose prince suffers from the sickly cast of individualist thought. The reader is treated to a sample of Ember's efforts, the first three lines of the play's most famous speech: "*Ubit' il' ne ubit'? Vot est' oprosen. / Vto bude edler: v rasume tzerpieren / Ognreprashchi I strely zlovo roka*" (118). Nabokov's introduction concedes that "the book teems with stylistic distortions," including "the hybridization of tongues" (xv). Nabokov scholars, such as Antonina Filonov Gove, have noted how this text probes the distinctions between languages for the polyglot mind. Gove points out that the repeated glosses mock institutional abuses of language (those of government bureaucracy, of academic writing) and can be misleading, blurring the differences between what is a "Russian word" and what is perhaps a wholly other word in a wholly other language: "the boundaries between real and invented language material in the novel are intentionally fluid" (Gove 85). Ultimately the reader of *Bend Sinister* cannot even say for certain whether the "default" narrative language of English should be understood as English, Russian, or the tongue of Sinisterbad. See also "Solus Rex."

References: Gove, Antonina Filonov. "Multilingualism and Ranges of Tone in Nabokov's *Bend Sinister*." *Slavic Review* 32.1 (1973): 79–90; Nabokov, Vladimir. *Bend Sinister*. New York: Vintage, 1990.

Blade

Blade is a 1998 action film based on a Marvel comic book character created by Marv Wolfman and Gene Colon in 1973. In this cinematic treatment, the protagonist, Blade, is a half-vampire who hunts down a vast hidden society of full-vampires who are threatening to take over the entire planet.

As the vampires are an ancient race, they have their own language, and for this film, UCLA Linguistics professor Victoria Fromkin was hired to design a **Vampire** language (Fromkin is also the creator of the Paku language from *Land of the Lost*).

Not enough of the language is provided in the film to construct a grammar or morphology, but phonetically the Vampire language sounds Slavic and is often mixed with Czech and Russian by the film's director, suggesting that the Vampire race is Eastern European in origin (perhaps Transylvanian?). *Krat* appears to mean "you" in Vampire, as in the phrases *krat pruchiri busistampol proto lukchano* ("you are a disgrace to the vampire nation") and *umfalat poskani krat kodobranku, chahaz kalinka paskolzo* ("you would understand this if your blood were pure"), but few other parts of speech can be discerned from such other Vampire expressions as *mabochachi mati a oranta orastu prakaritsa* ("the human politicians will make our lives very difficult") or *sika lupala tat kapro Blade?* ("don't we have enough trouble with Blade?").

There are two sequels to *Blade* (*Blade II* and *Blade: Trinity*), but they do not offer significant additional information regarding the Vampire language.

References: Blade. Directed by Stephen Norrington. Screenplay by David S. Goyer, 1998; see also J. Matthew Pearson's online transcription of Vampire phrases: listserv.brown.edu/archives/cgi-bin/wa?A2=ind0101c&L=conlang&F=&S=&P=25285.

Blade Runner

The setting of Ridley Scott's 1982 film treatment of Philip K. Dick's novel *Do Androids Dream of Electric Sheep?* (1968) is Los Angeles in the year 2019. While the narrative of the film adheres to the standard hard-boiled detective genre, *Blade Runner* has gained a cult following due to its vivid invocation of a future L.A., including its architecture, advertising, fashion, and urban design, as well as a populace that converses in its own argot, **Cityspeak**.

While the urban environment of the film houses a linguistically diverse community (Chinese and Japanese feature prominently, and street urchins speak German) the police officer known as Gaff (played by actor Edward James Olmos) communicates in Cityspeak, a combination of several languages in a single utterance. For example, Gaff's first command to fellow officer Rick Deckard (the Blade Runner) is "*Monsieur, azonnal kövessen engem bitte.*" This can be translated as "Sir, follow me immediately please," as it begins in French, continues in Hungarian, and concludes in German. In the dialogue that follows, Gaff also converses completely in Hungarian and in Japanese.

While the fact that the language is known as Cityspeak implies that it is an inner-city dialect (perhaps required by street-wise officers to communicate with members of the underworld or other informants) since only Gaff speaks it in such a manner, and most other characters speak English, it seems that it is more of an idiolect than a genuine language, similar to that of Salvatore in Umberto Eco's *The Name of the Rose.* Although based on Dick's book, as Cityspeak was an addition to Scott's script by Olmos (who is of Hungarian descent), there are no artificial languages in the original novel.

References: *Blade Runner.* Directed by Ridley Scott. Screenplay by Hampton Fancher and David Peoples, 1982; see also Director's Cut, 1993; Dick, Philip K. *Do Androids Dream of Electric Sheep?* Garden City, NY: Doubleday, 1968; Sammon, Paul M. *Future Noir: The Making of Blade Runner.* New York: Harper, 1996.

Buffy the Vampire Slayer

Although *Buffy the Vampire Slayer* first appeared as a film in 1992, it is the spin-off television series that began in 1997 that cultivated a devoted following. The premise for both is that a teenage American girl in the throes of high school's various turmoils discovers that she is destined to fight vampires and other evil, supernatural forces. The television show—as well as its own spin-off show, *Angel* (which first aired in 1999)—has a deeper sense of irony than the original film, and its brand of cultural awareness and critique has been further reflected in a surprising number of *Buffy* novels, comic books, academic studies, and Web sites. The show also, of course, depicts vampires and demons in a more complex light (there are good vampires, emotionally troubled werewolves, and so on).

This development of supernatural characters sometimes involves a distinctive language for them. Most of these languages, like the speakers themselves, are transitory, vehicles for a single episode, and not especially elaborated on. For example, "interdimensional" demons called Mok'tagar appear in one episode, speak a few lines with subtitles, and leave; in another, a human character is briefly turned into a demon and as a result speaks a demon language called **Fyarl** rather than English (luckily a vampire acquaintance also speaks Fyarl).

The world of *Buffy* is also of linguistic interest for the rich and original slang used by the vampire-fighting heroes. Sometimes called "slanguage" by fans, it includes such expressions as *guiltapalooza* (a festival of guilt or shame) and *vague that up* (to obfuscate something unduly).

Reference: *Buffy the Vampire Slayer.* Warner Bros. (WB)/United Paramount Networks, 1997–2003.

~ C ~

Carson of Venus

The third novel of Edgar Rice Burroughs's "Amtor" series, *Carson of Venus* (1939) expands the **Amtorian** vocabulary beyond what little appears in previous volumes and, albeit in an unsophisticated manner, some of the language's etymology. Amtorian nouns look to be readily compounded. For example, the measurement *klookob* is a compound ("*kob* being a unit of distance equivalent to 2.5 earth miles, the prefix *kloo* denoting the plural") and *anotar*, the name coined for Carter's flying ship, is a portmanteau: "*notar* means ship, and *an* is the Amtorian word for bird—bird-ship" (17). By contrast, the word *faltargan* "has an involved derivation"; indeed, the most complex expounded on in the novel: "*Faltar*, pirate ship, derives from *ganfal*, criminal (which is derived from *gan*, man, and *fal*, kill) and *notar*, ship—roughly, criminal ship. Add *gan*, man, to *faltar*, and you have pirate-ship-man, or pirate; *fal-tärgän*" (289). The similarity to German construction is worth noting, since the plot of this novel centers on a country called Amlot, which is commanded by the cruel Zanis (an anagram of "Nazis"). Zanis revile people called Atorians "because they have large ears" (134) and are given to intellectual pursuits; they abhor the contamination of "the pure blood of the super race" by Atorian blood; and they histrionically salute their leader Mephis with the words "Maltu Mephis!" (129). (However, Burroughs himself is not above anti-Semitism: see *Tarzan Triumphant*.)

The inside cover of this book includes a sketchy map of Amtor with some of the "strange Amtorian characters" (288) mentioned but not described in the novel in its labels and legend.

The entire Venus series includes five volumes: *Pirates of Venus* (1934), *Lost on Venus* (1935), *Carson of Venus*, *Escape on Venus* (1946), and *The Wizard of Venus* (1964).

Reference: Burroughs, Edgar Rice. *Carson of Venus*. New York: Canaveral Press, 1963.

Cat's Cradle

The American narrator of Kurt Vonnegut's 1963 novel identifies himself as a Bokononist, a disciple of the ideas and songs of Bokonon, the outlaw prophet of the

Caribbean Republic of San Lorenzo and author of *The Books of Bokonon*. Born Lionel Boyd Johnson, Bokonon took his new name from "the pronunciation given the name Johnson in the island's dialect" (108). Some examples of this fictional dialect, which the narrator describes as "both easy to understand and difficult to write down" (108), are provided in the novel (for instance, "Twinkle, twinkle, little star" is rendered as "*Tsvent-kiul, tsvent-kiul, lett-pool store*" [108–109]), but besides the dialect there are several words and expressions used in the novel that are identified as Bokononist, suggesting the possibility of a **Bokononist** language (though it may well be that the religion of Bokononism merely provides selected names for specific concepts, and there is no fully functional Bokononist language as such: *Cat's Cradle* is not clear on this point). Three of the four most important of these words appear as the title of Vonnegut's 1974 collection of essays *Wampeters, Foma and Granfalloons*, and the other important word is *karass*, a group of people whose destiny (or *zah-mah-ki-bo*) links them together and who effectively work as a "team" that unknowingly acts out "God's Will" (2). A *wampeter* is "the pivot of a *karass*" (52): any object about which the lives and destinies of members of a given *karass* revolve. "At any given time," Bokonon explains, "a *karass* actually has two *wampeters*—one waxing in importance, one waning" (52). (For the *karass* of the narrator of *Cat's Cradle*, the ultimate *wampeter* is ice-nine, a volatile chemical that brings about the end of the world.) A *granfalloon* is "a false *karass*" (91), a grouping or association of people that has no real meaning. Political parties, corporations, and most notably "any nation, anytime, anywhere" (92) are examples of *granfalloons* and are clearly objects worthy of derision for Vonnegut. Bokonon sings of such phenomena—"If you wish to study a *granfalloon*, / Just remove the skin of a toy balloon" (92)—neatly implying that they are nothing but hot air. Finally, the concept of *foma* is perhaps the epicenter of Bokononism. An epigraph to *Cat's Cradle* comes from *The Books of Bokonon*: "Live by the *foma* that make you brave and kind and healthy and happy"; and a footnote defines *foma* as "harmless untruths" (vii). Foma represent fictions, stories that though perhaps not scientifically true or demonstrable—Bokonon's enemy and a principal target of the novel's satire is the literal and morally unconcerned aspect of science—nevertheless express a kind of truth, often a moral truth.

Most of the other Bokononist words that appear in the novel do so only once, as part of a given satirical thrust appropriate to that moment in the narrative (e.g., when the dangerous presence of ice-nine is revealed, the reader learns that the word *pool-pah* may be translated as "shit storm" or "wrath of God" [244]). The ceremonial placing of one's bared soles against another's, "*boko-maru*, or the mingling of awareness" (158) can be compared to the communal act of *grokking* in Robert Heinlein's contemporary novel *Stranger in a Strange Land.

Reference: Vonnegut, Kurt. *Cat's Cradle*. New York: Dell Publishing, 1998.

Cathouse

Expanding on the narrative universe of Larry Niven's "Known Space" science-fiction series (see *Ringworld*), Dean Ing tells a story of the "Man-Kzin Wars" in his novel *Cathouse* (1990). A human named Locklear is stranded on a planet he nicknames "Zoo" for it is filled with living specimens of primitive creatures, including humans and Kzin, frozen in stasis. Out of loneliness Locklear thaws some of them and develops relations with them. There are two points of linguistic interest here, the first of which is the additional information about the **Kzinti** language that Ing provides. (The novel is inconsistent about whether the language is called *Kzin* or *Kzinti*.) Besides the insight that "to speak in Kzin, one needed a good falsetto and plenty of spit" (202), the novel introduces some new vocabulary, gives some impressions of what certain Kzin phrases sound like, and suggests some of the changes the language has undergone in the course of many centuries (abbreviation looks to be the major trend: for example, *kshauvat* ["dumb herbivores"] eventually becomes *kshat*, "a favorite cussword" [52]). Males of the species are *kzintosh*, females are *kzinrret*; a *prret* is a courtesan and a *wtsai* is a sort of ceremonial knife worn by a male to show authority. The traditional greeting translates as "the kzin is a mighty hunter!" (202). Judging from its use as a noun, verb, and expletive, the "blatantly lascivious" (80) word *ch'rowl* ("I am more skilled at *ch'rowl* than she" [79]; "would you ask me to *ch'rowl* a human female" [122]; "*ch'rowl* yourself" [104]) looks to be a plain metonym for "fuck." Kzin characters pronounce Locklear as "Rockear" (55).

The novel's second element of fictional language is less developed. Locklear also thaws some primitive humans, one of whom may be introducing herself as "Ch'roof'h" (142) and whom Locklear calls Ruth. Ruth is a telepath and so has little enough use for speech, but the subsequent generation of humans (called "the new") quickly begins to learn Locklear's language (presumably Interworld) but curiously does not achieve much sophistication: "Ruth not care. Like ugly man if good man, too" (189) is a typical example of one of the more complex expressions of feeling.

Reference: Ing, Dean. *Cathouse*. New York: Baen Books, 1990.

Changing Planes

"Interplanary travel" is the theme of Ursula K. Le Guin's 2003 book. The phrase refers to a form of travel available to otherwise bored travelers stuck waiting in airports; that is, imaginative people can "change planes" and visit fantastic places and cultures. Although the traveling narrator has recourse to a device called the "translatomat," some of these strange cultures' languages are described (often when they vex the translatomat's capabilities). Among these are **Asonu**, a language so little used by the people of the same name as to inspire wonder and even reverence at their devotion to silence, and the "cloudy language" of the Zuehe, whose reticent speakers use only the conditional, have no indicative or imperative, and "have a thousand ways of saying maybe, perhaps, lest, although, if . . . but not yes, not no" (232).

Paradoxically, the most vividly described language in *Changing Planes* is **Nna Mmoy** (also named after the people who use it), even though the language is apparently little understood, and what is understood is mostly educated guesswork. Learning the language is very difficult, even for native speakers, because it is anything but linear: indeed, written texts are "radial, budding out in all directions," and "literary texts carry this polydirectional complexity to such an extreme that they resemble mazes, roses, artichokes, sunflowers, fractal patterns" (167). Though there is a written vocabulary of several thousand characters, each of which represents a syllable, none of these syllables, though words in themselves, possesses any independent meaning.

All meaning in Nna Mmoy is potential meaning, for "the meaning of each word is continuously modified by all the words that precede *or may follow* it in the sentence (if in fact the Nna Mmoy speak in sentences)" (168). The Nna Mmoy individual does not have a name but is addressed with "ever-varying phrases which seem to signify both permanent and temporary relationships of consanguinity, of responsibility and dependence, of contingent status, of a thousand social and emotional connections" (177).

The syllable *dde* is presented to the narrator as an example of how protean such a syllable can be. Whereas in the phrase *A no dde mü as*, which roughly translates as "Let's go into the woods" (173), *dde* signifies "woods," in a completely different context, such as the phrase *Hse vuy u no a dde mü as hro se se*, meaning "The travelers came through the desert where nothing grows" (173), *dde* signifies "desert land." There is a limit to the possible meanings for any given syllable—which has no meaning on its own—but this seems to be a theoretical limit, or at least one difficult to compute. Le Guin's narrator finds puzzling the use of the syllable *nen*, whose central connotation might be "things that move fast" or "events occurring quickly" (170), yet *nen* is used by someone speaking indifferently of ancient ruins, cities, and sites of industrial technology.

These examples turn out not to be random. The Nna Mmoy, who live in a utopian garden engineered for them by their ancestors, have effectively compensated for the monotonously pleasant and dully utilitarian landscape in which they live, which is without animals or variation in natural surroundings. Their language and literature serve as a functional "endlessly proliferating ecology" (179).

Reference: Le Guin, Ursula K. *Changing Planes.* Orlando, FL: Harcourt, 2003.

Chanur's Legacy

Chanur's Legacy (1992) is the fifth of C. J. Cherryh's novels about the hani, a matriarchal, feline-type alien species, and their complicated dealings with other different aliens; it is also representative of the series as a whole. Often though the novel's heroine, Hilfy Chanur, claims to have learned many languages, she is just as often unable to make out what speakers of other languages are saying, apart from a few readily recognizable names. This contradiction is indicative of the treatment of and assumptions about language in the book: Cherryh drops occasional references to unspecified "dialects" and variations of **Trade tongue** and renders nearly all dialogue into English, with forms of pidgin English and decorative, sometimes syntactic mannerisms to distinguish speakers. A few terms and names and even fewer phrases in the languages outlined below may be found in *Chanur's Legacy*, but unlike some other Cherryh novels (see, for example, *Foreigner* and *Hunter of Worlds*), this volume includes no glossary.

Moreover, in *Chanur's Legacy*, language is inexorably, even biologically linked to its cultural (synonymous with species) worldview. Hilfy considers the "benefit to fluency in other languages. She could think in kifish [see below for more on this specific language]: see things from a kifish perspective—and, so doing, feel the shift in her heartbeat, the change from twice a month hunter to hair-triggered, hard-wired round the clock predator" (296). The expression "hard-wired" (used more than once in the novel to describe the habits and minds of aliens other than hani) marks how the philosophy of language here extends even further into determinism than most Sapir–Whorf-type conceptions dare to tread.

Hani, the name of the language of the protagonists as well as of their species, is understood to be the effectively invisible "default" language of the novel. As such it is hardly described at all: apart from occasional narrative clarifications that a given dialogue is being spoken in hani, the only distinguishing features of the language lie in the oft-employed curse *gods-be* (as in "I won't live with a gods-be fool" [256]). Hani males have such a lower status than females that it is considered impolite to use "the male pronoun in a message between clans [different Hani families]" (131).

The delicate creatures known as the stsho have a language, **Stshoshi**, that seems predicated on politeness, ceremony (called *liiyei*), and legal exactitude. One clear protocol concerns references to gender, an even touchier business for the stsho than the hani, if only because the stsho at times of stress are capable of changing from one sex to another. For a non-stsho, determining such differences are not easy, but they are finely made in pronouns: instead of "she" or "her," the stsho use *gtst* (as in the much-used honorific "*gtst* excellency"), while *gtsto* registers "something like male" (214) and *gtsta* refers to a kind of neutered shsto, an elder no longer able to procreate. The very signatures of stsho indicate "Mode, Phase, and Gender, among other Life Events of significance" (375).

The text repeatedly suggests that the degree of specific ornamentation in Stshosi makes it a formidable challenge to translation: "One did *not* translate a formal stsho contract into Trade tongue" as a matter of course because "it only developed ambiguities" (19). The word *kftli* means "awkwardness"—naturally, anathema to the stsho—but it has a "cognate relationship to 'foreignness' " (7). An even more complex word is *oji*, the name of a vase that operates as a MacGuffin in *Chanur's Legacy*: *oji* "means 'ceremonial object with accumulated value' and it's related to the word for 'antique' and 'relic' "; but an inquiry made to an automated translator produces an answer that is 532 pages long (24).

Mahendi is the language of the Mahendo'sat (sometimes called *mahe* for short, and *mahen* serves as an adjective), or at least so it seems—at one point in the novel there is a reference to Hilfy's knowing "two of the mahen languages" (102). The dialogue of the novel's primary mahe character, the unsavory Haisi, is almost exclusively rendered in a repetitive and slangy pidgin English, lacking in prepositions and conjunctions—for example, "Not need ask. Ask you: why be fool? Why make damn lot racket, attract notice? Ask you: what benefit you this stsho thing?" (102). Examples of mahendi phrases include *Rahe'ish taij meh, jai* (a command to a subordinate to move away from a door [100]) and *Silimaji nan nil Ja'hai-wa* ("through traffic prohibited" [173]). The Mahendo'sat have an undescribed formal style of writing or inscription, but there is also, somewhat confusingly, a "universal alphabet" (173) seen on signs.

The kif, who served as villains in the earlier novels of the series, like *The Pride of Chanur* (1982), appear in *Chanur's Legacy* as possible allies, despite the pointed fact that they have no word for "friend" (238). **Kifish** is described as a "language of clicks and hisses" (222). Hilfy is an "expert" when it comes to kifish, having "learned words she couldn't pronounce, lacking a double set of razor teeth, and words she couldn't translate, without resorting to words of psychotic connotation in every other language she knew" (259), though how one can be said to have learned words one cannot (physically) pronounce or translate seems paradoxical. That the novel has more samples of kifish than any of the other languages points to a narrative means of keeping the kif as alien to the reader. These examples include such words as *naikktak* (randomly or irrationally behaving [259]), *gakkak* ("herd creatures" [317]), and the all-important kif quality *sfik* ("elegance" [295]), as well as a few phrases, such as *Ssakkukkta sa khutturkht* ("hold your exact course" [344]).

Probably the most intriguing of alien languages in the Chanur series is that of the methane-breathing tc'a. The tc'a communicate in matrix formations, a form expressive of their multipartite brains. Although the component words of the matrix can be translated by computers, the meaning of a given message lies in understanding the order or pattern of those words, as the following example from the novel (283) demonstrates:

Tc'a	tc'a	tc'a	chi	hani	hani
birth	chi	rescue	birth	go	go
danger	danger	danger	danger	danger	danger
see	join	make	divide	danger	danger

The series also includes *Chanur's Venture* (1984), *The Kif Strike Back* (1985), and *Chanur's Homecoming* (1986).

Reference: Cherryh, C. J. *Chanur's Legacy.* New York: DAW Books, 1992.

A Clockwork Orange

From the Russian for "teen," **nadsat** is the slang used by the juvenile delinquent antiheroes of Anthony Burgess's novel *A Clockwork Orange* (1962) and Stanley Kubrick's subsequent 1971 film. It is also, as the narrator Alex attests, a "fashion": a codified rhetoric, a mode of dress, and a lifestyle that mark all constituents of the subculture. Alex and his *droogs* embroider their speech with a vocabulary drawn largely from Slavic roots to characterize their crimes and parts of the anatomy—theirs as well as, often less flatteringly, those of their victims (e.g., the Russian *grud*, "breast," becomes the plural *groodies*). Burgess, in his memoir *You've Had Your Time*, explains that the youths' vocabulary was designed as "a mixture of Russian and demotic English, seasoned with rhyming slang and the gipsy's bolo" (37). In addition to this etymological basis, nadsat words include instances of onomatopoeia (a *smeck* is a kiss, but it may also be any pursing of the lips, and Alex articulates the sounds of fighting as words: "ptaaaaa and grrrrr and kraaaaark" [51]) as well as the odd cultural mnemonic: *a pain in the gulliver* is a headache, with a nod to Swift's *Gulliver's Travels*, and the prison chaplain is called a *charlie*, an allusion to Charlie Chaplin very much in the manner of rhyming slang.

Nadsat speakers' syntax, interestingly, is English but archaic, even Shakespearean (as the conspiratorial Georgie puts it, "It was Will the English who like said" [46]), in contrast to the prosaic and common speech of the adults they encounter. Alex taunts the leader of another youth gang in a fashion reminiscent of the beginning scenes of feudal strife in *Romeo and Juliet*: "How art thou, thou globby bottle of cheap stinking chip-oil? Come and get one in the yarbles, if you have any yarbles, you eunuch jelly, thou" (16). The mock formality and euphemistic qualities of the argot bespeak the moral immaturity of its users. At its most remarkable level of construction, the nadsat lexicon interweaves these compositional strategies while the context of the utterance simultaneously undermines them, and usually Burgess thus makes a moral point. For example, to call something *horrorshow* is a favorable judgment rather in the same way, say, that slang can invert a word like "wicked" to mean "good," while the word also represents a transformation of the Russian *khorosho* ("good"). Yet what Alex describes as *horrorshow* is invariably connected with violence, and when he finds himself strapped in for a session of brainwashing, his use of the expression in the phrase "this must be a real horrorshow film if you're so keen on my viddying it" receives the ironic, corrective answer: "Horrorshow is right, friend. A real show of horrors" (81). He is then shown graphic films of atrocities while he is chemically induced to feel nausea and revulsion. In a sense, Alex's language is being as pointedly modified as the rest of his behavior is by drugs and audio-visual stimuli.

The brainwashing of Alex by psychologists and politicians is effectively reflected by the disorientation created by the narrative's use of nadsat. "The reader would be brainwashed into learning minimal Russian," Burgess recounts, revealing how subversive the novel really was within the Cold War years of its first appearance. "The novel was to be an exercise in linguistic programming. . . . I would resist to the limit any publisher's demand that a glossary be provided. A glossary would disrupt the programme and nullify the brainwashing" (Burgess 1990, 38). Despite Burgess's resistance, however, some editions of the novel did appear with a glossary, just as the original American edition of the novel—as well as Kubrick's film—actually omits the book's final chapter, even though it is this chapter that sounds the important Manichean note. Adults, including Alex's grown-up ("nearly twenty") former droog, Pete, do not speak nadsat, and many of them fail to understand it. Pete admits to his wife that, like the younger Alex, he, too, "used to talk like that," though now he enjoys "wine-cup and word games" as recreation: "Harmless, if you see what I mean" (146–147). Compared with the "harmless" and altogether bourgeois "word games" of socially well-adjusted and professionalized adults, nadsat is, for all its glorification of violence and misogyny, perversely poetic, and for this reason it is not surprising that it is frequently mimicked and burlesqued by readers and viewers of *A Clockwork Orange.*

References: Burgess, Anthony. *A Clockwork Orange*. London: Penguin, 1972; Burgess, Anthony. *You've Had Your Time: Being the Second Part of the Confessions of Anthony Burgess*. London: Penguin, 1990; *A Clockwork Orange*. Directed by Stanley Kubrick. Screenplay by Stanley Kubrick, 1971.

Close Encounters of the Third Kind

Steven Spielberg's 1977 film about efforts to communicate between human beings and unidentified aliens (the title refers to the classification of contact with UFOs) presents a simple musical phrase as a kind of key message with which to begin dialogue. In response to the alien music, scientists use both a system of colored lights and a gestural equivalent of the phrase: the latter is produced with the hand-sign notation designed by composer and ethnomusicologist Zoltán Kodály (1882–1967) for instruction of the deaf. The musical phrase is never itself translated, but the mimicry and adaptation (the aliens echo the hand sign at the end of the film) signify the beginning of communication. The invention of the film score composer John Williams, the catchy five-note musical phrase became a memorable trademark of the film.

   Reference: Close Encounters of the Third Kind. Directed by Steven Spielberg. Screenplay by Steven
   Spielberg, 1977.

Code 46

   The characters in the 2004 film *Code 46*, directed by Michael Winterbottom, speak a lively and somewhat startling blend of words and phrases in Arabic, Chinese, French, Italian, and Spanish within their English (which seems the dominant or at least metalanguage). This medley of tongues operates as a synecdoche for the themes of genetic and cultural mixing: the film's title refers to a law that prohibits couples who have similar DNA patterns. It is not clear how this apparently universal patois or lingua franca came about, particularly since the bio-technological advances of the globalized society depicted in *Code 46* include the manufacture of specialized viruses that can infect, as it were, a subject with new abilities. William and Maria, the main characters, have a brief and intriguing conversation about the effects of these viruses, in which Maria mentions that she once took a virus to learn Mandarin Chinese, but though she could consequently speak the language fluently, she did not understand what she was saying ("Chinese people knew what I was saying, but I didn't. Weird"). The cross-cultural linguistic transformation that may be either a symptom or an effect of this future civilization's structure bears contrast to the language deformations of other dystopian narratives, such as *Nineteen Eighty-Four*. A comparable, slightly earlier film, *Gattaca* (1997), offered a dystopian picture of a highly professionalized society that genetically determines the classes of its members; there public announcements are made in Esperanto.

   References: Code 46. Directed by Michael Winterbottom. Screenplay by Frank Cottrell Boyce, 2004;
   Gattaca. Directed by Andrew Niccol. Screenplay by Andrew Niccol, 1997.

Codex Seraphinianus

   It is difficult, if not impossible, to categorize Luigi Serafini's 1981 book. *Codex Seraphinianus* is an art object, a carefully crafted blend of surrealism and Hieronymus Bosch, made up of colorful drawings and text in a unique, totally untranslated script. (There are published "translations" of the *Codex*, but that simply means the copyright information has been translated: the rest of the book is exclusively in the unknown language. Even the page numbers are part of the conceit.) The book appears to be an encyclopedia (after the style of Diderot) in manuscript, though it is also remindful of a naturalist's sketchbook: its various sections proffer depictions of and notes on bizarre and fantastical flora, fauna, anatomies, dress, and foodstuffs. One section appears to be a discussion of the glyphs in which the book is written, including a picture of a kind of Rosetta Stone with another unknown script set beside that of the *Codex*. In another series of illustrations, a written word is shown ballooning off of the page while another parachutes onto it. It remains a mystery as to whether there is a breakable "code" within the *Codex*—that is, whether the glyphs can in fact be translated or whether the script is entirely without any "real" referent.

Reference: Serafini, Luigi. *Codex Seraphinianus*. New York: Abbeville Press, 1983.

The Color of Distance

In Amy Thomson's 1995 novel, Juna, a human xenobiologist, is marooned on a strange planet and spends years living with and learning about an amphibian species called Tendu. "Going native" is taken to its most extreme here, as the Tendu modify the ailing woman's biology and more or less incorporate her into their culture. Juna discovers that the **Tendu** language is primarily "skin speech" (107):

> The patterns on their skin seemed to carry information; the colors showed the emotional content of their words. Blues, particularly turquoise, were associated with pleasure, and greens with approval or agreement. Reds and oranges were related to anger and fear. Purple was connected with curiosity and questions. . . . "Yes" was a series of three horizontal bars. "No" was three vertical bars. Food was a colored dot or circle within a green oval. Water was a series of three vertical dots, usually blue or green. (38)

These early impressions are quickly confirmed by experience, and the text is flush with phrases like "he replied in soothing blue tones" (108) and "vividly pink with surprise" (193). Juna develops phonetic equivalents for names and words that do not correspond to alien subjects (i.e., things outside of her earthly experience). Twice in the novel a Tendu character employs an unknown name that the text represents as typographic symbols (126, 173), and the novel includes a "partial glossary" at the end. Although it seems that all Tendu, regardless of their region or tribal groupings, use the same language, Tendu young, called *tinkas*, are incapable of skin speech.

The Tendu have a couple of other forms of communication worthy of notice, however. One is called "linking" (*allu-a*), a process by which two or more Tendu can share or exchange emotion and energy, and which facilitates their extraordinary powers of healing. Juna thinks of it as "a deep awareness of another's physiology, a form of incredibly direct biofeedback" (275).

The other, which seems slightly out of place, is vocal expression. Tendu elders let out "a deep, booming call" (221) to signal for a meeting (since skin speech is obviously limited to face-to-face, or at least line-of-sight, encounters). When Juna begins to instruct the Tendu in her language—called **Standard**, though not specifically described, and markedly separate from Juna's mother tongue, Finnish—the Tendu find the vocalizations difficult but manage to simulate written characters on their skins right away.

Reference: Thomson, Amy. *The Color of Distance*. New York: Ace Books, 1995.

The Comical History of the States and Empires of the Moon and the Sun

Cyrano de Bergerac's *Comical History* is really a combination of two volumes, *Voyage to the Moon* (*Voyage dans la Lune*, 1657) and *The History of the States and Empires of the Sun* (*L'Histoire des États et Empires du Soleil*, 1662). There is speculation that a third volume may have been lost. Together these two books form an irreverent blend of philosophical story (*conte philosophique*), picaresque, and early science fiction (Bergerac has been credited with writing the first account of space travel using a rocket).

In the first volume, the narrator, Dyrcona, arrives on the moon to find that, as he had been telling his friends back on Earth, the inhabitants of the moon view the earth as a moon devoid of life. The lunar people use two different languages (Dyrcona calls them "idioms"): "one which serves the great and the other which is peculiar to the common people" (36).

The first is borrowed directly from Francis Godwin's *The Man in the Moon, published a few decades previously. (Dyrcona even meets and converses with Gonzalez, the hero of Godwin's book, while on the moon.) Described as "nothing else but a variety of non-articulated notes—more or less like our music when the words are not added to the melody," this language allows a great debate to become "the most harmonious concert" (37). All proper names of lunar people and places are transcribed as four- and five-note sequences. Books in this language are lovely, portable machines:

> When someone desires to "read," he winds up this machine with a great quantity of little threads of all kinds, then he turns the needle to the chapter he wishes to hear and at once there issue from it, as from the mouth of a man or from a musical instrument, all the distinct and different sounds which the great lunarians employ for the expression of their language. (89)

(Bergerac may thus also have a claim as the first writer to invent a sound recorder.) Small in size and light, as many as thirty of these books can be carried in pockets or on belts. Dyrcona describes one book he receives as having been "carved out of a single diamond" and another like "a monstrous pearl split in two" (88).

The language of the common people, who are habitually naked, is gestural. Their sentences are composed of every possible twitch, from "the shaking of the limbs" to "the agitation of a finger, a hand, an ear, a lip, an arm, an eye, or a cheek," while certain movements "serve only to express words, such as the wrinkling of the brow" (37). The name of one notorious lunar person's name, transcribed as a series of four rising notes, in "the common people's jargon was a fillip of the finger on the right knee" (89): this is the text's most specific example of the language's usage.

In the second volume, Dyrcona makes an even more improbable visit to the sun. He first lands on "one of the little earths which hover about round the sun (known to the mathematicians as *sunspots*)" (143) and there meets a little man who converses at length with him in a language "which I am perfectly sure I had never heard before and which had no connexion with any [of those of earth], but which, none the less, I understood more readily and more clearly than my mother tongue" (144). The little man explains that his language (which others whom Dyrcona meets on the solar surface proper also speak) is intrinsically "true," and that "the more a language departs from this truth, the more it falls short of the concept it seeks to express and the harder it is to understand" (144). This "perfect idiom" is "nature's own medium of communication with all the animals" (144–145) and may, Dyrcona speculates (but his interlocutor does not confirm or deny the idea), be the prelapsarian language of Adam. Precisely what "truth" is so central to this language is not revealed, and it may be that Bergerac is holding up the concept of an ideal language as an absurdity.

The sun offers more wonders than this. Dyrcona runs into trouble there with the kingdom of birds, but admits that the little man on the sunspot has equipped him only with a little of the vocabulary of "brutes," and so he has not "sufficient familiarity with the bird language" (158). Later still he socializes with a talkative forest (a forest on the sun!). The trees not only speak ancient Greek, which their oak forefathers acquired on earth ("the most universal language there was in those days" [189]), but they have other nonhuman modes of expression, too. The "soft and subtle breezes" and "low murmuring" of the woods are "to be precise, their language" (190). So diverse are the languages of the forest, Dyrcona is assured by certain oak trees, that each species of plant has its own: "thus the birch does not speak like the maple, nor the beech like the cherry" (190).

Reference: Bergerac, Cyrano de. *Other Worlds: The Comical History of the States and Empires of the Moon and the Sun.* Translated by Geoffrey Strachan. London: Oxford University Press, 1965.

The Coming Race

Lord Lytton's last novel, *The Coming Race* (1871), was published the same year as Darwin's *Descent of Man* and is dedicated to the Oxford philologist Max Müller (1823–1900), whose ideas Lytton drew on when describing the language of the subterranean people called the Ana (a general term for the species). An unnamed American narrator tumbles into an underground society with amazing resources: its citizens enjoy long lives in peace and harmony with one another largely thanks to the discovery of an energy called *vril*, a multipurpose sort of electricity of "natural" origin, in fluid form—the "all-permeating fluid" vril (55) is vaguely connected with willpower. The Vril-ya, as they call themselves (the term signifies "The Civilised Nations" [57]), use this energy to light their cities, to control the weather, to heal and preserve as well as to annihilate all potential threats to their society. The narrator discovers that his "language was much simpler than theirs, comprising far less of complex ideas" (47), and so members of the Vril-ya have mastered the former with ease.

The Coming Race dedicates an entire chapter to particulars of the language of the Vril-ya, explicitly taking its ideological framework from the work of Müller by hearkening to "the three main transitions through which language passes in attaining to perfection of form" (77). This chapter is profuse in vocabulary samples, interlinguistic analogies (*Gl* "is a single letter, as *th* is a single letter with the Greeks" [79]), demonstrations of an interrelation between words (e.g., "Ek is strife—Glek, the universal strife. Nas, as I before said, is corruption or rot; thus Glek-Nas may be construed, 'the universal strife-rot'" [81]), and unintentionally funny professorial histrionics ("what I have already said will perhaps suffice to show genuine philological students that a language which, preserving so many of the roots in the aboriginal form, and clearing from the immediate, but transitory, polysynthetical stage so many rude incumbrances" etc. [87]). There is a striking number of pejorative terms. From *Koom*, "a profound hollow, metaphorically a cavern" come such words as *Koom-zi* ("vacancy or void"), *Bodh-koom* (ignorance), and *Koom-Posh*, meaning democracy and understood to be a contemptible system of government (80–81). *Nax*, *Narl*, and *Naria* are terms for, respectively, darkness, death, and "sin or evil"; on the other hand, "the Supreme Being" cannot be named in writing and "is symbolised by what may be termed the hieroglyphic of a pyramid, Λ" (80). Largely populated by monosyllables, "which are the foundations of the language" (78), the Vril-ya tongue has in its history diminished the number of cases for the declension of nouns while it has multiplied explanatory prepositions. Lytton offers one full declension example (82):

	Singular		*Plural*	
Nominative	An	(Man)	Ana	(Men)
Dative	Ano	(to Man)	Anoi	(to Men)
Accusative	Anam	(Man)	Ananda	(Men)
Vocative	Hil-An	(O Man)	Hil-Ananda	(O Men)

Noting "how much the language of the Vril-ya is akin to the Aryan or Indo-Germanic" (86), the narrator takes pains to point out that his study is based on "literature of the past" (87). Indeed, there is no other kind of literature among the Vril-ya: plays, stories, and poems are at best children's pastimes, and the assured perfection of the society excludes the possibility of any "speculative theories" (134), in exactly the manner in which Plato excluded poets from his ideal Republic. The problematic style of feminism, if it may be so called, that Lytton gives his utopia (females are more clever and strong than males and initiate courtship, but upon marrying they become submissive) has its determinist roots in the language. For example, we are told that "the word Ana (pronounced broadly *Arna*) corresponds with our plural *men*; An (pronounced *Arn*) the singular, with *man*. The word for woman is Gy (pronounced hard, as in Guy); it forms itself into Gy-ei for the plural, but the G becomes soft in the plural, like Jy-ei. They have a proverb to the effect that this difference in pronunciation is symbolical, for that the female sex is soft collectively, but hard to deal with in the individual" (66).

The Vril-ya keep watch of numerous "barbarians" whom they barely consider to be fellow Ana. (The narrator is distinguished from both with the epithet *Tish*, which signifies a kind of pet.) It is not clear what their language is, or even what they might call themselves (the Vril-ya recognize their factious societies as *Koom-posh* or *Glek-Nas* [see above] and label them thus), but they are brought up by a Vril speaking of poetry, and when he disapprovingly refers to "their notions of Soc-Sec (money-getting)," he does not explain whether this is a Vril-ya expression or that of these "savages" (142).

Reference: Lytton, Edward George Earle Bulwer. *The Coming Race*. London: Routledge and Sons, 1871.

The Confidential Agent

In Graham Greene's espionage novel *The Confidential Agent* (1939), the hero D. encounters a collective of intellectuals bent on "communication instead of misunderstanding, strife" (127), which end they hope to achieve by promoting a new language. D. (himself a former professor of Romance languages) poses as a student in order to exchange information with a contact, one of the language's poorly paid instructors. The Entrenationo Language Centre represents a satire on L. L. Zamenhof's Esperanto ("one who hopes") and its international congress, which held its first meeting in 1905. The few samples of spoken **Entrenationo** in Greene's novel suggest that, like Esperanto, the language is an amalgam of European tongues: *bona matina* (good morning) and *bona nuche* (good evening), *tabolo* (table), *korda* (heart), and the numbers *una, da, trea, kwara, and vif*. Goldthorb, a made-up mystery writer, jokingly named as a writer of Entrenationo fiction, bizarrely anticipates the work of Diego Marani (see *Las adventures des inspector Cabillot*).

Reference: Greene, Graham. *The Confidential Agent: An Entertainment.* London: Penguin, 1971.

"Confluence"

Brian W. Aldiss's short story is simply a partial glossary of the language of the alien Myrinians (of the planet Myrin). This language, called **Confluence**, is more than eleven million (Earth) years old and is a "language-cum-posture": "meanings of words can be radically modified or altered entirely by the stance assumed by the speaker" (190). Thus, the definitions provided by the glossary are tentative and highly variable—there are nearly nine thousand permutations of posture involved in Confluent speech—but "they throw some light on to the mysteries of an alien culture" (190). The following selection of definitions from the story is illustrative of the clarity of that light:

INK TH O	Morality used as an offensive weapon
JILY JIP TUP	A thinking machine that develops a stammer; the action of pulling up the trousers while running uphill
JIL JIPY TUP	Any machine with something incurable about it; pleasant laughter that is nevertheless unwelcome; the action of pulling up the trousers while running downhill
KARNAD EES	The enjoyment of a day or a year by doing nothing; fasting
KARNAD CHESS	The waste of a day or a year by doing nothing; fasting (191–192)

These expressions have been recorded with a "romanised phonetic system" (190), but as some of the definitions reveal (e.g., YUP PA is "a book in which everything is understandable except the author's purpose in writing it"), the Myrinians do have writing and books. This fact immediately raises the question of the qualities of Confluent orthography and whether that writing somehow approximates or else neglects the posture element of spoken Confluence, but the text does not consider such a question.

Reference: Aldiss, Brian W. "Confluence." *SF12.* Edited by Judith Merril. New York: Dell, 1968. 189–196.

D

The Dark Crystal

This 1982 "live action animated film" (i.e., it employs models and puppets, with no visible human actors) has a fairly unremarkable story line—as in so much fantasy literature, an orphaned character is destined to save society by undertaking a quest—but is visually stunning, featuring a lush and highly imaginative world populated with numerous active flora and fauna as well as several humanoid races.

In the original script the villainous Skeksis (a repulsive group of vulture/reptile creatures) speak their own language (developed by linguist and children's author Alan Garner), which appears to be based on Egyptian and Greek. As test audiences responded unfavorably to the use of this language, it was replaced by standard English in the final film and can be found only in outtakes included in the 2002 DVD release of the piece. From the few examples given in the film, it appears that **Skeksis** is a fragmentary language based primarily on expletives, verbs, and noun clusters. Some phrases given include *haakskeekah* ("trail by stone"), *krakwhee* ("kill"), and *k'nim* ("dangerous"). The "g" sound appears to be rendered as "k" in Skeksis, as the race of Gelflings are known as *kelflinkh* in Skeksis.

One language that did appear in the original film is **Podling**, the language of the Pod People, a humanoid race of potato creatures, whose dress, music, and dance resemble that of the Celts or else that of the Roma. As they are earthy creatures, in touch with the land and its inhabitants, their language also seems to serve as a way to communicate with various animals. Some examples of Podling that appear in the film include the phrases *fala vam* ("thank you"), *avo yay* ("his name is . . ."), and *dobah* ("stay" or "don't move" to animal).

The aforementioned Gelflings, the ostensible heroes of the film, can speak various languages but appear to best communicate through a form of telepathy/empathy referred to as "dreamfasting." The Gelflings also appear to have a pictographic written language.

The novelization of the film, by A.C.H. Smith, provides some additional information regarding the culture of the world of *The Dark Crystal*, including more examples of Skeksis and Podling. It also includes a brief mention of an **urRu** language—the gentle and intellectual urRu are known as the Mystics in the final cinematic version—with the urRu language appearing to be related to Hebrew. The screenplay of *The Dark Crystal* has been transcribed unofficially by Laura Knauth.

References: The Dark Crystal. Directed by Jim Henson and Frank Oz. Screenplay by David Odell, 1982. DVD 2002; Smith, A.C.H. *The Dark Crystal.* New York: Henry Holt, 1982; see also Laura Knauth's Web site: www.lauraknauth.com/MovieCollectibles/DC_Screenplay.html.

Dark Skies

This short-lived science-fiction television series presents an alternative history of the United States in which an extraterrestrial race secretly arrived during the 1940s and has shaped the course of the twentieth century, including the orchestration of the Kennedy assassination and the downing of the U2 spy plane in 1960.

The alien race, known as the Hive, operates by implanting themselves in human hosts, yet they also have their own language, **Hivespeak**. This language, which was originally called **Thhtmaa** by its creator, linguist Matt Pearson, is a harsh and insect-sounding language that reflects the menacing and collectivist aspects of the Hive.

In phonology Hivespeak lacks initial vowel sounds and commonly utilizes trills and syllabic fricatives, while in morphology the language does not distinguish between nouns and verbs. Rather, words are formed from roots with prefixes and suffixes indicating part of speech and person. Thus, taking the root word *zaahh* (assimilation) and adding the prefix *gu* (a human) and suffix *a* (third person) creates the phrase *guzaahh'a* ("the human has been assimilated"). Other prefixes and suffixes can serve to indicate negation, repetition, pluralization, and other grammatical forms.

Some additional phrases of Hivespeak suggest the flavor of this complex language: *paabutmoo'gh, guukrr zataamuud'a* ("don't be afraid, soon you will understand everything"); *tmuugh'anlo zataamuud'a* ("I will return soon"); and *woogh daang'a'zh laawa* ("out of the many come one").

Reference: Dark Skies. Various directors and screenplay authors. Broadcast 1996–1997. DVD 1996.

"Day of Burning"

Originally published as "Supernova" in *Analog Science Fiction/Science Fact* in 1967, Poul Anderson's story is set on the planet Merseia, which stands to be severely affected by an approaching supernova. A group of aliens, called "galactics" by the Merseians, proposes to use their superior technology to assist the planet's population. These aliens speak something called **Anglic**, while the Merseians speak **Eriau**. Anderson's text offers no examples of either language outside of the English-language narration, but conversations in Eriau are rendered in an emphatically archaic, formal English. The persistent use of "thou" and "thee" and such phrases as "say on" (273), "smite this planet" (273), and "methinks" (295) seems parodic, though the object is not clear.

Reference: Anderson, Poul. "Day of Burning." *The Earth Book of Stormgate.* New York: Berkley, 1978. 270–310.

The Day of the Klesh

The third of what is sometimes referred to as the "Ler series" of novels, M. A. Foster's *The Day of the Klesh* (1979) is about an interstellar expedition to the planet Monsalvat. The purpose (and to a considerable extent, the result) of this trip is obscure, but involves cooperation between different species of sentient beings: humans, Spsomi, Vfzyekhr, and Ler. The Klesh, inhabitants of Monsalvat, represent a genetic experiment in human biodiversity, more or less abandoned by the Ler, who favor social and biological integration and a general narrowing of differences. The journey thus represents something of a visit to a shameful and troubling prehistory.

Their vessel, the *Ffstresha*, is run by the Spsom members of the expedition. Originally from the planet 'Rrtz, the Spsom are known for their spaceships and their strange sense of humor. The claim "Spsom distorted non-Spsom speech in numerous ways, not limited to grammar and phonetics" (12)—which appears in the first of several informational footnotes in the novel—is substantiated by examples of such distortions: "Very good" and "You want work?" become "Vv'ri gidd" and "Wirk yi went, yis?" (12–13). The **Spsom** word for "dream" seems to be *Mstli* (36)—apart from ship names, this is the only tangible example of the language in the novel. Ideograms glimpsed on the side of a Spsom spaceship are the only suggestion of a written language. When they meet Klesh warriors, the Spsom manage to communicate mostly through sign language, but the meanings or principles behind the signs, and even the signs themselves, are not revealed.

The Ler are to human eyes reserved in manner and fond of a certain decorum. *The Day of the Klesh* offers some samples of the ornate vocabulary of **Ler**, such as *Daorman* ("a temporary servant, hired for completion of a specific task or mission" [15]), *Liy* (a title implying nobility; applied to a young girl, it could be "rendered as Demoiselle" [17]), and *wurwan* ("a rare quality . . . best translated 'innocence'" [175]).

On Monsalvat, which they call *Aceldama* ("a place to bury strangers" [151]), the diverse peoples known as the Klesh originally spoke **Singlespeech**, "but with the changefulness of humans, it has undergone much development" (81). Foster is sporadically pedantic on certain points of translation and syntax, but the details offered tend to make even more obscure rather than clarify the workings of Singlespeech. The phrase *Zha' armeshero* is "approximately, 'It is indeed (most-)agreed.' Past Indicative Passive Participle, superior comparison. Zha' is emphatic" (150). There have evolved "many other variants" of this Ur-tongue, which a Ler member of the expedition classifies as "cult jargon, tribal lore-speech, and functional languages" (81). Most speakers are "fluent in at least three or four basic patterns appropriate to their station," and those intermediaries who communicate between groups hostile to each other are "conversant in more" (81). A footnote found later in the novel qualifies this information somewhat: in reference to the word *manefranamosi*, "which they [the modern Klesh] thought meant 'broadening' in the ancient Singlespeech of their once-masters," the note contends that

> what the Klesh thought was Singlespeech was actually the degenerate form
> of that tongue as spoken on the planet Dawn. The correct construction

would have been "mafranemosi (felor)," with the word for star, "felor," understood, but not said. (116)

Somewhat unclear distinctions are made between the *Radah* (the name of the original Klesh), for example, and the animalistic, "filthy" Derques. At one point in the novel an agitated Klesh "hunts-woman" forgets herself and lapses into "the secret hunt-language of the Haydars," uttering the untranslated sentence, "*O bi leberim, ao Dehir sherda!*" (138). Two significant terms in Foster's story are the Germanic-sounding *gorgensuchen* ("a word impossible to translate simply. It meant, more or less, 'the descendant of persons who deliberately perverted their racial ancestry and destiny.' It was a word filled with connotations of shivery horror and singularly repulsive deviance" [117]) and *Skazenach* (a "distorted Singlespeech" word that "means 'Behold-things.' The correct form is 'maskazemoni nakhon,' meaning those things which are spoken of in tales" [153]).

While on Monsalvat, the novel's human protagonist, Meure, becomes possessed by the spirit of an ancient Klesh rebel, Cretus, who threatens to "stir things up again" or to "say it the old way: *Tasi mapravemo zha*'" (156). A nebulous sort of revolution begins with the realization that the Vfzyekhr are not, as they have hitherto seemed, insensible animals or slaves, but are truly the remnants of an ancient and accomplished race. Their telepathic abilities allow Meure-Cretus to contact a distant ship in an "untranslatable" code and ask for rescue (215). From this point on, telepathic communication overrules questions of language, and the novel drives to a theologically charged conclusion.

The Warriors of Dawn (1975) and *Gameplayers of Zan* (1977) are the other novels in the "Ler series." *The Day of the Klesh* is of the greatest interest here because the Monsalvat scenario represents a reexamination (however convoluted) of the story of Babel.

Reference: Foster, M. A. *The Day of the Klesh*. New York: DAW Books, 1979.

The Day the Earth Stood Still

Klaatu is the name of a very human-looking alien who comes to Earth in the classic science-fiction film *The Day the Earth Stood Still* (1951) and addresses his traveling companion, the powerful but mute robot Gort, and the console of his spaceship in an unnamed language. Humans' discovery of "rudimentary atomic power" necessitates the visit, Klaatu explains, because the development requires that Earth either accept peace in accordance with interplanetary laws or be destroyed. For his trouble Klaatu is spurned, hospitalized, confined, hunted, and ultimately shot. An unchecked Gort threatens havoc ("There is no limit to what he can do. . . . He could destroy the earth") until Helen Benson, the kindly war widow, repeats to him the (now cultishly famous) phrase *Klaatu, Barada Nikto*. No direct translation is given in the film, but Gort responds by bringing the woman aboard the spacecraft and retrieving, even reviving, Klaatu. Other phrases heard in the film include *Gort, Baringa* (possibly "Gort, let's enter the spaceship") and a longer series of words, either commands to the ship's controls or a message to Klaatu's undisclosed home planet. The film is (rather loosely) based on Harry Bates's short story "Farewell to the Master," first published in *Astounding Stories* (October 1940), but there is no alien language in the text.

Reference: *The Day the Earth Stood Still*. Directed by Robert Wise. Screenplay by Edmund H. North, 1951.

"Death and Designation among the Asadi"

See *Transfigurations*.

"Decoding of the Martian Language"

Included in a 1965 issue of the University of Texas's *The Graduate Journal* dedicated to the topic of Mars, W. P. Lehmann's story poses as a kind of future report or history of how in the early twenty-first century humans learned to record and decipher melodies emitted by Martians. In this future scenario, the "indigenous languages" of Earth have been "displaced" (267) by a global language called **Earthtongue** (probably English, the language in which the story appears and which is mentioned as part of elementary education, but perhaps not). Yet it is the study of one such extinct language, a Mexican one exclusively composed of whistled melodies, that leads to a breakthrough in understanding **Martian** speech. Noting that a "full description of Martian requires considerable space" (268), Lehmann is able to confine his delineation to key details, though they are technical and precise.

The simplest manifestation of the Martian language, **Martian Plain-talk** is confined to five tones and is used for public announcements and by the young. In Plain-talk,

> nouns and their modifiers are, in general, characterized by upward movement, verbs by downward movement. In broken chords nouns are marked by repetition of the same initial tone. Adjectives resemble them by rising, but lack the repetition. Adverbs, even those modifying adjectives, descend to the third tone of five and then ascend. Prepositions have four descending tones. Verbs have five. (269)

Full Martian speech uses thirty tones, like a much larger alphabet. The first speaker establishes the musical key of the conversation. The vocabulary is (necessarily) limited, but the unusual grammar and form allow for a range of charged expressions. Redundancy is not a consideration of Martian speakers and changes to the language, such as the addition of new tones to accommodate new expressions and ideas learned from Earth, are made only by parliamentary decision. An example phrase of Martian Plain-talk (shown in the figure below), is recorded with attention to frequency in cycles per second, and translates as "Highly delightful floating in space" (269). Martians delighted to have been introduced to Beethoven's Fifth Symphony call it "a toying talk in praise of the ego" (269).

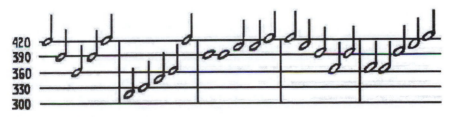

A phrase in Martian Plain-talk, from "Decoding of the Martian Language."

Lehmann ventures into satire in outlining the effects the study of Martian speech has on Earth. Besides the academic flurry that accompanies the discoveries, Martian visitors "upset the literary world"—meaning "Tape of the Day Clubs, bearded professors, *arrière garde* members" (271)—by inspiring experiments with Martian sounds in Earth-tongue literature. One vexed critic cries out for "adherence to the tried literary conventions, such as the delicate manipulation of consonants and vowels found in James Joyce" (271). Presumably the strangeness and musicality of Martian makes even *Finnegans Wake* look tame and prosaic.

The hero of this story of decipherment, Sensai, goes on to extend his research, studying light rays as a means for extraterrestrial communication and aspiring to develop a quantum theory of linguistic communication.

Reference: Lehmann, W. P. "Decoding of the Martian Language." *The Graduate Journal* 7.1 (December 1965): 265–272.

Devil of a State

Dunia, a fictional caliphate in Africa, is the setting of Anthony Burgess's novel *Devil of a State* (1961). The official "National Language" of Dunia is called **Sudu** (the word also apparently signifies an ethnicity), but it is not described and no examples are given.

Reference: Burgess, Anthony. *Devil of a State*. London: Heinemann, 1961.

"The Dialect of the Tribe"

A letter from a student of translation to a colleague provides the basis for Harry Mathews's 1980 short story, the title of which is an allusion to the poet's duty, expressed by both Mallarmé and T. S. Eliot, to "purify the dialect of the tribe." The translator has come across a vexing but fascinating language called **Pagolak**, "the speech of a small hill tribe in northern New Guinea" (8). His source is a transcription in an anthropology journal by Dr. Ernest Botherby; its (palindromic) title, *Kalo Gap Pagolak*, means "magic transformation of Pagolak" (8). The text comes from "an oral declaration by the *abanika* or 'chief word-chief' of the tribe" (9), but the fact that Botherby has provided no English translation of the declaration puzzles the story's narrator and prompts him to closer study. The "magic" of Pagolak is that it is untranslatable because Pagolak is itself a process of translation. Although the "final result of the transformation" of which the *abanika* speaks is "associated with the word *nalaman*" and "the means of achieving that result is *namele*" (10), ultimately "it must be that *namele* never be explained, or *nalaman* understood!" (For reasons that are unexplained, women of the tribe "are thought to create *namele* naturally, along with language" but have "no power of *nalaman*" [13].) As Mathews's narrator tries to explain the workings of Pagolak, for which dictionaries are useless because the problem is "not one of particular words" (9), he gradually falls out of English and fully into the obscurity of Pagolak. Offerings of vocabulary are muddled and uncertain (the phrase *sitokap utu sisi* "leaves an impression, approximately, of 'resettling words in [own] eggs': aptly enough, after the youngsters emerge from *afanu* through *sitokap utu sisi* into nuselek and its attendant privileges of *tun wusi* and *aban metse*" and so on and so forth, until the breakdown, "dear Christ, it doesn't *mean* that" [11]), while particular points of instruction and "helpful hints" are either incomprehensible or apparently contradictory (e.g., the reader is advised to repeat the phrase *amak esudupelu moke sadapalemuk use dup olemaka*, but is then told "don't bother with *amak*, a conventional opening *lan*; or with *dup*, which signals that an utterance is almost *nalaman*" [12–13]). The spontaneous and paradoxical nature of translation is the foundation of Pagalok, and only total surrender to one's inability to understand Pagalok seems to allow one to understand Pagalok. Thus, the narrator exhorts: "Do not think, do not care: Be!" (12).

Botherby, the Australian linguist, is a recurring character in Mathews's writings, usually involved with unusual linguistic problems. (The name "Botherby" is part of a game of literary variations played by members of Oulipo [short for *L'ouvroir de la littérature potentielle*]. "Botherby" is a variation on Georges Perec's Bartlebooth, the hero of his *Life A User's Manual* [1978], whose name is in turn a variation, a blend of those of the title characters in Herman Melville's "Bartleby the Scrivener" [1853] and Valéry Larbaud's *The Diary of A. O. Barnabooth* [1924].) Mathews opens an essay on Oulipian methods of translation with a reference to Botherby, "the scholar who founded the Australian ethno-linguistics" (67), as though he were a real person rather than an invention. Mathews describes Botherby's fascination with New Guinea and Pagolak and goes on to tell an anecdote about two tribes he discovers in the highlands, the Ohos and the Uhas (probably pronounced with a knowing tone as "oh-ho" and "ah-ha"). The **Oho** language has only one expression, a three-word phrase, "Red makes wrong" (68), and the **Uha** language is just as exclusively composed of one expression, "Here not there" (68). Botherby is faced with the problem of how to render the statement of one tribe into the language of the other, to which, says Mathews, there is only one solution: Botherby "grasped at once what all translators eventually learn: a language says what it can say, and that's that" (69). This "solution" is worth comparing with the total narrative immersion into Pagolak at the end of "The Dialect of the Tribe."

Interested readers should also see Mathews's "Remarks of the Scholar Graduate."

References: Mathews, Harry. "The Dialect of the Tribe." *The Human Country: New and Collected Stories*. Normal, IL: Dalkey Archive, 2002. 7–14; Mathews, Harry. "Translation and the Oulipo: The Case of the Persevering Maltese." *The Case of the Persevering Maltese: Collected Essays*. Normal, IL: Dalkey Archive, 2003. 67–82.

"Dialogue of the Greater Systems"

The title of Tommaso Landolfi's story (in the original, "Dialogo dei massimi sistemi," 1937) is an echo of a work by Galileo, *Dialogue Concerning the Two Chief World Systems* (1632), wherein the astronomer attempted to circumvent church censorship by presenting his arguments for a heliocentric planetary system as a drama with three characters. With its three characters—the narrator, a critic, and the unfortunate poet known as Y—Landolfi's story is also really a complex argument, though one of aesthetic principles rather than scientific theories. Y relates how he, having hit on the notion that the better vehicle for poetry would be a language the poet only partially knows, rather than one he knows very well, is taught rudimentary Persian by a visiting English captain. After the captain has left the country, however, and his pupil has spent years composing poems in his new tongue, Y discovers that he has learned and written in a language that speakers and readers of Persian, and indeed those of any language, do not recognize. Not even the English captain, when contacted, remembers the language (which he agrees is not Persian, and he remarks of the signs written for him that "on the one hand they resemble Amharic characters and on the other hand Tibetan ones; but you can be sure they are neither" [251–252]). "The saddest thing," laments Y, who has thrown out all his study notes, "is that this damn language I cannot name is beautiful, beautiful . . . and I love it very much" (252). His poems become the jumping-off point for a debate between the critic and the narrator concerning the nature of language, art, and criticism, and though the critic hurriedly concludes the meeting by assuring Y that he will undoubtedly become as great a poet as Shakespeare even if he can be read by no one else but himself, the narrator informs us that Y is always being turned away by editors and may be "slightly mad" (262). The text does include one of Y's poems and a translation that Y admits does the original poor service; it begins: *Aga magéra difúra natun gua mescíun / Sánit guggérnis soe-wáli trussán garigúr / Gꝋnga bandúra kuttávol jeriś-ni gillára* ("And her weary face wept with joy / as the woman told me of her life / and promised her fraternal affection" [258]).

> *Reference:* Landolfi, Tommaso. "Dialogue of the Greater Systems." *Words in Commotion and Other Stories*. Translated by Kathrine Jackson. New York: Viking, 1986. 248–262.

Dicamus et Labyrinthos

Admirers of R. Murray Schafer's epic "opera" cycle *Patria* (twelve sections, published as the complete sequence in 2002) will be aware of the acclaimed composer and musical theorist's interest in language, both artificial and actual, utilized throughout his self-denominated "theatre of confluence." It is therefore not surprising to find this linguistic interest, as well as Schafer's skills as a calligrapher, coming to the forefront in his pataphysical novel *Dicamus et Labyrinthos: A Philologist's Notebook* (1979/1984).

One might consider Schafer's text a prose analogue to Armand Schwerner's long poem *The Tablets* (1968–1999), but with less ironic authorial commentary. Rather, Schafer seems inspired by John Chadwick's historical narrative of translation and the classical world in *The Decipherment of Linear B* (1958) and creates a fictional narrative that recounts the struggles of an independent classical scholar to translate a series of tablets containing the hitherto unknown language referred to as **Ectocretan**. In the introduction to Schafer's novel—which takes the form of a photocopied notebook featuring the handwritten notes, deletions, and sketches of the unnamed translator—the "editor" recounts the history of the tablets and their relation to Linear A and B. Ectocretan, found at Magia Tribia in Sicily, appears to exist on a series of forty-seven clay tablets uncovered twenty years after Arthur Evans's discovery of the Minoan tablets. Like Linear A and B, the script is initially considered pictographic and believed untranslatable. In a playful intertextual gesture, Michael Ventris, the translator of Linear B, is quoted in the introduction as believing that Ectocretan is merely a further example of financial accounting in the ancient world.

Schafer's beautiful rendering of the philologist's notebook is extremely detailed and features complete reproductions of the tablets, comparisons of Ectocretan to various ancient languages, strategies and techniques of decipherment, and the eventual complete translation of the script. The cleverness of Schafer's enterprise is enhanced by the translator's realization that Ectocretan not only is an unknown language, but is written in code within that language. The act of decipherment therefore requires both a translation and a breaking of an encryption. The poem that is eventually revealed proves to be authored by Daedalus (the mythological artificer of the labyrinth and the wings of Icarus) and recounts the events at Minos leading to the birth of Minotaur, but unfortunately breaks off before Theseus's descent into the maze.

References: Chadwick, John. *The Decipherment of Linear B.* Cambridge: Cambridge University Press, 1990; Schafer, R. Murray. *Dicamus et Labyrinthos: A Philologist's Notebook.* Bancroft, ON: Arcana, 1984; Schafer, R. Murray. *Patria: The Complete Cycle.* Toronto: Coach House Books, 2002; Schwerner, Armand. *The Tablets.* Orono, ME: National Poetry Institute, 1999.

Dinotopia

Dinotopia began as a pair of lavishly illustrated young adult books by James Gurney and soon became a series of juvenile novels, a made-for-TV movie, and a short-lived television miniseries. All concern the island of Dinotopia, a society where dinosaurs and humans live in harmony, often in cities, marked by "utopian" beliefs and advanced cultural achievements.

As most humans residing in Dinotopia have arrived in shipwrecks from various nations over thousands of years, the human language is a mixture of multiple tongues resulting in a type of Esperanto. One word given of human **Dinotopian** is *cumspiritik*, a marriage or deep friendship, which translates literally as "breathing together."

The dinosaurs of Dinotopia all speak their own dialects and often require the service of a translating race of dinosaurs, the *Protoceratops multilinguous.* The only saurian phrase given in Gurney's books appears untranslated as *Ank—ayyank-lesh. Yank-ank-kee.* Certain dinosaur races, such as the sauropods, communicate in a "musical language" with "a downward glide indicat[ing] concern or distress. A rapidly rising and falling series suggests excitement or irritation. From these simple beginnings, a rich musical language has developed" (Gurney 1992, 104). There is also the gestural language of "pose dancing" in which paired dinosaurs and humans perform pantomimes or tableaux that also signify linguistically.

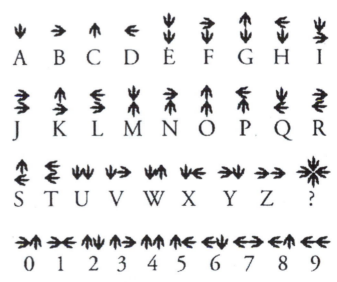

The alphabet common to all of Dinotopia. Based on the footprints of one of the many dinosaur races in Dinotopia, the Dinotopian alphabet can be transferred to scrolls or written in sand for temporary notation. Reprinted with permission from James Gurney.

While each dinosaur race has its own dialect, what all Dinotopians share is a single common alphabet, as shown in the figure. Permanent thought is transferred in this script to scrolls, with sandboxes serving as notepaper or jot pads. Although there are numerous dialects and languages in use in Dinotopia, all signage, in every region and every city, is printed using the same alphabet. Even more curious, in every example illustrated in Gurney's books, where a sign or scroll is depicted in the Dinotopian alphabet, translating these letters into roman script reveals that these messages are all written in standard English, a language that does not appear to be much used in the nation. Thus, while only a handful of dinosaurs can "speak" English, every one of them appears to be able to read it.

References: Dinotopia. Directed by Marco Brambilla. Screenplay by Simon Moore. DVD 2002; *Dinotopia: The Series.* Various directors and screenplay authors. Broadcast 2002. DVD 2004; Gurney, James. *Dinotopia.* Atlanta: Turner, 1992; Gurney, James. *Dinotopia: The World Beneath.* Atlanta: Turner, 1995.

The Dispossessed

Subtitled "An Ambiguous Utopia," Ursula K. Le Guin's 1974 novel dramatizes the cultural and ideological differences between two estranged worlds: Urras, a multinational, capitalist patriarchy, and its moon, Anarres, given in a past settlement to anarchist dissidents, now a poor, isolationist, and troubled sort of socialist environment.

Citizens of Anarres speak **Pravic**, a language constructed on antiauthoritarian principles. (Clearly its designers have bought into the Whorf–Sapir hypothesis wholesale, and Pravic bears interesting comparison to the socializing languages of *Utopia* and *Nineteen Eighty-Four*.) "The flexibility and precision of Pravic lent itself to the creation of vivid metaphors quite unforeseen by its inventors" (289), an observation made when a character is able to express the term "wallowing" by means of a kind of circumlocutory definition, even though there are no animals of any kind on Anarres. Metaphorical though it may be, this programmatic language also includes notable conceptual guidelines and strictures. Odonians—the unanimously held political creed of Anarres is named after its founder, Odo—reject "egoizing" and "propertarian" ideals; their bitterest insult is the term "profiteer." They espouse sharing and equality in all social exchanges. Accordingly, "singular forms of the possessive pronoun in Pravic were used mostly for emphasis; idiom avoided them. Little children might say 'my mother,' but very soon they learned to say 'the mother.' Instead of 'my hand hurts,' it was 'the hand hurts me,' and so on" (51). There are no official titles on Anarres, and *ammar* ("brother" or "sister") is the equivalent of an all-purpose appellation, like "comrade." Pravic lacks "any proprietorial idioms for the sexual act. . . . The word which came closest in meaning to 'fuck,' and had a similar usage as a curse, was specific: it meant rape. The usual verb, taking only a plural subject, can be translated only by a neutral word like copulate" (47). The word for work is the same word for play, though there are distinctive pejoratives for drudgery (*kleggich*) and for drifters who do not cooperate with the system of job rotations (*nuchnibi*, rendered in the singular as *nuchnib*). Pravic does apparently have a few unorthodox borrowed words from its oldest speakers' previous home world, such as "bet" and "hell" (a synonym for Urras), but because Odonians do not accept any spiritual or religious tenets and so do not believe in blasphemy, Pravic is "not a good swearing language" (225).

Language on Urras is a very different affair, divided as it is into nations and classes. **Iotic**, language of the powerful nation A-Io, has, in the eyes of Shevek, the novel's Odonian protagonist, a grammar that is "complex, illogical, and patterned" (94). Shevek is forced to learn Iotic so that he can write his scientific articles for journals and scientists on Urras; it is thus a language of official business and scholarship.

Iotic has an interesting alternative dialect, **Niotic**, used by the working classes, "as if the 'Nioti,' as they called themselves, did not want to be understood by outsiders" (169). A Nioti character named Efor makes pronouncements like "I make room set this tray down here" (169) and "Try manage things like you want sir without troubling for orders" (170). Shevek notes that this is "the verbal mode of the Nioti, past and future rammed into one highly charged, unstable present tense" (176). Just as Iotic is the language of, for example, scientific journals, Niotic is used by the "birdseed papers," the tabloid-style media deplored by the ruling classes and in which "spelling and grammar fell by the wayside" (176). Given the novel's historical context (specifically the cold war, but also its moment in the history of feminist thought and struggle), it makes some sense to read A-Io and its antagonist nation, Thu, as mirror images of the United States and the Soviet Union, respectively. Insofar as such a correspondence holds, it may be supposed that Niotic is a fictional metonym for a kind of pidgin English: there are times in the novel when Efor's dialogue sounds very like many other fictional renderings of African American speech (e.g., "They say, 'Old building, been a hospital six hundred years.' Stablishment of the Divine Harmony for the Poor, its name. An asshole what it is" [247]).

The languages of the other nations of Urras are not described, and the information about Pravic, Iotic, and Niotic is confined to the conceptual sort outlined here.

Reference: Le Guin, Ursula K. *The Dispossessed*. New York: Harper and Row, 1974.

A Door Into Ocean

Conflict opens between the peaceful inhabitants of the watery moon Shora and the imperial forces of a legendary "Patriarch" in Joan Slonczewski's 1986 science-fiction novel. Spinel, a young man from the planet Valedon, visits Shora as a kind of apprentice as the two different cultures uneasily seek mutual understanding.

Spinel is used to working with stone as a commercial trade and speaks **Valan** (a completely undescribed language). The alien people of Shora, called Sharers, are without exception female and generally reject inorganic matter such as stone in favor of water and life. Sharer speech, sometimes simply called **Sharer**, reflects their philosophy of free exchange and holistic interdependence, and both this language and the emphasis on "sharing" puzzle the various people who serve the Patriarch. One character who is hostile to the Sharers refers scornfully to "that cat's tongue they call a language" and adds, "with what passes for 'verbs,' you never know who's doing what to whom" (194). (It should probably not be inferred from this that Sharer speech sounds anything like a cat: "catfish" is a derogatory slur for Sharers.) In learning the language, Spinel is flummoxed by the reciprocal, inherently reflexive nature of Sharer vocabulary. For example, "wordsharing" is the word for speaking as well as for listening, and one meaning cannot be separated from the other. "Do you say 'hitsharing,' too?" asks Spinel in frustration.

"If I hit a rock with a chisel, does the rock hit me?" His teacher asks him whether he does not in fact feel it in his arm (34). There are no examples of Sharer in the text of the novel apart from these kinds of translated "-sharing" compounds.

Sharers have an interesting way of communicating across the endless ocean that separates each raft-bound community. A species of insect known as a clickfly is used to pass messages from group to group. The "colored ribs behind its head" tell the receiver where the clickfly comes from, and its "sound-scraper mandibles" click out the message (204). The novel does not make it clear what kind of code the clickfly's "perverse noises" are (34), nor are the history and full implications of this interspecies relationship revealed. In one scene, a Sharer is said to have "interpreted" a clickfly message with a little difficulty "because the code was in an unaccustomed dialect" (204). Whether there are Sharer dialects is unknown.

A Door Into Ocean mentions other planets and cultures, all either under the banner of the Patriarch or else destroyed by him, but few by name. Spinel finds out that there was once a planet "where they talk in birdsong" (i.e., whistled phrases), but it was presumably annihilated (140–141).

Reference: Slonczewski, Joan. *A Door Into Ocean.* New York: Arbor House, 1986.

Downward to the Earth

Robert Silverberg's 1977 science-fiction novel *Downward to the Earth* is both an investigation of spirituality (its title is taken from Ecclesiastes) and a loose retelling of Joseph Conrad's *Heart of Darkness* (featuring, for example, a tall and corrupt character named Kurtz who "goes native," a race of elephant-like creatures, and a journey through a tropical landscape in search of an earthly "agent" who needs to be retrieved). The narrative of the novel concerns a former colonist who returns to Holman's World (now known by its native name, Belzagor) to atone for his treatment of the intelligent inhabitants of that planet, the Nildoror. The Nildoror (singular: Nildor) resemble elephants, appear to have a near-Buddhist ideology, and possess a distinct language, **nildororu**.

Nildororu is an agglutinated language (words constructed by joining morphemes together) with a simple grammar. To human ears the language sounds like an unbroken nasal lowing. There is also a gestural element to the language that creates tone and other verbal subtleties. The most significant nildororu word given in the novel is *g'rakh*, which roughly translates as "soul," but the color of the language is also indicated by names and other proper nouns, such as the individual *Srin'gahar* or the Nildoror pronunciation of their planet as *Blls'grrr*.

The Nildoror also possess an ancient language used for liturgical purposes (analogous to Latin), but no examples of this obsolete language are given in the course of the novel.

Reference: Silverberg, Robert. *Downward to the Earth.* London: Victor Gollancz, 1977.

The Dragonbone Chair

The Dragonbone Chair (1988) is the first book of Tad Williams's fantasy trilogy, *Memory, Sorrow and Thorn*; the subsequent volumes are *Stone of Farewell* (1990) and

To Green Angel Tower (1993). Clearly inspired by as well as plotted and structured very like *The Lord of the Rings*, these novels are set in the lands of Osten Ard, populated by various tribes of men, such as Erkynlanders, Hernystiri, Rimmersmen, and Nabbanai, as well as Sithi (elves) and Yiquanic (trolls). The distinguishing traditions and beliefs of these factions are reminiscent of those of the peoples of medieval Europe and England in particular: the Rimmersmen are unmistakably Viking-like, the Hernystiri represent the Celts, the Erkynlanders the Anglo-Saxons, and so on. This parallel extends—to a limited degree, for unlike Tolkien, Williams is not a linguist—to their respective languages.

Erkynlandish is effectively the default language of *The Dragonbone Chair*: the reader understands that the dialogue presented in English signifies Erkynlandish, though this translation probably ought to be understood as nothing more than a modernization, in the manner that Old and Middle English texts may be carried into Modern English. The appendix's references to "Old Erkynlandish" and many easily recognizable elements of quotidian vocabulary, such as the months of the year (Jonever, Feyever, Marris, Avrel, and so on) and days of the week (Sunday, Moonday, Tiasday, and so on), support this interpretation. **Old Erkynlandish** is distinct from **Warinstenner**, a dialect that has presumably been imported from the island of Warinsten by one of its native sons, the High King of Osten Ard, John Presbyter (a.k.a. Prester John). This difference is evident in character names: according to the novel's appendix, Warinstenner names are "represented as variants on Biblical names (Elias—Elijah, Ebekah—Rebecca, etc.)," while Old Erkynlandish names have, with a few minor differences, Modern English pronunciations (778).

Rimmersmen speak **Rimmerspakk**, which has some longer vowels than Old Erkynlandish but is otherwise pronounced the same way and generally seems somewhat like Old Norse (and/or proto-Germanic). Only once in *The Dragonbone Chair* does Rimmerspakk dialogue appear untranslated (313), when one character asks, *Vawer es do kunde?* (the appendix renders this as "who is this child?" [782], but with the last word of the phrase spelled *ükunde*, possibly an error), and another answers, *Im tosdten-grukker* ("a grave-robber"; again there is a discrepancy: *todsten-grukker* [782]). One villainous character is said to speak "Black Rimmerspakk" (624), but it is not clear to what extent (if any) or how this variant differs from Rimmerspakk proper.

Hernystiri names and words share more or less the same pronunciation as Old Erkynlandish, though one of the exceptions—*ch* is "a guttural, as in Scottish 'loch' (779)—points to the mimetic source: just as Erkynlandish is a fictional reflection of English (ca. the tenth century), Hernystiri is a kind of fictional Gaelic. The novel contains only a few examples of untranslated Hernystiri dialogue. For example, the term *Feir* means "brother" or "comrade," and the phrase *E gundhain sluith, ma connalben* may be translated as "we fought well, my dear one" (781).

Once this medieval Europe analogy is identified, it comes as no surprise to read that the **Nabbanai** language "holds basically to the rules of a romance language" (779), for the Nabbanai people, who often have dark features and are said to have once had a great empire, are suggestive of Italians and/or Greeks. Their language is accordingly Latin-like: utterances like *Timior cuelos exaltat mei* ("Fear of death lift me"), *Oveiz mei* ("Hear me"), and *Aedonis Fiyellis extulanin mei* ("Faithful Aedon [God] save me") are illustrative (781). The "droning speech of Nabban" is synonymous with "the busy tongue of Mother Church and her Aedonite priests" (50), a religion that bears more than passing similarity to Christianity.

The analogy outlined above does not, it seems, extend to the languages of nonhuman characters. The mysterious Sithi, fairy folk who have little love for humans since the latter long ago drove them out of their lands, speak a language characterized as musical and "liquid" (628). *Sithi* is in fact a Hernystiri coinage, meaning "Peaceful Ones"; the Sithi know themselves as *Zida'ya*, "Children of Dawn" (783). The language known as **Sithi** (what the Sithi themselves call it is not revealed) is "virtually unpronounceable by untrained tongues" and includes clicking sounds (designated in the phonetic spellings with an apostrophe), which, the novel's appendix advises, "should not be voiced by mortal readers" (780). As this warning suggests, this language shares the vaguely mystical and dangerous qualities that are attributed to its speakers. Examples of Sithi words and phrases, which are few and infrequent in the text, include *Ine* ("it is"), *Skei'* ("stop"), *Sudhoda'ya* ("Sunset-children," the term for mortals), and *T'si im T'si* ("Blood for blood" [783]). The name of the arch-villain of the trilogy, Ineluki, is Sithi and means "here is bright speech" (533).

Qanuc, the language of the trolls, seems to be as rich in mordant proverbs as its speakers are superstitious. *Ko muhuhok na mik aqa nop*, for example, may be translated as "when it falls on your head, then you know it's a rock," and *Bhojujik mo qunquc* means "if the bears don't eat you, it's home" (782). Williams's notes on Qanuc pronunciation suggest that the *q* is consonantly equivalent to a *c* or a *k* except for "a slight clucking sound on the q" that "is not to be encouraged in beginners" (780); the *u* sounds as does a short *u* in English. Binabik, the novel's principal troll, has an interesting habit in his Westerling speech that may suggest a quality of Qanuc syntax. He consistently and wordily employs the continuous present tense, usually with the auxiliary verb "to be": for example, "this is being an example" (266). The enigmatic swear word *Kikkasut* (371) is not translated in the novel.

The novel's appendix includes notes on pronunciation and glossaries for select words and phrases for all of the languages named above, but there are a few loose ends and mysteries. Mentioned in passing are **Perdruinese** and **Harcha-tongue**, "Naraxi's rolling island speech" and "the singsong cadences of the Thrithings-men" (49–50), but nothing more tangible is revealed about any of these. Giants are described as "snarling their incomprehensible language" (757), without subsequent elaboration.

Reference: Williams, Tad. *The Dragonbone Chair*. New York: DAW Books, 1988.

The Dramaturges of Yan

John Brunner's 1972 science-fiction novel deals with the interactions between a small enclave of humans living among the natives of the planet Yan at an unspecified future date. The Yanfolk, a humanoid race, appear to have once had an extremely advanced civilization but throughout most of the novel live a simple, yet contented, existence in the shadows of gigantic monuments and appear quite uninterested in their eleven-volume literary masterwork, the *Mutine Epics*.

The difficulty that Marc Simon, a human fascinated with this alien culture, has in translating the *Epics* suggests the complexity of **Yannish**. While little detail is given of the language within the novel, various passages suggest the specificity of language use among the Yanfolk, such as when one responds to a human in the negative: "The word was far more forcible. It was in the philosophical negative mode, the mode of absolute denial reserved for such statements as universal categorical nulls" (110).

Beyond this evidence, readers are left with little sense of Yannish—including whether its script is alphabetic or pictographic—and less than a dozen words of vocabulary are provided in the novel. Some of the lexicon given include *elgadrin* ("one who speaks for" [43], or a representative), *heyk* and *welwa* (items of Yannish clothing), and *hrath* (an adjective used to describe one of the dominant class, or an "optimal" individual).

As the Yanfolk are a race that is able to enter into a collective consciousness, the Yannish word *shrimashey* is important in the novel as this single word signifies both as the name of the drug taken to induce this state and the ritual in which it is consumed and a communal consciousness is achieved.

Reference: Brunner, John. *The Dramaturges of Yan.* New York: Ace, 1972.

Dune

Before the popularity of *Star Wars* and *Star Trek*, Frank Herbert's *Dune* series was regarded as the closest science-fiction equivalent to *The Lord of the Rings*—a complete and detailed fictional universe to itself, featuring alternative histories, genealogies, and, of course, languages. Yet, rather than postulate new and invented languages, Herbert's novel implies that the core human languages merely evolve into new configurations over 8,000 years.

Although clearly belonging to the genre of science fiction, the action in *Dune* is based primarily on political intrigue and diplomacy, rather than battles or encounters with alien races, as is common in most "space opera" narratives. In this first novel, interplanetary noble houses vie for the control of the planet Arrakis, known conventionally as Dune, which is the universe's sole supplier of the spice *melange*, which is necessary for interstellar navigation.

That this spice is called *melange*, French for "mixture," alerts readers to the fact that "ancient" human languages are still in use (members of House Harkonnen also refer to each other with such endearments as *cher*). The sisterhood of the Bene Gesserit, responsible for training select women in almost superhuman mental and physical abilities, also routinely use Latin terms for their enterprises, such as the *missionaria protectiva* and the *panoplia propheticus*. Traces of many other languages can also be found throughout the novel, such as Hebrew (*kwisatz haderach* in the novel signifies a "shortening of the way" but is Hebrew for "jump ahead of the path") and Greek.

The lingua franca of all the Houses, however, is known as **Galach** (suggesting a phonetic modification of "galactic"), which claims to be "Hybrid Ingo-Slavic with strong traces of cultural-specialization terms adopted during the long chain of human migrations" (Herbert 1965, 518). Thus, like Anthony Burgess's **nadsat** from *A Clockwork Orange*, many of the untranslated Galach words appear to be Russian-based.

Here, a feud between houses is known as *kanly* (Islamic-Russian for "there is blood between us that is not revenged"), and other terms have Slavic-sounding roots, such as *chaumurky* (poison drink) or *chaumas* (poison food). The entry on Galach in *The Dune Encyclopedia* (1984) provides extremely detailed lists of sonic and morphological changes between Old to Early to Middle to Late Galach but does not provide a history of the language, nor an extensive lexicon. Galach is also the universal language in two of Herbert's other science-fiction novels, *The Whipping Star* (1970) and *The Dosadi Experiment* (1977).

Each noble house has its own language, and for the purposes of combat, many houses have also created **battle languages**: "any special language of restricted etymology developed for clear-speech communication in warfare" (Herbert 1965, 514).

The desert-dwelling inhabitants of Arrakis, the Fremen, speak a combination of two languages. The first, **Fremen**, derives directly from Arabic with many words surviving unmodified or with slight variation, such as *jihad* (holy war), *hajj* (pilgrimage), *kindjal* ("a knife," from the Arabic *khinjar*: "dagger"), and *usul* ("base of the pillar" in Freman, "principles" in Arabic). *The Dune Encyclopedia* entries on Fremen, by John Quijada and Alan S. Kaye, provide an extensive history of the development of the Fremen language, a list of its Arabic roots, and an alphabet (by Quijada, reproduced below). Khalid Baheyeldin has also written an excellent online source of Arabic and Islamic elements of Herbert's text with a focus on the Fremen.

For more ritualistic and military purposes, the Fremen utilize a language known as **Chakobsa**. This language is a dialect of an older, more formal language, **Bhotani**, that is not explored in Herbert's novel. More accurately, Chakobsa is a Bhotani-*jib*, with *jib* signifying a professional or trade-based jargon or cant. Chakobsa thus derives from the secret language of Bhotani assassins, suggesting that the Fremen descend from a ruthless and skilled warrior community. An example of Chakobsa from the novel, *cignoro hrobosa sukares hin mange la pchagavas doi me kamavas na beslas lele pal hrobas*, translates as "perhaps these are the strangers we are looking for" (Herbert 1965, 278). Unlike Fremen or Galach, finding the root languages here is more

The script of the Fremen people of Dune, created by John Quijada, suggests an Arabic origin. From *The Dune Encyclopedia* by Willis Everett McNelly, copyright © 1984 by Dr. Willis Everett McNelly. Used by permission of Berkley Publishing Group, a division of Penguin Group (USA) Inc.

difficult, although as in Esperanto there appear to be elements of many languages combined, including French, Spanish, and Roma.

Dune also contains a number of other languages, described but not detailed, that relate to diplomatic intrigue, such as Atreidean hand signals and a language of humming employed by some members of the House of Corrino that allows them to communicate privately during public functions.

While some additional elements of Galach and Fremen can be found in Herbert's sequels to *Dune* (*Dune Messiah, Children of Dune, God Emperor of Dune, Heretics of Dune,* and *Chapterhouse Dune*) and the numerous prequels authored by his son Brian, the essential elements of the Dune languages are all found in Herbert's first novel of the series. The cinematic versions of the book, David Lynch's *Dune* and the made-for-television series by John Harrison, give some indication of the sound of these languages, and the written scripts, particularly Galach, can be viewed in the background of some scenes.

References: Baheyeldin, Khalid. The Baheyeldin Dynasty: http://baheyeldin.com/literature/arabic-and-islamic-themes-in-frank-herberts-dune.html; *Dune.* Directed by David Lynch. Screenplay by David Lynch. DVD 1984; *Dune.* Directed by John Harrison. Screenplay by John Harrison. DVD 2000; Herbert, Frank. *The Dosadi Experiment.* New York: Putnam, 1977; Herbert, Frank. *Dune.* New York: Berkley, 1965; Herbert, Frank. *The Whipping Star.* New York: Putnam, 1970; McNelly, Willis E. *The Dune Encyclopedia.* New York: Putnam, 1984.

A Dweller on Two Planets

One of the more esoteric items in American arcana, *A Dweller on Two Planets* was first published in 1905, half a dozen years after the death of the young man who had written it but claimed not to be its author. Frederick S. Oliver contended that he was merely the amanuensis of a spirit named Phyllos the Thibetan (otherwise known as Yol Gorro), who dictated the book to him. Not surprisingly, the book is rather hard to categorize. By turns utopian fiction, spiritual-political manifesto, and New Age sourcebook (Shirley MacLaine is counted among its proponents), *A Dweller on Two Planets* describes the culture and civilization of Atlantis of several thousand years ago, with an implicit comparison with contemporary America, while it also maps out a "dividing of the way" (as the subtitle has it), essentially a strange prescriptive blend of religious ideas and doctrines.

The text offers some samples and a prefatory glossary of the **Atlantean** or **Poseid** language (whence comes this second [anachronistic] Greek name is not explained; the language is also referred to as **Atlan**). The degree of clarity varies in the translated definitions. Words such as *Astika, Incal,* and *Xioqene,* for example, are concrete nouns, "a prince," "the Supreme God," and "science student," respectively, but whereas currency like the Poseid gold coin the *Teka* is very precisely measured in "value about $2.67," an abstract term like *Maxin* is vaguely translated as "the Unfed Light" (11). A note to the glossary asks readers to "please remember" that suffixes of nouns designate number and gender: "the singular was indicated by the equivalent for 'a,' the plural by 'i,' feminine by 'u,' while the absence of this terminal indicated masculinity" (11). One of the only Atlantean phrases in the text is from a funeral oration for the Emperor (*Rai*)

Gwauxln, *Rai ni Incal, mo navazzamindi su*, which is translated as "To Incal the Rai; to the country of departed souls he is gone!" (161). Although the name *Gwaulxn* is said to be pronounced "Wallun," the text does not offer guidance on any other matters of pronunciation.

A few samples of "Poseid chirography" are provided: the numeral for two; an inscription on a vase that reads "To Ernon, Rai of Suern, I, Gwauxln, Rai of Poseid, return this in token of thy appreciation of the Posedi" (141); and the signature of Phylos the Thibetan (423).

The narrator of the first book of *A Dweller on Two Planets* also claims to be a student of other fantastical languages—he names the **Suerni** and **Necropanic** languages (59)—but nothing specific is said of them.

Reference: Oliver, Frederick Spencer. *A Dweller on Two Planets, or The Dividing of the Way, by Phylos the Thibetan.* Blauvelt, NY: Multimedia Publishing Group, 1974.

E

Earth: Final Conflict

The language spoken by the Taelon alien race in the science-fiction television program *Earth: Final Conflict* was created by Canadian poet Christian Bök in 1997 for Atlantis Productions. This series, concerning the arrival on Earth of a benevolent alien species during the early twenty-first century, was produced from notes left by the late Gene Roddenberry (the inventor of *Star Trek*) and was broadcast for five seasons.

The Taelons do not have a name for their language, as they believe that they are merely the hosts for a linguistic entity; that is, language speaks through them and is actualized in speaking rather than being viewed as a tool for communication. Named **Eunoia** by Bök, this language, unlike many artificial languages that generally follow the conventions of English syntax, was conceived as an absolutely alien expression with few recognizable cognates—"there are no nominate nouns, no transitive verbs" (70)—for example. Rather "sentences" are constructed by synthesizing noun and verb relations (a "nounverb" or "trait in action"). As the Taelons are conceived of as interstellar Buddhists, their language has no tense but the present and cannot express contrary positions (i.e., both the concept and its antonym exist simultaneously; "war" and "peace" are the same word, or at least both concepts are implicit within the word). The Taelon lexicon consists of "words" composed mostly of vowels, incorporating breath and aspiration, with occasional consonants; *sinaüi ëuhura* (pronounced "shee-nha-wheeee, yhoo-hurr-rha") translates as "we come in peace" (which also implies "we arrive fiercely"), while *ëeve ne-üevama* suggests "later, full of caring."

Bök has also titled a collection of his poetry *Eunoia* (Greek for "beautiful thinking"), but it bears little relation to his artificial language of the same name.

References: Bök, Christian. "The Alien Argot of the Avant-Garde." *Cabinet* 1 (2000): 70–71; *Earth: Final Conflict*. Atlantis Production, 1997–2002.

EggHeads

Emily Devenport's *EggHeads* is an awkwardly-paced science-fiction romance novel with a convoluted plot which includes the protagonist teaching her male partner to make love more gently. Beyond its sophomoric sex scenes, *EggHeads* recounts the adventures of a mercenary hired to locate the ruins of an ancient civilization known as the Earlies who have left evidence of their existence on numerous planets throughout the galaxy. Most valuable are the Early glyphs which are so densely packed with unknown technological advances that any race (of which there are several in the novel) who attains them will gain immense advantage and power over the others.

Most of the characters of various races in the novel speak **Standard** (presumably English) as well as having their own tongues and dialects. The giant race known as the X'GBri speak in a booming, or else subsonic, rumble, while the Vorn, insect-like beings, communicate in their own tongue through singing (by vibrating their carapaces) as well as through gesture or flight-pattern.

No account is given of the Early spoken language, but its written form appears to be kinetic. That is, Early glyphs move and change significance as the viewer approaches or apprehends them. A human linguist provides an example of this mutable writing when describing a glyph that signifies "information": "it looks like some sort of amphibian. When you first approach it, it's in the egg stage, and it progresses all the way to an adult stage as you get closer—then it shifts back again" (141). Devenport also makes William S. Burroughs's metaphoric concept of the "language virus" literal by depicting some glyphs which actually change the consciousness of those who read it, providing this recipient with new languages, skills, and knowledge instantaneously.

Reference: Devenport, Emily. *EggHeads*. New York: ROC, 1996.

The Embedding

Ian Watson's first novel is a fascinating exploration of applied linguistics to the science-fiction genre. Similar to Jack Vance's conscientious use of the Sapir–Whorf theory in *The Languages of Pao*, here Watson applies Noam Chomsky's theories of generative grammar to speculative fiction. Yet there are several languages and linguistic elements interrogated in the course of Watson's novel.

For example, an anthropologist in *The Embedding* encounters and attempts to describe the language of an Amazonian tribe known as the Xemahoa. This Brazilian culture has two forms of language, which the scientist categorizes as **Xemahoa A** and **Xemahoa B**. The first of these is the daily language of the Xemahoa and is relatively complex. Some vocabulary provided in the novel include *caraiba* (outsider), *bruxo* (chief), and *maka-i* (a sacred hallucinogen), but Watson also creates several unique linguistic characteristics of this tribe. For example, rather than having names for numbers (e.g., one, two, three), the Xemahoa use other nouns that have a quality that reflects that number (e.g., the name of a certain bird indicates a specific number based on the fact that the bird has that number of feathers). Another oddity is the use of tense, which is generated through the intensifier *yi*. In Xemahoa, one begins with a present-tense verb and then follows it with *yi* to indicate now, *yi-yi* to suggest the future, and *yi-yi-yi* to indicate the far future. Because of this sense of time, which is immediate and concrete, the Xemahoa language also has an elaborate vocabulary for sexual acts and processes: "the stages of orgasm in their love speech would have enchanted Wilhelm Reich. They can express the whole range from this microtime of orgasm, through the stages of embedding of the foetus in the womb" (75).

Xemahoa B sounds like babble to the anthropologist until he realizes that Xemahoa B is the language spoken by a *bruxo* under the influence of the drug *maka-i* and listened to by an audience that has also taken *maka-i*. Xemahoa B is a deeply embedded language with digressions and linguistic subroutines that cannot be grasped under normal circumstances, yet with the help of the drug, both the shaman and people can understand this convoluted utterance. It is used to recount deep myths and sacred concepts, and Watson suggests that this is a **Cratylean language** in which signifiers relate directly to signifieds:

> This embedded speech keeps the soul of the tribe, their myths, secret. But it also permits the Xemahoa to participate in their myth life *as a direct experience* during the dance chant. The daily vernacular (Xemahoa A) passes through an extremely sophisticated recoding process, which breaks down the linear features of normal language and returns the Xemahoa people to the space-time unity which we other human beings have blinded ourselves to. For our languages all set a barrier—a great filter—up for us between Reality and our Idea of Reality. (103; emphasis in original)

This is but one indication of the significance of the novel's title. A second trajectory explored in *The Embedding* is related to work of the surrealist and Oulipian writer Raymond Roussel. Chris Soles, a friend of the anthropologist, works as a linguist and has become deeply affronted by Roussel's long poem *New Impressions of Africa* (1932). This text, which took Roussel nineteen years to compose, consists of four primary cantos of less than ten lines, but within those lines are multiple embedded and parenthetical verses (as many as five embeddings—i.e., "(((((()))))") as well as numerous footnotes, making some individual cantos more than 600 lines long. Throughout the poem, even in the parenthetical sections, Roussel continues to utilize rhyme and alexandrine rhythm.

Annoyed at the arrogance of Roussel's enterprise, Soles experiments linguistically on juveniles in isolation, raising these feral children to speak an embedded form of syntax in English that Soles calls **Roussel Speech** and which would allow these children to comprehend and explain the multiply embedded phrases of *New Impressions of Africa*. However, clearly supporting Chomsky's theories of innate grammar, Watson demonstrates how this process drives these children insane—humans, it seems, are biologically and neurologically wired with deep linguistic structures that cannot be reprogrammed without causing psychosis.

These two storylines are linked through the arrival of extraterrestrial linguists known as the Sp'thra. Their language, also known as **Sp'thra**, is described as having a vast tonal range, including ultra- and infrasonic components (which are dropped where the apostrophe falls when speaking with humans), and their name literally translates as "signal traders." The Sp'thra travel the universe collecting language in all its forms in order to discover, by comparison and superimposition, a template for a universal language (or universal grammar, rather than an individual generative grammar) that would—again in an Idealist or Cratylean fashion—transcend perceived reality and access the universe without the mediation of representational language. This would allow them, the Sp'thra believe, to apprehend and communicate with pararealities in an act that they also refer to as an embedding. On Earth they wish to collect the brains of six different linguistic groups (in exchange for technological advancements) and are particularly interested in the embedded language of the Xemahoa.

Other languages are also mentioned by Watson in the course of the novel, such as **Gruebleen** (a sort of "Jabberwocky" language in which "grue" suggests something examined that is green or else not blue) and **Cetacean** (the language of dolphins and whales), but neither are explored in any detail.

Watson has written critically about several of the issues raised in *The Embedding* in a lecture, "Towards an Alien Linguistics." In it Watson argues that the importance of considering alien linguistics rests in the fact that as humans evolve, language will evolve, and there is a need to speculate about what might happen to a future humanity through language. Moreover, like an interstellar Lacan, Watson suggests that the universe is structured like a language, and that by understanding the underpinnings of human (both present and future) and alien language, one can begin to understand how the universe functions and "knows itself": "a topological grammar of the universe . . . reflects itself in the grammars of actual language" (58). This heady premise is summarized by Watson:

> we must be prepared to entertain the idea of a self-creating, self-examining cosmos, in which life is somehow involved in the very processes which bring it into being in the first place; and that the nature of life's involvement is, in the broadest sense, a linguistic one: its double role of message, and observer or messenger. Since language evolves, we must also entertain the idea that structural evolution of language is to some extent determined by the demands of this participatory role. (60)

Two other Watson short stories regarding artificial languages that are of interest are "The False Braille Catalogue" and "The Love Song of Johnny Alienson." In the former, Watson speculates about the possibility of developing a language that "would seem to say one thing while really saying another: one whose sounds, or shapes, would contradict the semantics" (64). As an example, Watson provides the example of Mallarmé's claim that *jour* sounds "dark" while *nuit* suggests "light."

The second story deals with how humans and aliens could learn each other's languages, faced with the problem that the alien's generative grammar would be fundamentally different than the human's. Watson's solution is to have children raised in alien communities so that their verbal patterning accepts both alien and human grammatical structures.

References: Watson, Ian. *The Embedding*. London: Victor Gollancz, 1973; Watson, Ian. "The False Braille Catalogue." *The Book of Ian Watson*. Willimantic, CT: Ziesing, 1985. 62–77; Watson, Ian. "The Love Song of Johnny Alienson." *The Book of Ian Watson*. Willimantic, CT: Ziesing, 1985. 78–88; Watson, Ian. "Towards an Alien Linguistics." *The Book of Ian Watson*. Willimantic, CT: Ziesing, 1985. 43–61.

"Enemy Mine"

Barry Longyear's short story "Enemy Mine," a thinly veiled depiction of the conflict between the United States and Vietnam, presents humans engaged in an interplanetary territorial war with a philosophical reptilian race known as the Dracs. When the narrator of this story, a fighter pilot named Willis Davidge, is stranded on an uninhabited and hostile planet with a Drac soldier, they become friends in their collective struggle for survival, with Davidge eventually assuming responsibility for the upbringing of the Drac's child.

Despite the fact that much of the story involves the learning of the **Drac** language, and a fair amount of the Drac lexicon is included in the tale, the language in this narrative is not particularly "alien." Indeed, Drac does not appear to differ significantly from many human languages in its grammatical structure, phonetics, or conjugation, and it seems a mere replacement of signifiers, rather than a unique language to itself. For example, many words appear to be slight variations of recognizable English words: the Drac *Irkmaan* is "Earthman" while its affirmative, *ae*, resembles "aye." A similar case might be made for French with the Drac negative being *ne*.

Notwithstanding the fact that there often appears to be a logic to the grammatical order of words and sounds—for example, *je* is "to teach," *jetah* "teacher," and *jetai* "teachers"—there are also numerous inconsistencies. While it might follow that since *vo* is "town" *vu* would be "city," there is no explanation given for why *vul* would thereby signify "one who loves perversely" (Is it merely "luv" spelled backwards?).

While this lack of grammatical consistency may be found in many human languages (and this may be Longyear's point), the logic and derivation of this language in the narrative appears to be more of a personal quirk of Longyear's (particularly in the case of *vul* above) than a rigorous linguistic system, and most exchanges require little mental effort on the part of the reader as they convey little sense of linguistic difference between these two cultures—for example, "[The Drac] pointed at its own chest. '*Kos va son* Jeriba Shigan.' It pointed again at me. '*Kos son va?*'" (113).

This short story, along with two book-length sequels, was collected in 1998 as *The Enemy Papers*. Also included in this edition is a Drac-English dictionary and an essay by Longyear recounting the development of language in his fiction, "On Alien Languages." Besides noting his admiration for *The Day the Earth Stood Still* for its use of an untranslated alien language, Longyear offers the following recommendation on the use of alien languages in fiction: "alien languages, as well as alien names, need to be understood and used by humans. . . . Movies can get away with a bunch of squeaks, glottal stops, clicks, grunts and whistles. . . . In print, however, names need to be remembered, and the alien words that appear at least need to be gotten through, if not understood and remembered" (631).

In 1985, "Enemy Mine" was also made into a popular film, which features the Drac language prominently as performed by actor Louis Gossett, Jr.

References: Longyear, Barry B. *The Enemy Papers*. Clarkson, GA: White Wolf, 1998; *Enemy Mine*. Directed by Wolfgang Petersen. Screenplay by Edward Khmara. DVD 1985.

"Enoch Soames"

In Max Beerbohm's classic 1912 short story, a failed Symbolist/Decadent poet sells his soul to the devil in exchange for being able to travel 100 years into the future (to June 3, 1997) in order to see what critical work has been written on him in the intervening years. A sly satire of literary fame, literary criticism, reviewing, journalism, science fiction, and tall tales, and featuring a generous amount of self-reflexivity (Beerbohm himself narrates and is complicit in Soames's fate), "Enoch Soames" is also a commentary on the decline of the English language. That is, in only 100 years, English has become completely phonetic in its spelling and usage.

This "new" language, which can perhaps be nominated **Inglish**, is a phonetic spelling, like that used by Russell Hoban in *Riddley Walker. For example:

> *Max Beerbohm, hoo woaz stil alive in the twentieth senchri, rote a stauri in wich an immajnari karrakter kauld 'Enoch Soames'—a thurd-rait poit hoo beleevz imself a grate jeneus an maix a bargin with th Devvl in auder ter no wot posterriti thinx o im!* (42)

Reference: Beerbohm, Max. "Enoch Soames." *Seven Men and Two Others*. London: William Heinemann, 1950. 3–51.

Eragon

An extremely derivative young-adult novel, *Eragon* is an overly long amalgam of *The Lord of the Rings and *Star Wars. Featuring elves, dwarves, dragons, and a young protagonist who has a destiny to fulfill by joining a rebellion against a corrupt empire (all the while aided by a wise old man and a short-tempered mercenary), this novel (the first of a projected trilogy known as *Inheritance*) follows the standard fantasy plotline relentlessly.

Three languages are mentioned in the course of *Eragon*, the first being the **Ancient Language**. This is the language of the elves, but it is also the language that is required to perform magic spells, for, following *The Cratylus*, author Christopher Paolini suggests that there are true names for objects and beings—signifiers that relate directly and ideally to signifieds. Thus, in the Ancient Language, there is no distinction between these two terms, and knowing the true name of objects gives one magical control over those items.

Paolini has noted that he based the Ancient Language on Old English, and there are a number of similarities, such as *wyrda* for "fate" or the phrase *stenr reisa* ("raise stone"), which is comparable to the Old English *stán* (stone). The author also borrows from French with his *arget* (silver) suggesting *argent* (money/silver), but much of this language is based on the sounds of Old English without an extensive or consistent use of grammatical rules. One of the longest sentences given in the Ancient Language is *Atra gülai un ilian tauthr ono un atra ono waíse skölir frá rauthr*, which translates as "Let luck and happiness follow you and may you be shielded from misfortune" (500).

The author also notes that the Ancient Language is runic, and this inscription is shared by the dwarves. The **Dwarf** language is given a less extensive vocabulary than the Ancient Language but also seems Germanic in its sound and structure as in the following: *knurl* ("rock"), *hírna* ("likeness"), and *Tronjheim* ("Helm of Giants").

The least-developed language is that of the orc or ogrelike creatures known as the Urgals. The **Urgal** language, as one might expect, is cacophonic in its sound, as in the words *drajl* ("spawn of maggots") and *ushnark* ("father") or the phrase *Kaz jtierl trazhid! Otrag bagh* ("Do not attack! Circle him") (503).

Reference: Paolini, Christopher. *Eragon.* New York: Knopf, 2003.

Erewhon

Samuel Butler's 1872 satire of utopian societies bears some resemblance to **A Strange Manuscript Found in a Copper Cylinder,* as it presents a civilization that is the inverse of Victorian England. In this case, what appears reversed is the Erewhonian treatment of illness and crime. Here, physical illness is punished with imprisonment and corporeal punishment, whereas the committing of a crime is viewed as an unfortunate circumstance that could happen to any citizen and is treated by the Erewhonian equivalent of a doctor known as a straightener.

Upon discovering Erewhon, the narrator Higgs quickly learns the language, **Erewhonian**, but gives few details of its structure, origins, or phonology beyond the fact that it bears no relation to any European language of which Higgs has knowledge. This leads him to speculate that Erewhonian is based on Hebrew (and that perhaps the Erewhonians are a lost tribe of Israel). However, if the Erewhonian language is anything like its proper nouns, it consists simply of anagrams and reversals of common English words. Hence the society's name, Erewhon, equals "nowhere," and some examples of Erewhonian personal names include Yram ("Mary") and Mr. Senoj Nosnibor ("Mr. Robinson Jones").

The scientists and philosophers of this society, in an striking parallel to Alfred Jarry's concept of 'pataphysics, are employed at the Colleges of Unreason, where they oppose progress and explore "hypoethics" (a philosophy whereby they seek intelligent answers to extremely improbable and fantastical problems). They also study an ancient and highly regarded language that all learned men speak known as the **hypothetical language**. These factors, as well as the fact that the hypothetical language is a "dead" language not commonly spoken by the populace, suggest that this is a parody of the use of Latin in higher education. As Butler writes:

> Thus they are taught what is called the hypothetical language for many
> of their best years—a language which was originally composed at a time
> when the country was in a very different state of civilization to what it
> is at present, a state which has long since disappeared and been super-
> seded. . . . The store they set by this hypothetical language can hardly
> be believed; they will even give any one a maintenance for life if he at-
> tains a considerable proficiency in the study of it; nay, they will spend
> years in learning to translate some of their own good poetry into the

hypothetical language—to do so with fluency being reckoned a distinguishing mark of a scholar and a gentleman. (186)

Reference: Butler, Samuel. *Erewhon*. 1872. London: Penguin, 1985.

Eye of Cat

Because the protagonist of Roger Zelazny's *Eye of Cat*, William Blackhorse Singer,
is Native American, the Navajo language features prominently in this 1982 science-
fiction novel. Singer is a retired hunter of nonsentient aliens (for zoological purposes)
and finds himself hunted by one of his acquisitions, who proves to be intelligent after
all. However, as this shape-shifting alien, known as a Torglind Metamorph, is telepathic, there is no description of this creature's own language. The closest Zelazny
comes to giving readers an insight into the sound or morphology of the language is
through the name of the Metamorph's natural predator, the *krel*. A second intelligent
humanoid race in the novel, the Strageans, make a brief appearance, but again, little
is given regarding the **Stragean** language beyond the fact that "the language of the
Strageans ranged into the ultrasonic on the human scale, and though they narrowed
their focus when speaking Terran tongues there were always some overtones. Too long
a conversation with a Stragean normally resulted in a headache" (35).

Reference: Zelazny, Roger. *Eye of Cat*. New York: Timescape, 1982.

The Eye of the Queen

A pair of human linguists find themselves confronted with a very complex alien
species and culture in Phillip Mann's 1983 novel. One of them, Dr. Marius
Thorndyke, gradually violates all of the central tenets of the "Handbook" that he
helped write for linguists studying extraterrestrials and effectively "goes native" with
his subjects, the Pe-Ellians. Despite the novel's premise and focus, however, the reader
learns remarkably little of the **Pe-Ellian** language, and the language itself seems somewhat redundant since the Pe-Ellians have telepathic abilities. Called "a language of
feeling" (219), Pe-Ellian has a very vaguely described gestural component but no written form. (This absence vexes Thorndyke, but again, the Pe-Ellian telepathic sharing
of thoughts and feelings would make a written literature unnecessary.) "Gesture," according to a preliminary report on Pe-Ellian speech, "seems to provide an emotional
modifier and is rarely, so far as we can judge, independent of the spoken language"
(41). The same report states that pronunciations differ between individual speakers,
though Thorndyke's assistant, Dr. Tomas Mnaba, points out that the authors of the
report were exposed only to "a purely ceremonial tongue" used by the first Pe-Ellian
visitors to Earth, "not used for ordinary communication" and consisting "mainly of
quotations" (41).

Throndyke and Mnaba visit the planet Pe-Ellia in the year 2076 to open communication with these aliens. The chief difficulty lies in the fact that humans are unaware that they are continually "broadcasting" thoughts and feelings and so affecting
the psychic environment about them as well as the dismayed Pe-Ellians themselves.
The Pe-Ellians appreciate the immediate and tangible power of *karit* (paradoxically

described by Thorndyke as "the word the Pe-Ellians use for thought and for which we have no equivalent" [204]); their greatest delicacy is called a *karitsa*, a kind of Pe-Ellian egg that tastes of consciousness itself. Central to the Pe-Ellian life cycle and culture is the attainment of *straan*, a word that Mnaba inadequately translates as "symmetry" (53). *Straan* is, a little more precisely, "the outward and visible sign of inward and spiritual fulfillment" (54).

The linguists' visit coincides with a debate among the Pe-Ellians about whether to continue with their traditional, self-reliant, and essentially incestuous way of life, or to integrate with other cultures and (literally) incorporate new consciousnesses into the so-called "melting pot" (257). Thorndyke is invited to the North, "old Pe-Ellia" (237), where the inhabitants speak "a new language, but with the Pe-Ellian feel to it" (243). The text offers no further elaboration or detail on this other language.

In the course of *The Eye of the Queen*, Throndyke makes mention of some other alien languages he has previously encountered and works he has taken to translating. Among these works are the epic poem the *Seliica* of the Archadians ("Thorndyke's pet name for the dominant race on [the planet] Orchid" [27]), the *Tapista Peru* ("a sequence of hunting songs from the planet Tiger Lily" [27]), the *Lantern Ballads* from the planet Persimmon, and a "collection of ballads and street songs" of "the Woodbinians of the Lethern race" (65–66). Quotations from these (translated) works appear in Thorndyke's diary, though only one excerpt, from the *Seliica* (89–90), appears in the original language.

Reference: Mann, Phillip. *The Eye of the Queen*. New York: Arbor House, 1983.

F

The Faded Sun Trilogy

Republished in an omnibus edition in 2000, C. J. Cherryh's *The Faded Sun Trilogy* comprises *Kesrith* (1978), *Shon'jir* (1978), and *Kutath* (1979). These science fictions concern the troubled interactions of five different species and cultures: humans, regul, mri, dusei, and elee. The first has just defeated the second in war, while the third, a matriarchy of mercenaries who hold honor above all and who did most of the fighting for the regul, have become something of a liability for their former employers. Duncan, the novel's human hero, "goes native" with the mri and leads the survivors of a regul act of genocide on the planet Kesrith to the mri homeworld of Kutath.

Humans in *The Faded Sun Trilogy* speak an entirely undescribed language simply called **Basic** (or even more simply, "human speech"); the beasts called dusei do not have a language, though they do have an empathic relationship with the mri; and the elee, who appear only briefly in the final volume, appear to converse with mri without translation, so it is not certain what language they speak. Regul and mri are the more developed alien cultures here, and both clearly have definite languages.

The regul have very long lifespans and long memories (at least, those few who survive the process of maturation do). A society of traders, their language and etiquette are both highly formal and, in a sense, exactingly honest: though they find strange the human concepts of lying and imagination, they are capable of deceit by indirect means, such as omission. Duncan finds studying the regul language a chore, as he learns the intricacies of a word like *Dag*, which means "favor, please, attention," can also be pronounced "with the timbre of a steam whistle" to mean "honorable" or, more shrilly, "blood" (47). *Dag su-gl'inh-an-ant pru nnugk* translates as "May I have indirect contact with the reverence" and *Dag nuc-ci* as "Favor, sir" (47). These isolated examples are clearly meant to be illustrative of the sycophantic and bureaucratic tendencies of **regul**, dialogue that almost always appears in English translation in the text. The question of regul literacy is somewhat uncertain. Though they do apparently have "an elaborate and intricate written language" (32), with an alphabet different than that used by the humans, the regul strongly prefer aural/oral communication and rely on their perfect memories rather than on external systems of documentation.

In contrast to the regul, mri are nomadic, and their only business with others involves service—that is, being hired out as warriors. There are two mri languages, **mu'ara**, or "the common speech," and **hal'ari**, "the High Speech" (377). The second of these is more esteemed and kept from outsiders (known collectively as *tsi-mri*). Most of the samples of words and phrases in these languages relate to rituals and titles, both of which are very important to mri. For example, the female leader of a group or tribe of mri is correctly called and addressed as *she'pan*; and *Shon'jir*, in the low language, is the Passing ritual (139), chanted at moments of transition for the mri, including deaths. Other mri words that arise in passing include *bu'ina'anein* ("presumptuous" [386–387]), *ka'ani-nla* ("arrogant" [394]), and *eshai'i* ("lack-honor" [63], an insult). Hal'ari has "four words for peace, and none of them meant or imagined what humans hoped for; one of them was sinister: the obliteration of potential threat" (623). The mri appear to have writing, possibly exclusively to record the history of the people (*mri* means "the People"), but *The Faded Sun Trilogy* is not very forthcoming on this aspect of mri culture.

Cherryh's characters both epitomize and themselves place full faith in the Sapir–Whorf linguistic hypothesis: conception is measured linguistically, and vocabulary defines one's actions, capabilities, and limits. A regul character observes, for example, that the mri have no word for "negotiation" and so concludes that the "concept does not exist with them" (667), while the regul, who have no term for "lie" in their language, can only approximate "honest" with *alch*, a business term that translates "evenly balanced" and "mutual benefit" (669).

Reference: Cherryh, C. J. *The Faded Sun Trilogy*. New York: DAW Books, 2000.

The Falls

Best known as a film director, Peter Greenaway has since 1980 been constructing a surreal multimedia project at once more ambitious and altogether stranger than any of his individual films. The extended investigation into the Violent Unknown Event (abbreviated as the VUE) and its bizarre repercussions began with the mock-documentary film *The Falls* and a book of the same name, and today continues to grow at Greenaway's Web site, *The Tulse Luper Suitcases: A Personal History of Uranium*. The film and book are ninety-two biographies, all of whose subjects have last names beginning with the letters FALL; they constitute "a reasonable cross-section of the nineteen million other names" of people listed in a directory compiled by the Committee investigating the VUE (5). Among the mutating effects of the VUE—all of which apparently relate to birds, flight, and water—is the spontaneous creation of ninety-two new languages. Those named in the book include the following (in alphabetical order): **Abcadefghan**; **Agalese**; **Agreet**; **Allow**, "terse and impersonal, full of abbreviations and imperatives as though invented for use on a parade-ground" (28); **Allow-ease**; **Althuese**; **Antoneen**; **Betelgeuse**; **Candoese**; **Capistan**, "a lazy, gentle language, spoken largely from the front of the mouth and requiring unusual amounts of saliva and an above average exposure of the tongue" (28); **Carn-est-aero**; **Carthaginian**, which evidently has a "prime version" (104); **Cathanay**; **Curdine**, "a cursive language that deliberately fosters ambiguities and encourages punning" (14); **Entree**; **Fallaver**, a language that "began and ended" with its one speaker, Agropio Fallaver (42); **Foreignester**, "a bastard language self-consciously devised by musicians" (111); **Glendower**; **Glozel**; **Hapaxlegomena**; **Instantaneous Dekis**, "a language better spoken with a beak than a mouth" (55); **Ipostan**; **Itino Re**; **Maudine**; **Metropolitan Kath-a-ganian**; **Mickel-ease** ("or Mickel," "a language full of alliteration and sudden turns of speed" [100]); **Kantan**, "one of the more popularly spoken of the mutant languages" (47); **Karnash**; **Katan**, the use of which "may or may not explain [the speaker's] nonchalance, his insouciance, and his equivocal grasp on the realities of gravity" (11); **O-Lev-Lit**, called a "primitive VUE language" (45); **Orthocathalian**; **Os-leet-er**, "a plain and rhythmic language suitable for the telling of a steady uncluttered narrative" (122); **Regest**; **Ringer**; **Sackamayer**; **U-thalian**; **Untowards**; and **Vionester**—not to mention various suggestions of regional dialects.

Of these VUE languages only a few are described, and the longest of such accounts are brief, usually fantastic sounding, and almost always without any example of the vocabulary. One exception to this last qualification is Allow: the word *guller* is defined as "those whose attempts to fly had taken place over water. Icarus had been a 'guller'" (22). Betelgeuse, by contrast, is "the language of unlimited vocabulary and rapidly changing grammar and syntax" (47). The Betelgeuse name *Adioner* could at one time "be translated approximately into Italian to mean 'yellow,'" but the meaning of the word changes (perversely reflecting the changes in a relationship between a fluent speaker and a student of the language) to "suggest the concept of yolk," then "embryo," and then "egg" (48). U-thalian has forty-seven different words for water, "each one describing, in less than three syllables, and under 14 letters, various of its states, like its purity, its scarcity, its temperature, weight, salinity, irridescence [*sic*], distance from the sea, height above sea level, colour, rapidity of movement and its age" (51); this characterization is obviously a refashioning of the (wrongheaded) bromide concerning the Eskimo horde of synonyms for "snow." Greenaway's text offers a few tentative, sometimes puzzling comparisons between elements of the VUE languages and real ones: Abcadefghan, for example, "is often used in the preparation of papers on engineering, metallurgy and radiophonics. It is said that Laps and Finns can understand Abcadefghan, which, in itself, is not that profitable since there are few technical-papers written in these languages" (71).

The "VUE gift of tongues and the fragmentation of language" (62) have been studied by a number of the odd characters profiled in *The Falls*, but no clear conclusions seem to have been agreed on. If anything, linguistics looks to have made matters more complicated. Philologist Anteo Fallapsy generates his own language, **Hartileas B**, in the hopes of "furthering communication with other vertebrates, mainly birds and their precursors, the reptiles"; to this end he has "undergone an operation on his tongue in order to reshape the acoustic spaces in his mouth that they might approximately coincide with the proportions of the singing apparatus of the starling" (35). Fallapsy's language has found converts ready for the necessary surgery.

Curious readers should definitely consult the DVD edition of the film as well as the extensive Web site on Greenaway, *The Falls*, and VUE-related matters provided by Chaotic Cinema.

References: The Falls. Directed by Peter Greenaway. Screenplay by Peter Greenaway, 1980; Greenaway, Peter. *The Falls*. Paris: Editions Dis Voir, 1993; see Chaotic Cinema's *The Falls* Web page: http://www .wayney.pwp.blueyonder.co.uk/falls.htm; Peter Greenaway's *The Tulse Luper Suitcases: A Personal History of Uranium*: www.tulselupernetwork.com.

Feersum Endjinn

Sections of Iain M. Banks's 1994 novel are narrated by Bascule the Teller, who writes in his journal in a crude phonetic English very reminiscent of Russell Hoban's *Riddley Walker. This idiosyncratic manner of writing, of which the title of the novel is an example, is not truly a functioning language but does signify the unique character and abilities of Bascule. He explains: "I alwiz felt I woz speshil—juss like evrybodi els—but unlike evrybodi els I got this weerd wirin in mi brane so I cant spel rite, juss ½ 2 do evrythin foneticly. Iss not a problim cos u can put eny old rubish thru practikly anyfin evin a chile's toy computir & get it 2 cum out speld perfictly & gramatisized 2 & evin improvd 2 thi poynt whare yood fink u waz Bill bleedin Shaikspir by thi langwidje" (78).

Reference: Banks, Iain M. *Feersum Endjinn*. London: Orbit, 2002.

The Fifth Element

A space-traveling race known as the Mondoshawans seek to ensure the safety of life in the universe against the periodic rise ("every five thousand years") of an apocalyptic evil in Luc Besson's 1997 film. In the twenty-third century, their weapon, the "fifth element" of the film's title, is a feat of genetic engineering, a "perfect" woman named Leeloo Minai Lekarariba-Laminai-Tchai Ekbat De Sebat, or "Leeloo" for short. She speaks a hurried, fluting, vowel-rich tongue, which Father Vito Cornelius, a member of an order that preserves the teachings of the Mondoshawans (whom such priests name "Guardians"), calls "the divine language, the ancient language, spoken throughout the universe before time was time." Cornelius provides a few translations before Leeloo manages, with amazing speed, to learn English. *Akta Gamat*, for example, means "never without my permission," and *San Agamat chay bet envolet* appears to mean "the case was stolen." Although there is no obvious basis language (i.e., a real-world language the filmmakers had in mind) for this "divine language," the grammar and some vocabulary (but not the pronunciation) is reminiscent of French (the root *vol* is in *envolet*, presumably "stolen") and, at times, Arabic.

There is a popular but incorrect notion among fans of the film that the cerulean-skinned Diva Plavalaguna, who performs an aria in a packed opera house, is uttering lyrics in an alien language. She is in fact singing in Italian ("Il Dolce Suono" from Donizetti's *Lucia di Lammermoor*), with some digital distortions to the voice. There is, however, another less conspicuous instance of a fictional language in *The Fifth Element*. On the back of the bulky uniforms of Earth's police officers is writing in an unknown script. Because this word appears beneath the legible English word POLICE and looks to have five distinct characters, it may represent a rendering of the same word in a new phonetic alphabet.

References: The Fifth Element. Directed by Luc Besson. Screenplay by Luc Besson and Robert Mark Kamen, 1997; see Christophe Rouchon's Web page on the "divine language" of *The Fifth Element*: www.thegeneric.com/Fifthelement/language.html.

Finders Keepers

Linnea Sinclair's 2001 science-fiction/romance novel draws on many conventions from movies and TV shows like *Star Trek* and *Star Wars*. Three languages are at work in the story, though two of them are only mentioned. The (presumably human) heroine, Captain Trilby Elliot, and most of the characters speak **Standard**, an undescribed space travelers' lingua franca, rendered without elaboration as English in the text. The enemy aliens, called the 'Sko, speak **Ycskrite**. Only one word of Ycskrite appears in the text: *Ren'zorc'a*, the name of a poison loosely translated as "blood boil death" (273).

The heroine's love interest, T'vahr, is a Z'fharin and speaks **Z'fharish**. The Z'fharin have "a linear society, patriarchal" (13) and are known for their pride and arrogance. Z'fharish characters occasionally utter a word or phrase in their language, but the novel contains no detailed comments about grammar, syntax, or pronunciation. The samples of vocabulary given in the text suggest a fanciful Russian or Slavic basis: *vad* (yes), *nav* (no), *lutsa* (lights), and *S'viek noyet* (I am sorry). One of the stranger linguistic moments in *Finders Keepers* occurs when T'vahr translates the phrase *dravda gera mevnahr* into an altogether anachronistic idiom: "ass over teakettle" (101). The most important Z'fharish phrase in the novel—and in fact the novel's last sentence—is the passionate declaration, *Yav cheron*: "I want you" (spoken to a male; to a female one would say *Yav chera*).

Reference: Sinclair, Linnea. *Finders Keepers.* Douglas, MA: NovelBooks, 2001.

"First Contact"

Murray Leinster's much-republished short story, "First Contact," originally appeared in the pages of *Astounding Science Fiction* in 1945. In many respects it has become a template for science fictions dealing with the problems of one space-traveling species meeting another for the first time: mutual suspicion, linguistic barriers, and the search for common ground. A number of episodes of the television series *Star Trek*, for example, pay homage to Leinster's story.

Somewhere in the Crab Nebula, a spaceship of researchers from Earth encounters a somewhat larger ship from an unknown planet. Both ships are adequately armed to destroy the other; both humans and the very humanlike aliens breathe oxygen; both acknowledge that their uncertainty as to whether the other ship might follow them to their home planet (perhaps worthy of later plunder) leaves them at an impasse. Eventually, however, an ingenious compromise is hit upon: the humans and the unnamed aliens trade ships, with weapons dismantled and records removed, and return to their respective home planets with evidence of their new discoveries.

Leinster's story has a very interesting approach to the problem of representing an alien language. Whereas so many other science fictions revert to the cliché of telepathy, Leinster gives his aliens the ability to communicate by projecting microwaves: "they use frequency-modulation plus what is probably variation in wave forms—like our vowel and consonant sounds in speech" (569). Thus, while from a human perspective the speechless aliens effectively have a form of "telepathy," the aliens, who apparently cannot perceive and do not use sound, may well suppose the human use of speech to be itself an otherwise incomprehensible kind of "telepathy" (570). Dialogue between the two species, one human character explains to another, is based in an ad hoc "sort of code which isn't the language of either set": "They shoot over short-wave stuff with frequency-modulation, and we record it as sound. When we shoot it back, it's reconverted into frequency-modulation" (569–570). The story does not offer any specific details about the grammar, syntax, or vocabulary of the alien language itself, but the conceit of a soundless language (it is unclear whether there is a written component, though the story alludes vaguely to "the alien equivalent of a ship's library" [582]) is insightfully deployed here.

Reference: Leinster, Murray. "First Contact." *The Best of Science Fiction.* Edited by Groff Conklin. New York: Crown Publishers, 1946. 559–583.

The First Men on the Moon

When Mr. Cavor, one of the two protagonists of H. G. Wells's 1901 novel, is abandoned on the moon, he teaches his lunar captors English but apparently learns nothing of the **Selenite** language. The narrator, the rash Mr. Bedford, refers to "a slight elusive twittering" (120) and Cavor's later similar descriptions of Selenite speech include terms like "shrieks" (238). The Grand Lunar, the Master of the Moon, addresses Cavor with "a faint wheezy noise" (240), which is then translated into mannered English by a Selenite named Phi-oo: this arrangement purposefully keeps honest Cavor at a disadvantage, though he is unaware of it. The Selenites have no written language, since a special class of intellectuals are bred and raised specifically to house within their memories the complete history of the Selenites.

Reference: Wells, H. G. *The First Men on the Moon.* London: Collins, 1970.

Forbidden Planet

A unique "adaptation" of Shakespeare's *The Tempest*, the classic science-fiction film *Forbidden Planet* (1956) is set on the planet Altair-IV in the year 2257. A rescue ship looking for survivors of a lost team of scientists finds only the reclusive Dr. Morbius, his daughter Altaira, and their robot servant, Robby. The other scientists, Morbius explains, were violently killed by unknown forces. Commander John J. Adams and the crew of his rescue ship are subsequently attacked by an invisible being of great power, which, they ultimately discover, is a projection of Morbius's id, a "monster of the unconscious."

The monster is a result of Morbius's research into the culture of the previous inhabitants of Altair-IV, a long-lived and technologically advanced species called the Krell. A philologist, Morbius has studied **Krell** writings: "It took months to decipher their huge logical alphabet." The film offers a glimpse of one document, but its meaning is not established. Morbius has in fact misinterpreted the history and technology of the Krell—they did not succeed in banishing primal impulses and unconscious urges, but effectively gave them incredibly strong and tangible form when they endeavored to transcend their own corporeality and were themselves wiped out in the process—and his own misreadings lead him to repeat the error of the Krell by releasing his own personal demons into the physical world.

Morbius suggests that there are many Krell manuscripts, but he says nothing more specific about their language and does not utter any Krell-language words or phrases in the film.

Reference: Forbidden Planet. Directed by Fred McLeod Wilcox. Screenplay by Cyril Hume, 1956.

Foreigner (C. J. Cherryh)

Taller and stronger than humans though less technologically advanced, the **atevi** (singular: *ateva*) in C. J. Cherryh's novel *Foreigner* (1994) are an extraterrestrial race whose thought is rich with numbers (there is no obvious separation between mathematics and numerology, and they esteem *agoi'ingai*, "felicitous numerical harmony" [376]) and whose culture centers on schemes of duty and treachery. Their language has fourteen different words for "betrayal," and "one of them double[s] for 'taking the obvious course'" (314). Human language (English?) is called *Mosphei'*, after the human settlement on the island of Mospheira, and an interpreter is a *paidhi* (pronounced "pait'-(h)ee"). The apostrophe, found in a word like *man'chi* ("primary loyalty to association or leader" [377]), represents a pause, and syllable stress is dependent on vowel pronunciation. A sample declension is given for the noun *aiji*, "lord of central association" (375–376):

Singular	Non-specific plural
aiji Nominative	aijiin Nom pl. Subject The aiji
aijiia Genitive	aijiian Gen pl. Possession's [*sic*], The aiji's [*sic*]
aiji Accusative	aijiin Acc. Pl. Object of action (to/against) the aiji
aijiu Ablative	aijiiu Abl. Pl. From, origins, specific preposition often omitted: (emanating from, by) the aiji

Only a few examples of complete phrases and sentences can be found in *Foreigner*: for example, *Man'china aijiia nai'am.* . . . *Nai'danei man'chini somai Banichi?* ("I'm the aiji's associate, foremost. . . . Whose associate are you and Banichi, foremost of all?" [89]). In keeping with atevi fascination with numbers, there are "pluralities more specific than simply singular and more-than-one, such as a set of three, a thing taken by tens, and so on, which are indicated by endings on a word" (374). Formality is crucial in all addresses, and abruptness in speech may be insulting or embarrassing. The vocabulary given here is presumably the result of transliterations, since atevi text is read from right to left and down, and books are read from back to front. The novel includes a short glossary and some notes on pronunciation.

Foreigner is the first volume of a long series; it is followed by *Invader* (1995), *Inheritor* (1996), *Precursor* (1999), *Defender* (2001), and *Explorer* (2002).

Reference: Cherryh, C. J. *Foreigner.* New York: DAW Books, 1994.

Foreigner (Robert J. Sawyer)

Foreigner is the third novel in Robert J. Sawyer's Quintaglio Trilogy (which also includes *Far-Seer* [1992] and *Fossil Hunter* [1993]) in which dinosaurs that were transported from Earth to a moon in the Quintaglio system by an alien race are given time to evolve into sentient and technologically advanced beings. The trilogy recounts various paradigm shifts these dinosaurs, known as Quintaglios, experience, drawing parallels to the earthly Copernican revolution as well as to the discoveries of Darwin and Freud.

Various unique nouns and phrases from the **Quintaglio** language are presented in these books, such as *dagamant* ("bloodlust") and *hahator pas da dan* (a standard greeting, allowing a friend to approach within an individual's personal space), but there is not a great deal of vocabulary or grammar provided by the author in the trilogy. The only grammatical rule appears to be that related nouns share suffixes, such as *-pel* indicating planets (e.g., *Kevpel* or *Carpel*) or *-'toolar* indicating provinces (e.g., *Fra'toolar* or *Kev'toolar*). In both these cases, the prefix *kev-* implies "brightness." Proper names can also function as adjectives in Quintaglio, so that the scientist Afsan's name translates as "meaty thighbone" while another proper name, Afdool, suggests "meaty legbone."

The Quintaglio written language is pictographic or glyphic and is produced on strips of leather by ink and claw. As the Quintaglios lack an alphabet, knowledge is not organized alphabetically, but rather through classifications based on physical properties arranged linearly known as "the Sequence."

In *Foreigner*, the Quintaglios also have their first encounter with another intelligent dinosaur race living on the same moon but at a far remove. Throughout the novel, they are referred to as the Others, and they have a distinct culture and language. The **Other** language is similar enough to Quintaglio so that an explorer from the latter race is able to develop a standard vocabulary and grammar in a matter of days. One interesting quality of the language includes using *na* as a negative, although placed within a word cluster rather than preceding or following a noun or verb; for example, *hoos-ta* is "good" while *hoos-na-ta* is "bad," and *sek-tab* is "correct" while *sek-na-tab* "incorrect." Another unusual element is the lack of superlatives; rather, intensity is conveyed by repetition so that *hoos-na-ta hoos-na-ta* is "very bad." Finally, as well as utilizing the standard interrogatives of who, where, why, what, and how, the Others employ two other forms of questioning: *glees*, meaning "how righteous?"; and a second unnamed phrase asking "with what degree of certainty?" Like Quintaglio, the Other language is pictographic in its written form.

The aliens who transported the dinosaurs from Earth to the Quintaglio system, the **Jijaki**, also have a language, although the only words noted are *kiit* (the material from which their spaceships are constructed) and *Kijititatak Gikta* (the name of a Jijak television program).

Reference: Sawyer, Robert J. *Foreigner*. New York: Ace, 1994.

～G～

Galactic Pot-Healer

Philip K. Dick's 1969 novel *Galactic Pot-Healer* has many points of linguistic interest, including a book that prophesies in a patchwork of passages in different tongues, a robot who pointedly adopts an African American slave dialect when conversing with its human master, and an alien's troubles with translating Goethe's *Faust*. Part of the difficulty of this latter project lies in the fact that the original text "was written in a language which has died out" (90). (Russian and English, at least, are still extant.) In this future scenario, there are apparently many languages from many different planets available to the humans who live in a tyrannical and demoralizing sort of global socialism. None of these is presented or discussed in any significant depth, and when characters of varied species and languages do confer in central scenes of the novel, their discourse is instantaneously translated by the telepathic abilities of a powerful being known as the Glimmung. In the story, the Glimmung contacts a number of individuals whose unique talents will assist his efforts to reshape his planet, and he offers a payment sum of "thirty-five thousand crumbles" (18). When Joe, the novel's hero, tries to determine what a *crumble* is, he is given a bizarre array of possible definitions by "the twenty-four-hour-a-day dictionary service": in the **Udrian** language spoken on Betelgeuse seven it means "a small opening of a temporary nature"; it is "a small life-form which scuttles" in an unnamed language from Rigel two; and in the **Plabkian** tongue of the Glimmung's home planet, Sirius five (or "Plowman's Planet"), it is a monetary unit of extraordinary exchange value on Earth (19). These are the most detailed and specific instances of alien languages.

The novel also has its fair share of neologisms (e.g., *squimp*, *pidnid*, and the color *rej*), almost all of which appear without definition or identified source language. *Tóojic* is an intriguing exception: this word is brought into focus by a character who (rather imprecisely) translates for Joe a section of the Kalends' multilingual prophetic book pertaining to the fates of those recruited to help the Glimmung. At first she says "destroyed" but then "corrected herself. 'Tóojic. Damaged or made to unexist. Maimed, that's it. They will be permanently altered, beyond immediate repair'" (77–78). The ultimate fortunes of the recruits does not clarify or narrow the definition significantly, since the authority (not to mention the motives) of the Kalends' pronouncements is cast into serious question and the recruits arrive at different, ambiguous endings; while "permanently altered" seems apt, "destroyed" may be an overstatement for those who incorporate themselves into the Glimmung.

Reference: Dick, Philip K. *Galactic Pot-Healer*. New York: Vintage, 1994.

Galaxy Quest

A parody of both *Star Trek and the persistent subculture that has accrued around it, *Galaxy Quest* (1999) is a film about a group of out-of-work television actors who are mistaken for real space travelers by an alien race, the Thermians, who have intercepted transmissions of their show's reruns and have misidentified them as "historical documents," evidence that these humans are heroes. The Thermians have such names as Mathesar, Teb, and Laliari. Although they affect a human appearance so as not to disturb the actors, when their "appearance generators" lapse, they reveal themselves to be blinking and large-eyed, multicolored squidlike creatures. In a likewise fashion, it is only when Laliari's "translator" device "is broken" that we first hear the **Thermian** language. It is a mix of shrill ululation and scratchy barks, and given the penchant they have for waddling and arm's-length clapping, the sound is probably meant to be reminiscent of seals. No translation is given for Laliari's outburst or for any of the subsequent dialogue squealed in Thermian. However, the DVD edition of *Galaxy Quest* offers the viewer the unusual option to watch the entire film dubbed in Thermian (with or without English subtitles).

In the course of their adventure with the Thermians, the would-be heroes encounter one other alien species with a distinctive tongue. These fanged little creatures "look like little children" to human eyes, though they make the same assessment of a full-grown human male. At first glimpse their manner is mild and their speech a chirping, whispering sort of infantile chatter. The innocent appearance is quickly belied by their vicious cannibalism. A few phrases ("Hit it with a rock and we'll eat it!") are translated by subtitles, but otherwise no indications of how the language is structured are given. Only one word is singled out: the aliens chant and repeat *Garignak*, translated by the Thermians' "translation circuit" as "rock," though this may only be the name of a gigantic rock creature that they summon. Watching the Thermian audio version provides no further insights on this point.

Reference: Galaxy Quest. Directed by Dean Parisot. Screenplay by David Howard and Robert Gordon, 1999.

Gargantua and Pantagruel

When in the second book of Rabelais's *The Histories of Gargantua and Pantagruel* (1532–1551) Pantagruel first encounters Panurge, the latter responds in several languages, some of them fictional. Besides demonstrating fluency in German, Italian, English, Basque, Dutch, Spanish, Danish, Hebrew, Greek, Latin, and French, Panurge confuses Pantagruel's company no less with three other pronouncements in invented languages. The first begins, *Al barildim gotfano dech min brin alabo dordin falbroth ringuam albaras* (197), and leads Pantagruel to remark, "I think that it is the language of the Antipodes. The devil himself couldn't get his teeth into it" (198). Emile Pons (the French translator of *Gulliver's Travels*) has suggested that "ringuam albaras" may be read as a kind of anagram of "linguam arabas"; this "language of the Antipodes" is thus a sort of pidgin Arabic.

Panurge's second address in a fictional language reads in full: "*Prug frest frins sorgdmand strochdt drhds pag brlelang Gravot Chavigny Pomardière rusth pkalhdracg Devinière près Nays. Bouille Kalmuch monach drupp delmeupplist rincq dlrndodelb up drent loch minc stz rinquald de vin ders cordelis but jocststzampenards*" (199). Pantagruel's friend Epistemon doubts that this is "a human Christian language" and calls it "Lantern-language" (199). From the context (i.e., Panurge's previous statement in Basque and his next one in Dutch) as well as incidences of recognizable French words like *vin* (wine), we can at least understand that the speaker desires food and drink. (Umberto Eco gives this "Lantern-language"—indeed, Panurge's exact words here—to eunuchs in his novel *Baudolino*.) The reader again encounters **Lanternese** in the third book, which Panurge claims to understand "like a native" of Lanternland (416), and he gives an offering of verse: "Briszmarg d'algotbric nubstzne zos, / Isquebfz prusq: alborz crinqs zacbac. / Misbe dilbarlkz morp nipp stancz bos; / Strombtz, Panrge walmap quost grufz bac"; this is translated as "All miseries attended me whilst I / A lover was. I had no good thereby. / The married folk of better fortune tell; / Panurge is one of them and knows it well" (417). Panurge promises to make Pantagruel "a smart little dictionary" of the language but claims that it willl not last him "much longer than a pair of new shoes" (417), suggesting that Lanternese is indeed an improvisational style of nonsense.

Panurge also says to Pantagruel, in his third unknown language, "*Agonou don't oussys vou denaguez algarou, nou den farou zamist vou mariston ulbrou, fousquez vou brol tam bredaguezmoupreton den goul houst, daguez daguez nou croupys fost bardou noflist nou grou*" (200), and Pantagruel thinks he understands: "for either it is the language of my native Utopia, or else it has a very similar sound" (201).

It is worth noting that Panurge's fanciful polyglottism bears contrast to other occasions in Gargantua and Pantagruel when characters make verbal displays of their education. Pantagruel is less tolerant of the affectations of a Limousin, whose grotesque answers to such similarly straightforward questions as those later posed to Panurge are characterized as "some devilish new language" but are later judged to be an overwrought effort by the speaker to sound like a well-educated Parisian (184–185). For uttering such pretentious Latinate nonsense as "I latrially venerate the supernal astripotent" and "my genius is not aptly nate, as this flatigious nebulon asserts, to excoriate the cuticle of our vernacular Gallic" (184–185), Pantagruel threatens to skin him alive, though he releases the Limousin when at last he speaks "the language in common use" (185). In another incident, a scholar from England named Thaumaste (conceivably a lampoon of Sir Thomas More, author of *Utopia*) holds a learned argument against Panurge conducted "by signs only, without speech" because "these matters are so difficult that human words would not be adequate to expound them" (231). The ridiculous gestures and noises that follow, ranging from humming and waggling of fingers to Panurge's removing an orange from his codpiece and throwing it repeatedly into the air, represent another of Rabelais's satires on abstract pseudoerudition, though Thaumaste, for his part, seems to take them seriously, for he concedes defeat and goes on to publish in London "a great book" (239) in which he explains the meaning of every sign used in the argument (to which Rabelais's narrator can refer without further elaboration).

References: Pons, Emile. "Les langues imaginaires dans le voyage utopique: les 'jargons' de Panurge dans Rabelais." *Revue de Littérature Comparée* 2.11 (April–June 1931): 185–218; Rabelais, François. *The Histories of Gargantua and Pantagruel.* Translated by J. M. Cohen. London: Penguin, 1955.

"The Gift of Gab"

In Jack Vance's 1955 story, human workers in Bio-Minerals on the planet Sabria discover that the ten-limbed marine species called dekabrachs are "intelligent autochthons" (129). However, to prove to authorities that the dekabrachs are intelligent and thus grant them protection from another industrialist who is killing them for the rare chemicals their bodies contain, the men at Bio-Minerals must demonstrate that the dekabrachs can communicate. Yet any communication between dekabrachs is indiscernible to human observers, prompting the speculation that dekabrachs "work on a basis of communal empathy" and do not require speech or language as such (135). This hypothesis is, unfortunately, unprovable, and the protagonists of the story hit upon another way of revealing dekabrach intelligence: they manufacture a rudimentary language with which humans and dekabrachs can intercommunicate. Nouns, adjectives, and verbs are expressed with arm positions, taught to a captive dekabrach with a pliable model. Specific words taught include "water," "food" (148), and "null-zero" (the number or a negative response [157]). Eventually the captive dekabrach articulates its own statements and is released back into the ocean with a message to take to other dekabrachs, offering to teach them the sign language. At the story's end, the "first class" (160) of students arrives, proving that the dekabrachs have an unknown means of complex communication—possibly a language—amongst themselves as well as an interest in developing the improvised sign language between humans and dekabrachs.

Reference: Vance, Jack. "The Gift of Gab." *Future Tense.* New York: Ballantine, 1964. 105–160.

Glory Road

Oscar, the hero of Robert A. Heinlein's *Glory Road* (1963), is transported from a luckless life on Earth to heroic adventures in other worlds and other universes (the "glory road" of the title). In the course of these adventures, he is taught a few strange languages via a very fast-working form of hypnotic instruction.

Nevian is both the first language Oscar learns by this method and the only one of which the reader glimpses a direct (i.e., not paraphrased) though minimal example. When Oscar is told, "*Erbas*, Oscar, *'t knila voorsht*," he answers, "I am getting up. Don't rush me" (61). Named after the world Nevia, where it is spoken, the Nevian language seems to reflect the kind of fantasy that Oscar's adventures there represent. Admittedly unable to "launder" a Nevian idiom that he translates as "Bless your bouncy little bottom!" (93), Oscar describes Nevian as "rich in profanity and in words for making love, and richer than English in some technical subjects—but with surprising holes in it. There is no word for 'lawyer' for example" (61). This example of a "hole" is not really a surprise at all, once the reader understands that *Glory Road* is the narrative of a Vietnam veteran soured on bureaucracy and government, a man whose only success (or glory) outside of the interplanetary voyages, battles with dragons, and sex with the Empress of Twenty Universes recounted in the novel has been in high school football. Seen in balance with the readiness with which he accepts the fact of being in an alien world or fights inanimate foes, Oscar's near-obsessive efforts to avoid American taxation points to the quixotic nature of the novel. *Glory Road* is an escape from the very concepts of lawyers, taxes, and estrangement, so the Nevian language is an obliging vehicle for fantasies of empowerment. That these fantasies are aggressively masculine may go without saying, but Oscar makes a point of mentioning that some Nevian words can possess a "feminine ending" (97) at the same time that he encounters a local custom that sees male guests offered the sexual favors of any of the females of a given household. Although Nevian has what seems to be a highly mannered speech (Oscar likes to supply repetitions of "milord"), its "politest endearments . . . would win you a clout in the teeth in the U.S.A." (98).

By contrast, the mixed peoples of the world called Center, where the Empress resides, speak "a pidgin language with thousands of years of imports and changes and is uninflected, positional, and flat" (222). Center is the capital world of the Twenty Universes and thus the site of a lot of politicking and parties, a place of formality and diplomacy. To speak to another person, one simply says "Self" and waits to be answered, though one may be ignored (as Oscar sometimes is). Oscar's frustration with the language parallels his dissatisfaction with domestic married life with the Empress. A good and colorful example of the differences between the narrator's American idiom and the sterile quality of Center's language may be found in Oscar's rebuke to a communication officer, spoken over a visual sort of telephone:

> Hold it, you overpaid clerk! Switch me off and you'll be in charge of smoke signals in Timbuctu an hour from now. Now listen. This bloke is elderly, bald-headed, one of his names is 'Rufo' I think, and he is a distinguished comparative culturologist. *And* he is a grandson of Her Wisdom [an honorific for the Empress]. I think you know who he is and have been dragging your feet from bureaucratic arrogance. You have five minutes. Then I talk to Her Wisdom and ask *her*, while *you* pack! (258–259)

In the language of Center, the above would literally be rendered like this: "Stop! Danger you! Other old bald Rufo (?) Top comp-culturist. Wisdom egg-sperm-egg. Five-minutes. Liar and/or fool. Wisdom? Catastrophe!" (259).

The novel contains hints of other languages and other worlds, but they are neither named nor described.

Reference: Heinlein, Robert A. *Glory Road*. New York: G. P. Putnam's Sons, 1963.

"Grammar Lesson"

One of Larry Niven's stories about Draco's Tavern, a bar located in the Mount Forel Spaceport, "Grammar Lesson" (1977) presents a dialogue between the bartender-narrator and an alien customer of the species chirpsithra. They converse in **Lottl**, a language that the narrator admits to having no mastery of despite nearly thirty years of study. The chipsithra tells a story of how the chipsithra empire vanquished an enemy empire to make a point about the importance of what might otherwise seem peculiar or minor variations in possessives in spoken Lottl. No samples of Lottl are represented in the text.

Reference: Niven, Larry. "Grammar Lesson." *Niven's Laws.* Philadelphia: Philadelphia Science Fiction Society, 1984. 13–16.

The Gray Prince

The portrayal of the world of Koryphon in Jack Vance's 1974 novel *The Gray Prince* implies that the diversified residents use at least one unearthly language, but no names are given. Footnotes define certain but by no means all strange words uttered by characters of different species and classes, though these definitions can be somewhat puzzling. For example, the Germanic-looking word *weldewiste* comes from "the lexicon of social anthropology" and refers to someone's "cosmic consciousness; his perception of self vis-à-vis the universe; his character and personality from the purview of comparative culture" (21). The precise currency of this term is problematized by the fact that it is used by a member of a privileged human class, an *eng'sharatz* ("literally: the revered master of a large domain" but loosely translated as "landbaron" [3]), who subordinates other sentient beings, such as the Uldra, and the narrative voice that writes the book's prologue and footnotes is not identified. Other words, such as *aurau*, *sarai*, and *xheng* are described as "untranslatable" just before a provisional explanation of each is nonetheless provided (37, 105, 205). Add to such inconsistencies the mention of a character uttering "a soft Uldra curse" (128) and the reader cannot conclude how many languages are in use on Koryphon.

Reference: Vance, Jack. *The Gray Prince.* New York: ibooks, 2003.

Gulliver's Travels

Jonathan Swift's 1726 satire (the full title of which is *Travels into Several Remote Nations of the World, in Four Parts*) finds the hapless (and eventually embittered) ship's surgeon Lemuel Gulliver cast away in one fantastic country after another. Gulliver acquires the language of each country's inhabitants, "having from [his] youth a great facility in learning languages" (188), and in some instances the specific details of a given language play a part in the satirical designs of a given chapter. Certainly, Swift's attention to spoken language and his fondness for word games and puns, evidenced in writings ranging from *Polite Conversation* (1738) to the so-called little language he used in his *Journal to Stella* (1779), suggest that the linguistic inventions of *Gulliver's Travels* were hardly arbitrary.

Gulliver's first and probably most famous journey is to Lilliput, where he is christened by the tiny bellicose people living there *Quinbus Flestrin*, "the Great Man-Mountain" (27). He is taught **Lilliputian** by six of the nation's greatest scholars and, occasionally, the emperor himself, who requires that Gulliver *lumos kelmin pesso desmar lon emposo*; "that is, swear a peace with him and his kingdom" (27). Conditionally released from the bonds in which the Lilliputian army had ensnared him, Gulliver curries favor with the emperor while studying the culture. He learns about the internal division between *Tramecksan* and *Slamecksan*, the political parties whose names mean, respectively, High-Heels and Low-Heels (38), and the religious strife over the proper way to break one's egg before eating it, rules for which may be found in the holy text known as the *Brundecral*. Many titles of prestige are enumerated, such as *Snilpall*, *Legal*, *Galbet*, *Clumglum*, and *Nardac* ("the highest title of honour" [42]), as are some various measurements, such as *drurr* ("about the fourteenth part of an inch" [39]) and *glumguff* (seventy *glumguffs* of depth "is about six foot of European measure" [41]): surely the point to be drawn here is that the Lilliputians revel in meaningless distinctions and are "small" in more than height. Gulliver calls Lilliputian writing "very peculiar, being neither from the left to the right, like the Europeans; nor from the right to the left, like the Arabians; nor from up to down, like the Chinese; nor from down to up, like the Cascagians, but aslant from one corner of the paper to the other, like ladies in England" (46)—further evidence of their trivial manners and habits.

Gulliver is drawn into Lilliput's war against the inhabitants of the Island of Blefuscu and notes how "the languages of both empires [differ] as much from each other as any two in Europe, and each nation [prides] itself upon the antiquity, beauty, and energy of their own tongues, with an avowed contempt for that of their neighbour" (44). He offers one example of the difference of vocabulary—"a most delicious wine, called *glimigrim* (the Blefuscudians call it *flunec*, but ours is esteemed the better sort)" (45)—though it suggests that the differences are little more than caprice and chauvinism. We may accordingly understand the thus briefly described **Blefuscudian** language to be more or less a cipher for the French language, for insofar as Lilliput is a satirical portrait of a corrupt England, its constant enemy would be its neighbor, France.

Gulliver's second voyage reverses the physical situation of the first. Among the giants of Brobdingnag, he is called *Grildrig*: "the word imports what the Latins call *nanunculus*, the Italian *homunceletino*, and the English *mannikin*" (77). He in turn calls the nine-year-old girl responsible for his care and safety "*Glumdalclitch*, or little nurse" (77), and she is also his instructor in the **Brobdingnagian** language. Gulliver is treated like a doll or toy and is compared to a *splacknuck*, "an animal in that country very finely shaped, about six foot long" (79). Later, attempting to categorize the strange, tiny Gulliver, who is much smaller than their queen's dwarf, scholars from the metropolis "called in their language *Lorbrulgrud*, or *Pride of the Universe*" (80) declare him "*relplum scalcath*, which is interpreted literally, *lusus naturæ*" (84), or a freak of nature. Swift's use and accounting of the giants' language are generally similar to his scheme in Part One, but where the Lilliputians' speech and writing betoken parvanimity and ambition, those of Brobdingnag suggest judiciousness and toleration. As in the voyage to Lilliput, the exaggerated scale of the place is emphasized in the given vocabulary: for example, the term *glonglungs*, three of which "make about fifty-four English miles" (90). The Brobdingnagians have had print since "time out of mind" but, to Gulliver's mind, not a great number of books, though those they have are written in "clear, masculine, and smooth, but not florid" style, and even their written laws do not "exceed in words the number of letters in their alphabet, which consists only of two and twenty" (110). It is worth noting here that in a prefatory letter to later editions of the *Travels*, Gulliver complains that Brobdingnag is a printer's error for Brobdingrag, "for so the word should have been spelt" (5).

In the third part of his *Travels*, Gulliver encounters a number of peoples with languages and linguistic concepts appropriate to their unusual customs and philosophies. Swift's primary targets in this section of the satire are dubious intellectual enterprises, and though the languages of such places as Laputa and Maldonada are the most cursorily described in the book, they are (as the expression by which reason may be judged) significantly nuanced. The citizens of the floating island of Laputa, for instance, speak "in a clear, polite, smooth dialect, not unlike in sound to the Italian" (127); but the language is clearly not Italian, for no one understands Gulliver's attempts to communicate in Italian, and Swift may be implying that this imperfect relation to the relation of Latin, the classical tongue of reason, reflects the remove of the Laputans' abstruse ideas from pragmatic science. No sooner does Gulliver get a footing in the **Laputan** language than he assumes the air of a philologist: "The word which I interpret the *Flying* or *Floating Island* is in the original *Laputa*, whereof I could never learn the true etymology. *Lap* in the old obsolete language signifieth *high*, and *untuh* a *governor*, from which they say by corruption was derived *Laputa*, from *Lapuntuh*. But I do not approve of this derivation, which seems to be a little strained. I ventured to offer to the learned among them a conjecture of my own, that *Laputa* was *quasi Lap outed*; *Lap* signifying properly the dancing of the sunbeams in the sea, and *outed* a wing, which however I shall not obtrude, but submit to the judicious reader" (130). That Gulliver is here himself engaged in as ludicrous an academic sort of pseudoproblem as any of the natives he encounters points to both his inability to recognize himself in what seemingly foreign things and persons he observes around him and his tendency to try to conform, even toady, to the powers about him. Part of Swift's joke here lies in the most obvious etymology for the name of the country: *la puta* is Spanish for "whore," and the word "academy" has some history as a slang term for brothel or insane asylum.

Gulliver notes that Laputan phraseology is dependent on understandings of mathematics and music, and that "their ideas are perpetually conversant in lines and figures. If they would, for example, praise the beauty of a woman or any other animal, they describe it by rhombs, circles, parallelograms, ellipses, and other geometrical terms, or else by words of art drawn from music" (131). Ever distracted and clumsy, the Laputans are "wholly strangers" (131) to imagination and fancy, but their schemes are imperial in scope. The Balnibarians, by contrast, whose continent lies beneath the floating island, are ruled by the Laputans and have a less abstract if equally risible interest in the applied sciences, inspired by their misinterpretation of the Laputans' studies. In the Grand Academy of Lagado of Balnibari, one professor's project is a book-writing machine, worthy of note here because the illustration provided in the original publication (it may have been drawn by Swift himself) depicts squares on which are written "all the words of their language in their several moods, tenses, and declensions, but without any order" (148). This matrix thus provides evidence of a variegated writing and the suggestion that words, for the scholars of Lagado, are merely "laborious" tools (148) that may be heedlessly yoked to mechanical strictures. By contrast, another professor at "the school of languages" proposes a "universal language" that contains no words at all, since "every word we speak is in some degree a diminution of our lungs by corrosion" (150–151). Swift mocks the aspirations to a universal language of John Wilkins and the debates on rhetoric within the Royal Society by having his academics (altogether impractically) replace words with things and thus effectively equate a universal language with having no language at all.

Exactly what distinction there is, if any, between the Laputan tongue and "the language of Balnibarbi" (164) is not clear, but in his travels after Lagado, Gulliver remarks in passing on how different are the languages of Glubbdubdrib (meaning "The Island of *Sorcerers* or *Magicians*" [157]) and **Luggnagg**, though only the latter is presented in any detail. Described as "a polite and generous people" (167), the people of Luggnagg have a culture apparently rich in supplication and obsequies. To visit the king is to "have the honour to 'lick the dust before his footstool'" (165), an expression that turns out to be entirely literal. Gulliver is taught to utter the ordained compliment to the king, *Ickpling gloffthrobb squutserumm blhiop mlashnalt, zwin tnodbalkguffh slhiophad gurdlubh asht* ("May your Cœlestial Majesty outlive the sun, eleven moons and a half"), after striking his forehead "seven times against the ground" (166). Gulliver does not understand the king's rejoinder but does know to answer it with a formal request to have his interpreter brought forth and introduced: *Fluft drin yalerick dwuldum prastrad mirplush*, "which properly signifies, My tongue is in the mouth of my friend" (166).

Houyhnhnmland is the last place Gulliver visits, and the one he least cares to leave. Its inhabitants are of two altogether different species, the rational equine Houyhnhnms and the barbarous Yahoos. Only the former has a discernible language, and they are amazed to meet Gulliver, who to their judgments is a Yahoo inexplicably capable of speech and reason. Because they "have no letters" (220), Gulliver recounts what he hears in "English orthography" (184), though he observes "that their language expressed the passions very well, and the words might be with little pains resolved into an alphabet more easily than the Chinese" (183). The appellation "*Houyhnhnm*, in their tongue, signifies a *horse*, and in its etymology, *the perfection of nature*" (190), and besides admiring them for their moral virtues and physical elegance, Gulliver bestows great praise on the Houyhnhnms for their poetry: "the justness of their similes, and the minuteness, as well as exactness of their descriptions, are indeed inimitable" (220). "In speaking," reports Gulliver, the Houyhnhnms "pronounce through the nose and throat, and their language approaches nearest to the High Dutch or German, of any I know in Europe; but it is much more graceful and significant" (189). Swift provides the reader with samples of a vocabulary indicative of clear-headed pragmatism and a serene relationship with the environment: besides names for food (*hlunnh* [oats]) and local animals (*luhimuhs*, "a sort of wild rat" [215]), the Houyhnhnms refer to the death of one of their number with the verb *lhnuwnh* (221), a word that is "strongly expressive in their language, but not easily rendered into English; it signifies, 'to retire to his first mother'" (221).

What is most interesting about **Houyhnhnm** as a fictional language is not what expressions it contains but rather those it explicitly does not. Gulliver finds himself "at much pains" to explain such terms as "begging, robbing, stealing, cheating, pimping, forswearing, flattering, suborning, forging, gaming, lying, fawning, hectoring, voting, scribbling, star-gazing, poisoning, whoring, canting, libelling, free-thinking, and the like occupations" (203). The Houyhnhnms, in short, "have no word in their language to express any thing that is evil," though they can refer to their neighbors the Yahoos: "Thus they denote the folly of a servant, an omission of a child, a stone that cuts their feet, a continuance of foul or unseasonable weather, and the like, by adding to each the epithet *yahoo*. For instance, *hhnm yahoo, whnaholm yahoo, ynlhnmawihlma yahoo*, and an ill-contrived house *ynholmhnmrohlnw yahoo*" (222). Particularly foreign to the Houyhnhnms is the human capacity to speak "*the thing which is not*" (199)—that is, to lie or fabricate. For the Houyhnhnms, "the use of speech was to make us understand one another, and to receive information of facts" (193). This famous satirical ploy of Swift's, by which human iniquity serves as a defining characteristic of the species in contrast to some other to whom it is alien, has in subsequent centuries of fiction (particularly science fiction) become a standard device and even a cliché. It may well be the most scathing indictment of humanity in *Gulliver's Travels*.

Reference: Swift, Jonathan. *Gulliver's Travels and Other Writings.* Edited by Louis A. Landa. Boston: Houghton Mifflin, 1960.

ᕥ H ᕤ

Haroun and the Sea of Stories

When the hero of the title of Salman Rushdie's 1990 novel visits an area called the Twilight Strip, he and his allies encounter a Shadow Warrior who "speaks" the "Language of Gesture" (130). Haroun's father Rashid is able to translate the language he calls **Abhinaya**, which Rushdie explains in a note is the Hindustani for the communicative element of Indian classical dance. In the novel, the Shadow Warrior's every twitch and glance, the exact position of every limb, can be rendered as complex verbal statements. This language is of great significance in a story in which the villains (who live in darkness) seek to destroy narrative and possibly language itself, opposed by those who live in light and enjoy tales, chatter, and all manner of verbiage.

Reference: Rushdie, Salman. *Haroun and the Sea of Stories.* New York: Penguin, 1991.

"The Haunter of the Dark"

In this 1935 short story, H. P. Lovecraft's protagonist, Robert Blake, discovers a book of ancient writing in an abandoned church that is first assumed to be written in code. As Blake has a literary and artistic interest in the occult, he soon realizes that the tome is actually written in **Aklo**, "the dark . . . language used by certain cults of evil antiquity, and known to him in a halting way through previous researches" (230). Little detail is given of this language beyond the fact that it is pictographic—resembling alchemical and zodiacal signs.

Aklo is also briefly mentioned in Lovecraft's "The Dunwich Horror" (1929) but was adopted from Arthur Machen's short story "The White People" (1906), where it is also referred to as the **Chian** language.

References: Lovecraft, H. P. "The Haunter of the Dark." *The Best of H. P. Lovecraft.* New York: Random, 1987. 218–238; Machen, Arthur. *The White People and Other Stories.* Silverton, CO: Chaosium, 2003.

Hellflower

Hellflower (1991) is the first of Eluki bes Shahar's trilogy of novels about "dark-traders," interplanetary smugglers, and its darktrader narrator, Butterfly St. Cyr, who narrates in a patchwork idiom evocative of hard-boiled detectives and, to a lesser extent, urban African American slang. For the most part, Butterfly communicates in **patwa**, apparently a patois variation of the more formal and standardized **Interphon**, "the lingua franca of deep space" (77: its written glyphs are called **Intersign**). It is not always clear which alien words are originally Interphon, a language that has broken down "along lines of profession, not lines of astrography" (77). An artificial intelligence named Paladin considers the variations a symptom of "the organic [i.e., not a computer's] love of novelty for its own sake, even when it is not particularly desirable" (77). The accent and idiosyncrasies of patwa can vary, and even Butterfly is a little confused by another speaker's stylings, "thick enough to slice and ship, but the tune was simple to follow" (201). Butterfly's patwa can be "broad," as when she calls out to see if the owner of an office she is visiting is there: "Yo, che-bai, je tuerre? Art t'home, forbye?" (80). Some terms are recognizable from repeated use, such as *je* and *ne* (yes and no, or yeah and nah), *oke* (okay), *por'ke* (why), *tronics* (robots), and *trufax* (presumably "true facts," the truth).

Butterfly's indifference to the niceties of grammar (she regularly says things like "they'd gave" [174] and will use a verb's singular form with a plural subject) stands in contrast to the rectitude of Paladin's occasional log entries and thus should probably be understood as the novel's English approximation of her patwa. However, Butterfly's habit of blending real languages besides English into her speech (in, for example, phrases like "beaucoup-illegal" [40] and variations on a theme: "You got a name? T'name-je, bai? Namaste'amo?" [47]) may suggest that patwa (or even Interphon) is itself the result of such blending, a projection of a future Babel. The history of Interphon is not clarified when Butterfly mentions that "Imperial records are kept in Standard, not Intersign. It might as well of [*sic*] been Old Federation Script for all I could make of it" (135), for the novel includes no further details about either of these languages/scripts.

The plot and title of Shahar's novel concern an alien culture colloquially known as Hellflowers. These honor-obsessed people call themselves alMayne and speak a language that Paladin identifies as **alMayne Common Tongue**, known to Butterfly as **helltongue** or **helltalk**. Very little about this language is revealed to the reader apart from the definition of a few significant words and phrases, including *Dzain'domere* (this reportedly sounds like "jane-doh-meer" [35]: "I pledge and give my word" [59]), *chaudatu* ("outlander" or "anyone who is no alMayne and therefore not a real person" [34]), and *higna* (prey).

Reference: Shahar, Eluki bes. *Hellflower*. New York: DAW Books, 1991.

Herland

In Charlotte Perkins Gilman's 1915 feminist utopia, three "modern" men—representing, by their occupations, engineering, medicine, and sociology—discover, explore, and are eventually expelled from a completely female society. In the course of learning about this matriarchal civilization (no male has been born in Herland for close to 2,000 years and the women reproduce "parthenogenetically"), the men learn the unnamed language of its inhabitants. According to the novel's narrator, the women of Herland have worked over centuries to make their language simple, clear, and unambiguous: "it was not hard to speak, smooth and pleasant to the ear, and so easy to read and write that I marveled at it. They had an absolutely phonetic system, the whole thing was as scientific as Esparanto yet bore all the marks of an old and rich civilization" (31). Unfortunately, beyond this one description, there is little indication of the language's lexicon or grammatical system. The closest glimpse readers get of the language is when the men are told that Odumera, the leader of Herland, is so called due to the fact that *mera* means "thinker" and *du* means "wise." There are also no equivalents for the words "virgin," "wife," or sexual love in the tongue of Herland.

Reference: Gilman, Charlotte Perkins. *Herland*. New York: Pantheon, 1979.

An Historical and Geographical Description of Formosa, An Island Subject to the Emperor of Japan

The real place of birth and perhaps even the real name of the man who called himself George Psalmanazar (1680?–1763; sometimes spelled Psalmanaazaar) remain historical mysteries, although he is best known for the fantastical provenance he claimed for many years and the odd celebrity that came with it. Psalmanazar took great advantage of eighteenth-century Europe's febrile imaginings of an exotic "East" when he published his account of his purported homeland, Formosa.

It is as easy to see why contemporary readers of his *Historical and Geographical Description of Formosa* (first printed in 1704 and revised in a second edition the following year) might become absorbed in his account of such an amazing place (the Bishop of London was very public in his support of Psalmanazar's claims) as it is to understand why many were highly skeptical. According to Psalmanazar, the Formosans went without clothing and practiced both polygamy and cannibalism. His own pale skin was not at all a contradiction, he said, but rather a confirmation of his own class of privilege in Formosan society, which kept him from having to labor in the sun. He claimed to have been smuggled out of Formosa by Jesuits when he was nineteen years old, and he pointed to this young age as a means of defending any weaknesses or vague points in his descriptions of his homeland.

Psalmanazar dedicates one chapter of his *Description* to the **Formosan** language, which he begins with a comparison: "The Language of *Formosa* is the same with that of *Japan*, but with this difference that the *Japannese* do not pronounce some Letters gutturally as the *Formosans* do: And they pronounce the Auxiliary Verbs without that elevation and depression of the Voice which is used in *Formosa*" (266). By identifying Japanese as his sole point of linguistic reference—and to which, of course, this Formosan bears no genuine resemblance—Psalmanazar could be fairly confident that no European of his day could contradict him with any authority.

Most of Psalmanazar's notes on the language focus on pronunciation, how "elevation and falling of the Voice is observ'd" in this or that verb tense, as he does "not intend to write a Grammar of the Language but only to give some Idea of it" (267). He makes one "general Observation": Formosan is "very easy, sounds musically, and is very copious" (267).

Such generalities notwithstanding, Psalmanazar does include a complete Formosan alphabet, made of twenty letters, "which are to be read from the right Hand to the left" (268), and phrase-by-phrase translations of "The Lord's Prayer" (below), "The Apostle's Creed," and the Ten Commandments into Formosan.

Phrase-by-phrase translation of "The Lord's Prayer"

The Lord's Prayer	*Koriaka Vomera*
Our Father who in Heaven art,	Amy Pornio dan chin Ornio viey,
Hallowed be thy Name,	Gnayjorhe sai Lory,
Come thy Kingdom,	Eyfodere sai Bagalin,
Be done thy Will as in Heaven,	Jorhe sai domion apo chin Ornio,
also in Earth so,	kay chin Badi eyen,
Our bread daily give us to day,	Amy khatfada nadakchion toyeant nadayi,
and forgive us our trespasses,	kay Radonaye ant amy Sochin,
as we forgive our trespassers,	apo ant radonem amy Sochiakhin,
do not lead us into temptation,	bagne ant kau chin malaboski,
but deliver us from Evil,	ali abinaye ant tuen Broskaey,
for thine is the Kingdom,	kens sai vie Bagalin,
and Glory, and Omnipotence,	kay Fary, kay Barbaniaan
to all ages. Amen.	chinania fendabey. Amien.

Reference: Psalmanazar, George. *An Historical and Geographical Description of Formosa, An Island Subject to the Emperor of Japan.* London: Printed for Dan. Brown, 1704.

The History of the Sevarites or Severambi

Attributed to Denis Vairasse d'Allais, this account of a voyage to *Terrae Australis Incognitae* (as the title page has it) was published in two parts, the first in 1675, the second in 1679. Its preface (signed with the initials "D. V.") bemoans the fact that, in the wake of books such as Thomas More's *Utopia, the reading public can hardly tell the difference between fact and fiction when it comes to tales of voyages to unknown countries. This ironic complaint marks *The History of the Sevarites or Severambi* as a contemporary of such works as Gabriel de Foigny's *The Southern Land, Known* (1676) and a forerunner to Jonathan Swift's *Gulliver's Travels* (1726). Captain Siden, the "Worthy Person" who narrates the book, describes Sevarambi as a most exotic and wondrous country. All of the laws and institutions of the Severambi are based on reason and monotheism, including sex slavery and what seems to be magic, and the diverse wildlife includes lions, bears, jackals, camels, and even unicorns.

Unlike the works of Foigny and Swift, however, *The History of the Sevarites* contains strikingly little information about the language encountered in the fictional place that the narrator hazards on. Conversations with the Severambi are held in Dutch or Spanish or French, which the local speakers know as well as they know the whereabouts and affairs of Europe. In the only clear observation of its kind in the book, a companion of Siden reports that **Sevarite** speech sounds "much like the Greek or Latine, as I have sometimes heard it spoken in Holland, and ran very smooth and Majestical" (73). Only two examples of the language appear: the word *Marabi* ("Justice" [124]) and a strange chant that may or may not be a magical spell of some sort (it is never confirmed as such, nor is it translated): *Bomralok Kostraborab Abrolakar Bourakabou Branbastrokobar Abrovora Birikabu* (94).

Reference: Vairasse, Denis. *The History of the Sevarites or Severambi.* London: Printed for Henry Brome, 1679.

The Hitchhiker's Guide to the Galaxy

Douglas Adams's science-fiction comedy has several incarnations—five books (nevertheless called a "trilogy") as well as radio and television programs—and unflagging cult status. The far-out and often ridiculous scenarios and characters encountered by mild-mannered Englishman Arthur Dent include some accounts of far-out and often ridiculous languages, though Adams gets around the difficulty of having to detail or explain almost any of the alien languages he mentions by introducing a unique version of the "universal translator" conceit. The Babel fish, according to "the wholly remarkable book" (12) that is *The Hitchhiker's Guide to the Galaxy,* is a "small, yellow and leechlike" creature, which, when inserted into a person's ear, enables the carrier to "understand anything said to you in any form of language" (42). However, the narrator's archly informative digressions, some of which are borrowed or paraphrased from the *Guide,* supply occasional remarks on linguistic oddities. For example, a hitchhiker called Ford Prefect is said to have never learned to pronounce his original name "in the ancient Praxibetel tongue"; this "obscure Betelgeusian dialect" has largely vanished since the Great Collapsing Hrung Disaster on Betelgeuse Seven. Ford's schoolmates "nicknamed him Ix, which in the language of Betelgeuse Five translates as 'boy who is not able satisfactorily to explain what a Hrung is, nor why it should choose to collapse on Betelgeuse Seven'" (34).

Besides the eponymous first volume (first published in 1979), the series includes *The Restaurant at the End of the Universe* (1980); *Life, the Universe and Everything* (1982); *So Long, and Thanks for All the Fish* (1985); and *Mostly Harmless* (1992).

Reference: Adams, Douglas. *The Hitchhiker's Guide to the Galaxy. The More Than Complete Hitchhiker's Guide.* New York: Wings Books, 1986. 1–143.

The Hobbit

See *The Lord of the Rings.*

Hunter of Worlds

In an introductory note to a 2003 republication of her early novel, C. J. Cherryh explains that *Hunter of Worlds* (1977) "involves perception and language and what's truly alien. . . . The language freights the mental differences. If you don't catch a word at first, look at the situation in which it's used" (5). This advice seems of little help to a reader confronted by a sentence like the following, indicative of the dense use of alien terminology: "Perhaps to ease the sting of it a *nas-katasakke* of Kharxanen could be requested for *kataberihe*, for *Tashavodh*'s *m'melakhia* to gain *sra* within the *orith-sra* of *Ashanome* was of longstanding" (454). Even after having read many chapters and being able to consult the "Glossary of Foreign Terms" provided at the novel's end, it can be difficult to follow this kind of prose.

There are four sentient species active in the novel—iduve, kalliran, amaut, and human—and each has its own language (though the human language is undescribed and unnamed, and the other three all happen to translate as "people" or "men and women"). Yet the aspect of these languages revealed to the reader is conspicuously slight: highly conceptual terms pepper the English syntactic structure of the narrative and all dialogue between characters.

The **kalliran** language is described as similar to that of humans, but "a fossilized Ethical" is retained as an adjective (531). Besides being but one example of Cherryh's reliance on an essentialist and Sapir–Whorf kind of approach to the relationship between culture and language, this unusual phrase may be understood as a description of the importance of moral philosophy to the kalliran people. Of paramount significance for kalliran are the concept words *giyre* (pronounced "GIU-rey": "recognition of one's proper place in the cosmic Order of things; also, one's proper duty toward another" [531]) and *kastien* (pronounced "KAHS-tee-yen": "being oneself; virtue, wisdom; observing harmony with others and the universe by perfect centering in one's giyre toward all persons and things" [532]). To disregard these qualities—to presume, whether by deciding for others or by killing another living creature—is to be *ikas*.

The **amaut** language is similar to kalliran speech and employs many kalliran words and mannerisms. Cherryh's glossary makes the puzzling assertion that the amaut "alphabet is native [though, disappointingly, the reader encounters no new alphabets in *Hunter of Worlds*], but literature as such dates from first contact with the iduve" (539). The amaut are not flattered by their portrayal: in the drama between predatory iduve and enslaved humans and kalliran who strive for their dignity, the amaut constitute servants and toadies, untrustworthy and in all respects inferior. The limited sampling of amaut vocabulary pertains to ancestry and drink, but the most intriguing expression is *shakhshoph*, literally "hiding-face. Politeness to hide true feelings from outsiders" (540).

Much more "alien" to humans is the **iduve** language, in which there is "no clear distinction between the concepts of noun and verb, between solid and action" (532–533). Cherryh's glossary includes several details about the language concerning such matters as prefixes, suffixes, and loose gender designations, not explored in the novel itself. Technologically and physically powerful, divided into clans and essentially predatory, the iduve have terms for specific binaries, such as mating for pleasure (*katasukke*) and mating for procreation (*katasakke*), or the state of freedom (*arrhei-akita*) and the state of being bonded (*akitomekkhe*, as the space-traveling iduve recognize humans and kalliran by their terrestrial nature). There are no curses in iduve (386) but the exclamation *tekasuphre* ("stupidity, irrationality, nonsense" [538]) may be used if the iduve speaker opts not simply to kill the addressee. Iduve culture revolves around the notions of *nasul*, one's clan, and *vaikka* (pronounced "VAI-k*hah" [538], where the asterisk "indicates a guttural sibilant . . . a throat-sounded hiss" [533]), an extraordinary drive for revenge in reaction to any sense of dishonor or embarrassment.

Reference: Cherryh, C. J. *Hunter of Worlds. At the Edge of Space.* New York: DAW Books, 2003. 283–540.

I

I Never Promised You a Rose Garden

Hannah Green (the pseudonym of Joanne Greenberg) published her semiautobiographical novel *I Never Promised You a Rose Garden* in 1964; a film version, directed by Anthony Page, was released in 1977. Sixteen-year-old Deborah Blau is diagnosed with schizophrenia (a diagnosis that has been questioned by contemporary readers) and is institutionalized. Her mental illness manifests itself as a division between the hurtful real world and an imaginary world called Yr. The latter is a world inhabited by capricious, sometimes cruel gods and a being known as the Censor, and their language, **Yri**, is presented as a gift to Deborah. When Deborah's psychiatrist, Dr. Fried, pronounces the language's name "Eerie," she is corrected, though apparently the two words sound similar; Dr. Fried also learns that this secret language is so powerful that Deborah occasionally employs another "Latinated cover-language," which she describes as "a screen" and "a fake," because speaking in Yri all the time "would be like powering a firefly with lightning bolts" (55–56). For Deborah, English or real-world language is little more than a means for deceit, while Yri expresses true statements and genuine feelings.

As Deborah's treatment progresses, she provides the doctor (and the reader) with greater insights into Yri as well as more examples of its vocabulary and grammar. Yri appears to be given to formality, even ceremony, as may perhaps befit a divine language, but it is replete with formulations for alienation, loneliness, and agitation. For example, Deborah thinks of another patient in her ward, a woman who seldom speaks, as a *nelaq tankutuku*, one who is "eyeless" and "unhidden" (89). She later rages in full Yri sentences that display the arch (and archaic) tone that the other Yri speakers, those gods that beleaguer her, adopt: *Recreat xangoran, temr e xangoranan. Naza e fango xangoranan. Inai dum. Ageai dum* (" 'Remember me in anger, fear me in bitter anger. Heat-craze my teeth in bitterest anger. The signal glance drops. The Game'— Ageai meant the tearing of flesh with teeth as torture—'is over' " [177]). Where certain words and idioms are polyvalent (for instance, "in Yri the word that means death also means sleep, insanity, and the Pit" [60]), there is at least one explicit gap: "there was no Yri word for 'thank you' " (180). There is also a nonverbal element to Yri: the text makes passing reference to "the Yri hand-gesture of compliance" (162) and "the gesture of turmoil and renunciation that was Yri hand-language for the world" (241), but these are not described or analyzed in any further detail.

Dr. Fried, to whom Deborah gives the Yri name Furii, makes the significant point that Yr and Yri are not themselves Deborah's affliction, but rather it is the possessive claims they make on her that need be overturned.

Reference: Green, Hannah. *I Never Promised You a Rose Garden.* New York: Signet, 1964.

Icosameron

The complete title of Casanova's 1788 novel is *Icosameron, or, The Story of Edward and Elizabeth, Who Spent Eighty-One Years in the Land of the Megamicres, Original Inhabitants of Protocosmos in the Interior of Our Globe.* (The original French text, *Jcosameron, ou Histoire d'Edouard et d'Elisabeth qui passerent quatre vingts un ans chez les Mégamicres habitans aborigènes du Protocosms dans l'intérieur de nôtre globe,* appeared in five volumes and runs over 1,700 pages. Rachel Zurer's translation, cited here, is also a severe truncation.) In the course of twenty conversations (the word *Icosameron* is Greek for "twenty days"), Edward relates his adventures with his sister and wife, Elizabeth, among the Megamicres to a group of idle lords and ladies. The Megamicres are tiny creatures, approximately twenty inches tall and of different colors, which signify social status, and live within the Earth but worship the sun—this apparent paradox is but one of the puzzling aspects of *Icosameron.* Edward and Elizabeth learn these creatures' language and set about revolutionizing their society.

Megamicran is principally a "singing language" (37), though it is sometimes accompanied by dance and gesture. It is made up exclusively of six vowels—"consonants are apparently too harsh for their delicate eardrums" (29)—though only *a, e, i, o,* and *u* appear in the novel's few examples of names (a Megamicre doctor is identified as Aaaau Eooo Eiiio) and phrases. Elizabeth gives a demonstration of spoken Megamicran, represented in the text thus, without translation (97):

```
                                                              u
  ———— i ————————— i ——— u ————————————— u ———

     e        e         a      a         o         u

  ———— u ————————— i ————————————— o ——————————

            u ———        ——— i o

  ————————————————— o ————————— o ——————————
```

Each vowel of the alphabet has seven "colorations": "these forty-two sounds are the base upon which a vocabulary of almost thirty thousand words is formed" (50). Megamicran writing, accordingly, requires seven colors of ink, but eventually Edward introduces into the culture a printing press that employs just one color (and which demands undescribed "accents, punctuation, capitals" [103]).

Learning to speak Megamicran is difficult, Elizabeth explains, because it requires much practice and close attention to nuances, including "the gestures and the facial expressions" of the speaker (49). The language is also necessarily formalized: "the first speaker in a company sets the conversational tone. This is the key note which determines the meaning of a great number of words. Once begun, this tone must be maintained. A change in tone may be regarded as rudeness or may occasion laughter" (50).

The Megamicres also employ a "mute language" when they are underwater. Elizabeth claims this is a simple but useful method of expression, akin to pantomime, but "it is a poor language and has no intrinsic value since it depends on a give and take relationship" (49). Exactly what she means by this last phrase is unclear.

Reference: de Seingalt, Jacques Casanova. *"Icosameron," or, The Story of Edward and Elizabeth.* Translated by Rachel Zurer. New York: Jenna Press, 1986.

If on a winter's night a traveler

The reader of Italo Calvino's 1979 novel is, perversely, the hero of a story about frustrated attempts to read "Italo Calvino's new novel, *If on a winter's night a traveler*" (3; the original Italian title is *Se una notte d'inverno un viaggiatore*). In the course of misadventures with faulty editions, scurrilous translations, misleading dust covers, and stolen books, "the Reader" is exposed to a controversial series of texts, among them *Outside the town of Malbork, Leaning from the steep slope,* and *Without fear of wind or vertigo.* The first of these three is initially thought to have been translated from Polish but includes the untranslated word *schoëblintsjia*: "But on reading *schoëblintsjia* you [the Reader] are ready to swear to the existence of *schoëblintsjia*, you can taste its flavor distinctly even though the text doesn't say what the flavor is, an acidulous flavor, partly because the word, with its sound or only with its visual impression, suggests an acidulous flavor to you, and partly because in the symphony of flavors and words you feel the necessity of an acidulous note" (35). Guessing that *Outside the town of Malbork* may not be Polish at all but actually a translation from **Cimmerian**, a "Bothno-Ugaric" language, the Reader consults one Professor Uzzi-Tuzzi, who paradoxically refers to Cimmerian as "a modern language and a dead language at the same time . . . a privileged position, even if nobody realizes" (51). The Reader describes the novel he has been unable to finish and Uzzi-Tuzzi zealously identifies it as "unquestionably *Leaning from the steep slope*, the only novel left us by the most promising Cimmerian poets of the first quarter of our century, Ukko Ahti" (53). Because this book "has never been translated into any other language" (53), Uzzi-Tuzzi narrates one on the spot, but the story bears no resemblance to that of *Malbork* apart from the use of the character name Zwida, and is incomplete. Uzzi-Tuzzi says that "the wordless language of the dead" is all that comes after that point in the story, where the author fell into a deep depression and ultimately committed suicide: "Cimmerian is the last language of the living, the language of the threshold" (71).

Uzzi-Tuzzi's despair is abruptly answered by his colleague, a "chair in Erulo-Altaic languages" named Galligani, who contends that not only is the novel in question not unfinished, it has a different title, a different author, and is written in an altogether different language (73). According to Galligani, "the vast novel *Without fear of wind or vertigo*, whose opening chapter apparently also exists in a first draft in Cimmerian, signed with the pseudonym Ukko Ahti" is a work written in **Cimbrian** (sometimes called **Cimbric**) by Vorts Viljandi, who wrote in both languages (75). When *Without fear* is read (though only in part) in Galligani's pretentious seminar, the Reader finds no *schoëblintsjia*, no Zwida, nothing like the previous two texts.

The confusion looks to be the effect of a conspiracy, in which the translator Ermes Marana is trying to disrupt all narrative continuity; but what "reality" value the Cimmerian and Cimbrian languages have within the world of these characters cannot be finally determined. When the Reader, whose own "reality" and relationship with the events of the fiction are most pointedly questioned here, tries to seek out an author for explanation, "you" arrive in Ataguitania, a nation with an authoritarian government. The book-banning police there have, significantly, a language that is unnamed and unknown to the Reader, but which "your" protean nemesis, the hegemony-loving Nonreader, can speak (213).

Reference: Calvino, Italo. *If on a winter's night a traveler.* Translated by William Weaver. San Diego: Harcourt, 1981.

Immortal—Ad Vitam

Based on his graphic novels, Enki Bilal's 2004 film *Immortel—Ad Vitam* (the original French title) defies simple description, involving as it does mutants and eugenics, flying cars and flying sharks, and a giant floating pyramid. Such as it is, the story revolves around the Egyptian god Horus, who is for reasons not explained in the film given seven days of freedom in late twenty-first-century New York by his fellow gods, Anubis and Bastet. (Horus uses the time to seek out a blue-haired woman to procreate with, again for unexplained reasons.) The gods speak to one another in a fanciful kind of ancient Egyptian, with subtitles provided (compare with **Stargate*). There are also phantasmal little creatures who perform various menial and household functions: they speak a high-pitched jabber that the film viewer cannot make out but that characters in the film appear to comprehend. And the aforementioned sharklike monster has a few lines of its own in a flat, growling language (also subtitled).

Reference: Immortal—Ad Vitam. Directed by Enki Bilal. Screenplay by Enki Bilal, 2004.

The Infernal Desire Machines of Doctor Hoffman

Reason and reality come under attack in Angela Carter's novel *The Infernal Desire Machines of Doctor Hoffman* (1972), and Desiderio, the narrator, encounters many fantastic peoples and places in his quest to defeat the title character. Three of their unusual languages are worthy of inclusion here.

Two of them are the stuff of Orientalist fantasy, exotic-sounding languages of the mysterious "East," with some strange, potentially mystical properties. The River People, among whom Desiderio settles for a while, "speak in a kind of singing," which Desiderio supposes is on the one hand "a version of one of the Indian dialects" and, on the other, the effect of the speakers being "altered descendants of the birdmen of the swamps" (70). Their language has neither general forms of pluralization, "only an elaborate system of altered numerals for denoting specific numbers of given objects," nor, more vexingly, a verbal equivalent for "to be," though one demanding aria "could roughly be translated as 'one finds oneself in the situation or performance of such and such a thing or action'" (71). Living with "a complex, hesitant but absolute immediacy," the River People have (and have little need for) abstract nouns, and their verbs are tensed in either the simple past or the continuous present, with a future tense noted by "various suffixes indicating hope, intention and varying degrees of probability and possibility" (71). The River People name Desiderio *Kiku*, which means "foundling bird" (77).

The language of a crew of pirates that later captures Desiderio is less detailed. A "clicking, barking, impersonal language" (149), its vague connections to "the East" are suggested by the semisuccessful efforts to communicate made by another hostage (who has "picked up a smattering of many tongues" during "his adventures in the East" [150]).

The third and most unusual of the fictional languages in *Doctor Hoffman* is the musical, wordless one used by centaurs. Lacking both grammar and vocabulary, the language of the centaurs is described by Desiderio as "only a play of sounds. One needed a sharp ear and a keen intuition to make head or tail of it and it seemed to have grown naturally out of the singing of [their] scriptures" (173). The centaurs have no word for "guest" or "visitor," but "they had many words to describe conditions of deceit; they were not Houyhnhnms" (187; see *Gulliver's Travels*). A cuneiform writing, "based on the marks of their own hooves" (184), is a method of expression exclusive to one designated member of the society, the Scrivener, used to paint "The Books of the Sacred Stallion" and tattoos.

Reference: Carter, Angela. *The Infernal Desire Machines of Doctor Hoffman*. New York: Penguin, 1994.

The Interpreter

An interpreter at the United Nations overhears an assassination plan in this 2005 film. The ostensible target is President Zuwanie, the leader of a fictional African nation, the Democratic Republic of Matobo. (The resemblance of prospective war criminal Zuwanie to President Mugabe of Zimbabwe is difficult to miss, and Matobo is the name of a national park in Zimbabwe.) Using Swahili and Shona as templates, linguist Said el-Gheithy devised **Ku**—short for **Chi'itoboku**—as the language of this country, which actress Nicole Kidman was made to study. There is not very much Ku spoken in the film, unfortunately, and its presence here seems principally to be a means of avoiding lawsuits.

Reference: The Interpreter. Directed by Sydney Pollack. Screenplay by Scott Frank, Charles Randolph, and Steven Zaillian, 2005.

Islandia

A utopian novel by American lawyer and legal professor Austin Tappan Wright (1883–1931), *Islandia* (1942) is the stuff of literary cults—a massive text (2,000 pages in typescript, later edited by his daughter to half that length) that includes extremely detailed imaginary geographies, histories, customs, and cultures. This detail does, of course, include a fictional language (**Islandian**), but although Wright is said to have amassed a complete dictionary and grammar for his language, it does not appear as an appendix or as footnotes in a Tolkien-like manner. Rather readers are left to piece together the language through natural usage and from the notes of the novel's American protagonist, John Lang.

Islandia is an isolationist agricultural nation with little technological development, but at the beginning of the novel is beginning to consider opening itself up to foreign interaction and investment. Lang arrives as an American "ambassador" but soon finds himself rejecting his American values for that of Islandia. Through a series of political, but mostly romantic, events that constitute the bulk of the novel, Lang learns to appreciate the tri-part nature of Islandian love represented by the words *apia*, *alia*, and *ania*, which correspond to erotic love, love of place, and marital or familial love, respectively.

Equally important is *tanrydoon*, which translates directly as "soil-place-custom" (51) but refers to a room in a home that is set aside exclusively for a close friend. To be given tanrydoon is considered among the highest honors an Islandian can bestow on another.

Islandian appears remarkably consistent in its construction; for example, *-ta* is always a diminutive so that a romantic crush is *apiata*. Similarly, once a root word has been established, variations of that noun are generated by prefixes: for example, *win* (river) can become *matwin* ("broad-river") or *alwin* ("swim-river"). Hence, knowing the roots *ry* or *tan* from *tanrydoon* explains *elainry* (city) as "place-of-many-people" and *tanar* (proprietor) as "one-who-owns-soil."

As demonstration of some of the complexities of Islandian, an example is given of a green-eyed girl who is referred to as *solvadia*. Lang attempts to translate this adjective into English terms thusly: "*Sol-* was an intensive prefix; *di* or *dee* was green; the final *a* was feminine; but the *va* puzzled me until I had a happy thought. *Va-* or *van* was the word for eye; a far-seen thing was *vant-*; *Vantry* was the place seen far away. . . . The idea conveyed to me . . . the girl with the very green-green eyes" (221).

Some indication is also given regarding pronunciation and general rules of the language, such as the lack of gendered common nouns, declensions, tenses, or moods, while in verbalizing all vowels and consonants are articulated with no silent letters. Another interesting deviation from many languages is the Islandian use of two first-person plural pronouns, one that refers to the speaker and his or her family (and by implication his or her ancestors), the other that is the more conventional use of "we" to mean several unrelated members.

As in many other cases, the words that a society lacks reflect cultural and ideological aspects of that community. In addition to not having a single term for "love," the Islandians are unable to express equivalences for "diplomatic," "business," "fatalist," or "jealousy." In contrast, Lang also notes that "perhaps it takes a farmer really to learn Islandian, for its vocabulary as to all matter of husbandry is rich and various with several words where we make one do" (208).

In an afterword to *Islandia*, Wright's daughter makes mention of an Islandian alphabet and its lack of philological connections ("Islandian is not a European language and its origins remain obscure" [1023]), but there is no indication of the appearance of its script in the course of the novel.

Islandia continues to be the subject of contemporary inquiry as enthusiast Mark

Saxton (1914–1988) has written a trilogy of sequels that recount the adventures and tribulations of the descendents of the protagonists in Wright's original novel: *The Islar: A Narrative of Lang III* (1969), *The Two Kingdoms: A Novel of Islandia* (1979), and *Havoc in Islandia* (1982).

Reference: Wright, Austin Tappan. *Islandia.* New York: Overlook, 2001.

J

Jem

In Frederik Pohl's relentlessly pessimistic science-fiction novel, humanity encounters, and subsequently exploits, three intelligent races on a newly discovered planet known as Jem.

The first race encountered are crablike beings known as the Krinpit that maneuver through their world by sonar and also communicate by using the same principle. In motion, each Krinpit is constantly sounding his or her name, and variations in this perpetual sonic field function as language. As Pohl writes of the Krinpit:

> Their main auditory apparatus was the drum-tight undersurface of the belly. It possessed a vent like a dolphin's that could produce a remarkable range of vowel sounds. The "knees" of the double-boned legs could punctuate them with tympanous "consonants." They walked in music wherever they went. They could not move silently. The exact sounds they produced were controllable; in fact, they had an elaborate and sophisticated language. The sounds which became their recognition signals were probably the easiest for them, but they could produce almost any other sound in the frequency range of their hearing. In this their voices were quite like humans'. (41)

While the **Krinpit** language has no visual component, their communities do have signage in the form of whistles, Aeolian harps, and chimes, which indicate places of business or personal lodgings.

A second purely aural language is that of the Balloonists, large floating beings, like aerial jellyfish, who fly and sing by releasing hydrogen from their bodies. Variously described as sounding like bagpipes, cellos, birdsongs, or Hawaiian, the **Balloonist** language is given the most attention in Pohl's novel. Besides noting that *h'aye'i* is a predator in Balloonist, several other phrases are given, such as *Ma'iya'a hi'i hu'u ha'iye'i* ("These creatures unlike us are vicious animals" [170]) and *ni'u'a mali'i na'a hu'iha* ("they have killed my song" [171]). While there is no official lingua franca of

Jem, when members of the three races wish to converse with each other they often use Balloonist.

The least-described language in *Jem* is that of the Burrowers, a subterranean race of mole or ferretlike creatures. The only "word" of **Burrower** that is given by Pohl is *tssheee*, which is an interjection that is comparable to "humph." A sense of the sound of the language might also be derived from the proper names of various burrowers, such as dr'Shee, t'Weechr, and qr'Tshew.

Reference: Pohl, Frederik. *Jem.* New York: Bantam, 1980.

Journal from Ellipsia

In *Journal from Ellipsia*, Hortense Calisher applies her naturalist style to the science fiction genre through a first person account of an extraterrestrial's attempts to understand earthly life and to actually become human. Comparable to the Martian poetry of Craig Raine, the alien in Calisher's book describes his/her experiences on earth with a considerable amount of defamiliarization.

Life on the alien's home planet, Ellipsia, is also recounted in some detail. As a spheroid race of energy beings, who at some point in their evolution relinquished the concept of gender and individualism (as well as their material bodies), their language also lacks the first person pronoun or gendered terms. At this stage in their evolution the Ellipsians appear to have also given up the need for written or spoken language, although they have existed in the past.

At this point in time, the Ellipsian language also appears to be minimalist, although not restrictive, with the narrator noting: "at home, what we use for language *begins* with monosyllable, and thereafter concentricates inward, while Your Babel proliferates every which way [*sic*]" (109).

Reference: Calisher, Hortense. *Journal from Ellipsia.* Boston: Little, Brown, 1965.

The Journey of Niels Klim to the World Underground

The hero of the title of Ludvig Holberg's fictional voyage (first published in Latin as *Nicolaï Klimii Iter Subterraneum* in 1741) discovers a solar system within the Earth itself, and in his travels on the world of Nazar and beyond encounters many fantastic creatures and societies. For the first half of the book, Klim lives with the Potuans, mobile, and sentient trees and shrubs, who classify him as a *pikel emi*, "a monkey of an odd shape" (17), in their **Subterranean** language (later called **Nazaric**). Klim learns the language without difficulty and for the most part only presents certain titles (e.g., *Kadoki* signifies High Chancellor, and *Kiva*, Secretary) and technical terms in his narrative. He does explain the Potuan legal and political system with some care and admiration, and remarks on the term *Rip-fac-si* (indifferent), the rarely given and harshest judgement upon a departed monarch (i.e., the monarch is said to have performed his duties "indifferently"). Rather strangely, the Potuans have books and a sophisticated textual culture: Klim names titles such as "*Sebolac Tacsi, or, The True Remarks of a Religious Tree*" (56) and *Mahalda Libab Helil*, "which in the Subterranean language signifies *A Key to Government*" (66) and approvingly notes the state-appointed censors, "*syla-macati*, that is, 'purgers of book-sellers' shops'" (77).

The Subterranean language is not confined to the Potuan region, and lengthier, more colorful samples of the language occur during Klim's travels about Nazar. When he takes public employment among the tribe known as the Nagiri, an oval-eyed people "to whom consequently all objects appear to be oval" (85), he takes the oath *Kaki manasca quihompu miriac Jacku mesimbrii Caphani Crukkia Manaskar Quebriac Krusundora*: this is to swear that "the sacred tablet of the sun appears to me to be oval, and I promise that I will persist in this opinion to my last breath" (86). In the Philosophical Region, Klim is rudely called *kaki spalaki*, "ungrateful dog" (98), despite the lack of evidence of dogs on Nazar.

Although Klim contends that "the same language obtains everywhere" (48), this eventually turns out to be incorrect when he is banished by the Potuans and forced to live in Martinia among clothed and vain monkeys who speak an entirely different language. Klim refers to the language as **Martinese** or **Martinian** but gives no information about it apart from a few samples of vocabulary, such as *maskatti* (valets or footmen) and *stercolates* (units of currency), and a description of the sound of the monkeys' speech as "chattering" like the beating of "so many drums" (130). When Klim sails from Martinia, he mentions an encounter with sirens, whose language "resembled the Martinese" (153), but he gives no further details.

When Klim lands on the shores of Quama, the technologically primitive and somewhat fearful inhabitants there repeat to him the words *Dank, Dank*, but when Klim tries to speak to them in High Dutch, Danish, and Latin without success, he tries "the Subterranean languages, namely, the Nazaric and the Martinian, but all to no purpose" (172). Klim learns to speak **Quamitic**, and at the very end of his narrative he employs the phrase *Jeru pikal salim* ("show me the way" [223]) and is mistaken for the mythical Wandering Jew. Apart from this phrase, however, Klim limits his description of the language to explanations of the very grand titles he himself assumes as he leads the Quamites into imperial wars. He begins as *Pikil-Su* ("Ambassador of the Sun" [173]), becomes *Jachal* ("generalissimo" [180–181]), and finally *Koblu* ("Great" [214]). As a warlord, Klim subdues many other countries (Martinia among them), though only one of them is explicitly said to have a foreign language. Remarkably, the **Canaliscan** language is its people's weapon: they attack the Quamite invaders with "a volley of curses and hard names," and an interpreter informs Klim that they are "perfect masters of their weapons, and not inferior to the grammarians of our world" (206). The Canaliscans also have a written language, for the defeated people satirize their new and unwanted emperor with a book whose title translates as *The Happy Shipwreck*.

An "Apologetic Preface" to the *Journey*, purportedly written by Niels Klim's grandsons, certifies that Klim's manuscript had attached to it "a Subterranean grammar, together with a dictionary in two languages, Danish and Quamitic" (2) and suggests that a "grammar of the Quamitic language" will be published in the future, with an account of Klim's son Thomas and his own adventures underground (4).

Reference: Holberg, Ludvig. *The Journey of Niels Klim to the World Underground.* Edited by James I. McNelis Jr. Lincoln: University of Nebraska Press, 1960.

Julian the Magician

Canadian poet Gwendolyn MacEwen's first novel (published in 1963 when she was twenty-one) concerns a medieval magician who begins to believe himself Christ, which causes his life to unfold in such a way that he reenacts the Passion. Julian is crucified halfway through the novel, and an epilogue follows that contains pages from a journal kept by Julian in his youth and early manhood.

Late in the journal, Julian begins to write in an unknown language, which the fictional editor of the collection claims is "[a]n esoteric dialect which we have not been able to decipher. Its content and motive are yet unknown, but we are working on it" (137).

Two examples of this language are given: *Blith ga reztrono, has eem no halek ronom; kalooth kalooth, haara natzeem onboi ts oom oomvo* (137) and *ghoum rajh hibau* (146). It appears that this language is solely MacEwen's invention, relying on sound effect to replicate "speaking in tongues" or else an invocation of casting magical spells.

Reference: MacEwen, Gwendolyn. *Julian the Magician*. Toronto: Insomniac, 2004.

The Jupiter Theft

Much is made in early chapters of this 1977 novel of the astronaut protagonist's perfect sense of pitch and ability to play music. Readers curious as to why are rewarded when Tod Jameson encounters the aliens, known as the Cygnans (so named by humans as they are believed to originate from the constellation/black hole of Cygnus X-1), who are attempting to steal the planet Jupiter's hydrogen for fuel. The language of these creatures, **Cygnanese**, is primarily musical, and Jameson learns to communicate with them by whistling and by using a Moog synthesizer.

The "voices" of the Cygnans are described as sounding somewhat like bagpipes, harmonicas, or chirping and are used to communicate through pitch and scale, with each tone representing an individual phoneme. Capable of two octaves of expression, as well as half tones, multinoted tones, and glissandos, there are thus thousands of phonemes in Cygnanese. Words can be produced by sequences of tones, and larger concepts are often produced by making these tones into chords in a seeming parallel to the visual concept of the ideogram.

At the beginning of the novel, the Cygnanese script appears cursive and is written in a sine-wave pattern rather than in parallel lines. Later it is described as looking clawlike and is compared to Greek and Hebrew letter forms. The Cygnans also communicate through gestures, such as a mock rush to indicate a violent disagreement or the assuming of a submissive posture to signify an apology. Perhaps indicating the single-minded and purposeful lifestyle of the Cygnans, there is no word in their language for "please."

Reference: Moffitt, Donald. *The Jupiter Theft*. New York: Ballantine, 1977.

Jurgen

In James Branch Cabell's episodic and baroque satirical fantasy novel (1919), the roguish forty-something Jurgen is given his youth back and sets out on a series of amorous and mythological adventures, including encounters with gods, a descent in to hell, and an "escape" to heaven before returning to Earth and his shrewish wife.

While there appears to be no artificial languages presented in this text, Cabell does utilize several spells and magical charms in "unknown" languages, including such phrases as *a ab hur hus, eman hetan, temon,* and *arigizator.* According to James P. Cover, these spells are taken from Reginald Scot's *Discovery of Witchcraft* (1584).

References: Cabell, James Branch. *Jurgen: A Comedy of Justice.* New York: Dover, 1977; Cover, James P. *Notes on* Jurgen. New York: McBride, 1928.

K

Kingdoms of Elfin

In Sylvia Townsend Warner's 1977 collection of tales of fairy lives and adventures, a Scottish professor of rhetoric, James Sutherland, has occasion to meet Elfin, as they are called, and eventually becomes a welcome visitor to their society. Their speech, also called **Elfin**, "resembled no civilized mortal language; slurred and full of hushed hisses, it was more like some dialect of Gaelic" (214). When Sutherland has acquired conversational Elfin, he contemplates writing "a treatise of Elfin Grammar" (217), a notion altogether alien to the unlettered fairies, but nothing comes of this project. Nothing more is revealed in Warner's text about this language.

Reference: Warner, Sylvia Townsend. *Kingdoms of Elfin*. London: Chatto and Windus, 1977.

L

Land of the Lost

A relatively complex children's television program, produced by brothers Sid and Marty Krofft (*H. R. Pufnstuf*; *Sigmund and the Seamonsters*), *The Land of the Lost* concerns the Marshall family (a father and two children), who are transported to a primitive world through a "time doorway." This land features dinosaurs, civil war veterans, an alien race known as the Sleestak, and the Pakuni, who are Neanderthal-like humanoids.

It is the Pakuni, rather than the Sleestak, who are given their own language in the program. Developed by the Californian linguist Victoria Fromkin (see also *Blade*), the **Paku** language is based on the Kwa languages of southwest Africa. Fromkin created approximately 200 words of Paku and, in general, they are less than three syllables and are dominated by vowel sounds: for example, *amasu* (love), *onam* (food), and *yo* (yes). The grammar of Paku appears consistent with pluralization and adjective creation following set rules—the verb *mund* (to scare) becomes *mundi* (frightened), while *abu* (child) has clear connections to *abuni* (children) as well as *abusa* (small) and *abosa* (short). Paku also appears to follow English syntax, with the exception of adjectives following the verb. Rather than "strange noise," in Pakuni it is "noise strange" (*oje rocasa*).

Not only is Paku the first artificial language created for a children's program, it is also one of the earliest examples of television producers hiring a professional linguist to design a language, a practice that has become much more common today.

References: The Land of the Lost. Produced by Sid and Marty Krofft. NBC, 1974–1976; "*The Land of the Lost* (1974 Television Series)": en.wikipedia.org/wiki/Land_of_the_Lost_%281974_television_series%29; Pakuni Dictionary: members.aol.com/PyrateScum/pakuni.html.

The Land That Time Forgot

Edgar Rice Burroughs's *The Land That Time Forgot* is in fact three novellas, *The Land That Time Forgot*, *The People That Time Forgot*, and *Out of Time's Abyss*, all of which were published in *Blue Book Magazine* in 1918 before being collected under the one title in book form in 1924. Together they tell of the adventures of various American, English, and German characters who discover the South Pacific island of Caprona and, within it, Caspak, a place where prehistoric beasts yet thrive. Besides pterodactyls and sabertooth tigers, Caspak also contains a number of tribes of humanlike beings. Although each tribe is differentiated from the other by degrees of physical and intellectual evolution, "the tongues of the various tribes are identical except for amplifications in the rising scale of evolution" (168). Thus, with a single **Caspakian** language, Burroughs directly connects linguistic competence and ability with biological evolution. At the lowest rung of this hierarchy, the *Alu* tribe are hairy and without tools, weapons, or words (their name means "speechless"), while the *Galu* (literally "ropeman" [257]), who have woven blankets, ornaments, and weapons, such as the bow and arrow and the noose with *honda*, "a golden oval about which is braided the rawhide [rope], making a heavy and accurate weight for the throwing of the noose" (256–257), enjoy the enviable status of "golden race" (168). Between these extremes are such variations as *Bo-lu*, *Sto-lu*, *Band-lu*, and *Kro-lu*: club men, hatchet men, spear men, and bow-and-arrow men, respectively. The Bo-lu have "the simplest form of speech known to Caspak" (172–173), and each successively developed tribe is more linguistically expressive and articulate than the last. Burroughs takes this concept to the most elementary limit by suggesting that members of the Band-lu, for example, generally have two-syllable names and words, whereas the Sto-lu generally have words and names of one syllable (126).

It is interesting to note the implication that, judging from the meanings of these tribes' names, the word or root *lu* connotes, apparently simultaneously, "speech" and "man": this interpretation is corroborated by the definitions of compound words like *coslupak*, "unpeopled country, or literally, no man's land" (209), and *jaal-lu*, "hyena-man, an appellation of contempt" (325). Besides the altogether macho tenor of the novel, patriarchy looms large in Caspak, and the Caspakian language reflects the poor situation of females. The word *lu* is more often used in *The Land That Time Forgot* than *lo*, the word for woman. To the consternation of one of Burroughs's easily flustered male heroes, "there is no Caspakian equivalent" for the term "young lady," and "to speak always of a beautiful young girl as a 'she' may be literal; but it seems far from gallant" (230). Women in all of the tribes are possessions, and men unhesitatingly fight for ownership of an attractive "she." Women also participate in a strange ritual that turns out to be central to (if not exactly explanatory of) the mysteries of Caspak: why the heroes see no children among the tribes, for example, and how individual members may graduate from one tribe to the next above it on the evolutionary ladder. This ritual, called *Ata*, involves women of every tribe immersing themselves in warm pools of water ("filled with billions of tadpoles" [119]) nearby their habitations every morning. The Caspakian life cycle is one of a highly accelerated evolutionary pattern, beginning with the transformation of female eggs into tadpoles within these pools (whether the eggs are first inseminated is not altogether clear, and Burroughs is notoriously, often comically squeamish when it comes to sex). These tadpoles may become fish or reptiles, some of them then amphibians, and then very few may develop "into the lowest order of man" and begin the ascent from Alu to Galu (351). This life cycle explains why "from the Bo-lu to the Kro-lu there is no word which corresponds with our word *mother*. They speak of *ata* and *cor sva jo*, meaning *reproduction* and *from the beginning*, and point toward the south; but no one has a mother" (199). The phrase *cor-sva-jo* (the use of hyphens for such constructions is inconsistent in the text) may thus be used as a specific geographical location but also serves as a metaphor, so a speaker in *The People That Time Forgot* may say that his dog "came to me *cor-sva-jo*" (245). There is an important distinction, however, between someone's being *cor-sva-jo* or *cos-ata-lu* (if the someone in question is male; if female, *cos-ata-lo*). The term *cos-ata-lu* has the literal meaning "no-egg-man, or one who is born directly as are the young of the outer world of mammals"; such births among the Galu only result after seven generations of the same ancestral line (351–352).

John Bradley, the hero of *Out of Time's Abyss*, is captured by yet another tribe or race, the *Wieroo*. They have developed wings and can fly at great speeds, but they can only produce *cos-ata-lu*, "so they prey upon the Galus for their women and sometimes capture and torture the Galu men who are *cos-ata-lu* in an endeavor to learn the secret which they believe will give them unlimited power over all other denizens of Caspak" (351). Murderous, imperialistic, and sun-worshipping (they call their god *Luata*), their culture is based on the principle of *tas-ad*: "doing everything the right way, or, in other words, the Wieroo way" (385). The Wieroo are also distinctive in that they have a written language: Bradley discovers paper with "strange hieroglyphics" on it and surprises his Wieroo captors by signing his name and so demonstrating his own written language (327–328).

The few other items of Caspakian vocabulary presented in the novel, such as *kazor* (beware) and *jo-oos* ("flying reptiles—pterodactyls" [222]), suggest its functional but simple design. The commemorative edition of *The Land That Time Forgot* published by University of Nebraska Press includes a Caspakian glossary, but Burroughs did not provide samples of the written Wieroo language.

Reference: Burroughs, Edgar Rice. *The Land That Time Forgot*. Lincoln: University of Nebraska Press, 1999.

"The Language of Love"

In Robert Sheckley's 1957 story, a young lover frustrated by his inability to articulate his love fully and precisely endeavors to learn the "Language of Love" of the peoples of the planet Tyana II. Rather than relying on such bland formulations as "I love you," the Tyanians "would use a phrase denoting the exact kind and class of love they felt at that specific moment, and used for no other purpose" (41). Although the Tyanians are extinct, one researcher from Earth remains there and after some hesitation accepts the hero as a pupil.

The "Language of Love" is taught alongside "a technique of love-making quite incredible in its perfection" (41–42); there is no clear separation of the two in the story, just as there are no unmediated examples of the language at all. The story concludes with ironic bathos: having learned this amazingly precise and honest manner of expressing one's feelings, the hero tells his patient beloved that he is "rather fond" of her. Having lost her, he is able to deduce that the reason for the Tyanians' extinction is that they "had been so preoccupied with the science of love, after a while they just didn't get around to making any" (50).

Reference: Sheckley, Robert. "The Language of Love." *Galaxy* (May 1957): 39–50.

The Languages of Pao

Jack Vance's novel *The Languages of Pao* (1958) is unusually rich in the number of invented languages it boasts, and it is on the question of how language conditions thought and ability, and thus power and freedom, that the plot turns. Walter E. Meyers rightly called the book "the fullest exposition of the [Sapir–] Whorf hypothesis" (166).

The fifteen billion placid humans who live on the planet Pao speak a language "derived from Waydalic" and expressive of the typical Paonese feeling of being "a cork on a sea of a million waves, lofted, lowered, thrust aside by incomprehensible forces" (3). Without verbs, adjectives, or even "formal word comparison such as *good, better, best*" (3), **Paonese** favors declaration over description, straightforward avowal (a non-Paonese in the novel remarks on "the Paonese concepts of 'trust,' 'loyalty,' 'good faith'" [160]) over critical assessment. Literally translated, the Paonese for the statement "There are two matters I wish to discuss with you" would read "*Statement-of-importance* (a single word in Paonese)—in a state of readiness—two; ear—of Mercantil [see below]—*in a state of readiness*; mouth—of this person here—*in a state of volition*," where the words in italics "represent suffixes of condition" (10). Similarly, the Paonese sentence "The farmer chops down a tree" would be literally rendered "Farmer *in state of exertion*; axe *agency*; tree *in state of subjection to attack*" (57). Although this "necessary paraphrasing" may seem to complicate utterances, Vance observes, "the Paonese sentence, '*Rhomel-en-shrai bogal-Mercantil-nli-en mous-es-nli-ro*' requires only three more phonemes than, 'There are two matters I wish to discuss with you'" (10). This is the novel's lone sample of a full Paonese sentence, and only a few other terms are mentioned, such as *Bereglo* ("applied to an unskillful slaughter-house worker, or a creature which worries and gnaws its victim" [38]) and *praesens* (called "the Paonese vitality-word" [91]). Students recite the numbers *Ai, Shrai, Vida, Mina, Nona, Drona, Hivan*, and *Imple* (83), but it is not certain what amounts these terms represent: we do know that the Paonese system of counting "is based on the number 8," and so "a Paonese 100 is 64, 1000 is 512, etc." (11).

Unfortunately for the citizens of Pao, they are at the mercy of the demanding and militant people of the planet Batmarsh. Little is revealed about their language, **Batch**, apart from the fact that in Batch "the word 'friend' could only be interpreted as 'companion-in-arms'" (169). These people are presented in contrast with the **Mercantil**, interplanetary traders who "express themselves in neat quanta of precise information" (10). The same phrase in Mercantil which may be translated into English as "I am at your orders, sir" may be literally translated as "I—Ambassador—here-now gladly-obey the just spoken-orders of-you—Supreme Royalty—here-now heard and understood" (10). The Paonese are squeezed between the belligerent Batmarsh armies and their Mercantil suppliers of arms and goods, and the heir to the Paonese throne, Beran, is forced into hiding.

Beran seeks the help of Lord Palafox, a megalomaniacal linguist (also called a wizard) whose home planet and mother tongue are both called **Breakness**. Called "the language of insulated intelligence," Breakness is "basically 'isolative,'" unlike the "polysynthetic" language of the neighboring planet Pao; the speaker of any utterance in

Breakness is "the frame of reference upon which the syntax depended, a system which made for both logical elegance and simplicity" (81). The literally self-centered essence of the language is reflective of the central principles of (explicitly patriarchal) personal interest that govern the people of Breakness: a great number of Paonese conceptual expressions (such as trust, cooperation, loyalty, anger, and love) find no equivalents or counterparts in this language. Not only is there no "I" in its usage, there are no personal pronouns at all, "except for third person constructions—although these actually were contractions of noun phrases" (82). Nor is there a passive voice, as verbs are "self-contained: 'to strike,' 'to receive-impact'" (82). Polarities ("such as 'go' and 'stay'") are employed rather than "negativity," but the language is rich in words "for intellectual manipulation" and "to define a hundred types of ratiocination" (82).

In laying out his strategies for Pao, Palafox cites as an instructive example the people of the planet Vale, who "give the impression of insanity," while in truth they are "complete anarchists," and their language reflects this philosophy of "complete spontaneity." "Language on Vale," explains Palafox, "is personal improvisation, with the fewest possible conventions. Each individual selects a speech as you or I might choose the color of our garments" (63). No examples of Vale speech are provided in the novel. Palafox explains that language can be used as a vehicle for social and ideological change, and attitudes on Pao may be changed if they are instructed to speak languages that embody the desired values of the new attitude.

Following the advice of Palafox, the people of Pao are divided into labor-specific classes and taught new languages—**Cogitant**, **Technicant**, and **Valiant**—to facilitate their skills in their assigned tasks. Vance gives no specific examples of these languages' vocabularies or grammars, but the ideological differences of their construction are outlined. Cogitant is a "simplified" version of the language Breakness and is designed for the managerial and intellectual classes of the planet Pao. The modifications from Breakness are against "the solipsism latent in the original tongue" (84) and include "considerably looser use of pronouns" (131). Technicant, meanwhile, is designed for and used by the technician classes and accordingly has a grammar that is "extravagantly complicated but altogether consistent and logical" (78). The newly formed warriors of Pao speak Valiant, utterances that are "based on the contrast and comparison of strength, with a grammar simple and direct" (77). In stark contrast to its basis language, Paonese, whose characteristics are passivity and dispassion, Valiant is "rich in effort-producing gutturals and hard vowels" and makes synonymous notions like "pleasure" and "overcoming a resistance," "relaxation" and "shame," and so on (77).

The situation grows more complex when language students generate **Pastiche**, a workable blend of these and other tongues, and one student remarks how "on Pao one must know five languages merely to ask for a glass of wine" (109). By the end of the novel, Pastiche becomes the Paonese lingua franca. "A tongue used by men dedicated to human service" (214), Pastiche is a blend or "bastard mish-mash" (117) of the languages of the planets Breakness, Mercantil, and Batch, and, primarily, the Paonese language and Paonese sublanguages Technicant, Valiant, and Cogitant. The novel gives no direct examples of Pastiche utterances, and it is unclear how the considerable hegemonic contradictions between these component languages are transcended.

References: Meyers, Walter E. *Aliens and Linguists: Language Study and Science Fiction.* Athens: University of Georgia Press, 1980; Vance, Jack. *The Languages of Pao.* New York: ibooks, 2004.

"The Last Castle"

Jack Vance's 1966 novella "The Last Castle" tells the story of an insurrection against human aristocrats, given to the theoretical sciences and daintier arts, by a species formerly kept as slaves, the Meks, who are mechanically proficient and methodical. Although one of the humans is inclined to study Mek "physiology, linguistic modes, and social patterns" (150), Vance's text gives no definite signs of a unique **Mek** language per se. Rather more strangely, there is some suggestion that the castle-inhabiting humans themselves have a distinctive language, whose "pungency" is remarked on in a footnote. Little is known about this language apart from a few definitions of terms, such as *volith* ("to toy with a matter, the implication being that the person involved is of such Jovian potency that all difficulties dwindle to contemptible triviality" [153]) and *sthross* ("indicating a manner flawed by an almost imperceptible slackness and lack of punctilio" [156]), which reflect the patricians' affectations and their fixation on dignity.

Reference: Vance, Jack. "The Last Castle." *The Dragon Masters.* New York: ibooks, 2002. 139–233.

The Last Hawk

The third in Catherine Asaro's "Skolian Empire" series of science-fiction novels, *The Last Hawk* (1997) is set on a planet named Coba. Kelricson Garlin Valdoria kya Skolia, a member of the technologically superior Empire, crash-lands on Coba and there becomes a pawn, then a significant player in its politics. Kelric (as his name is abbreviated) speaks **Skolian**, a language generally unknown on Coba because the planet has wholly rejected the Empire. Written Skolian is described vaguely as "hieroglyphics," and the only significant sample of Skolian is the word *pug*, a multipurpose "cuss-word" (440) that seems to have the same polymorphous applications as "fuck" (a common example of its usage: "for pugging sake" [385]). Also spoken within the Skolian Empire, though "only by scholars and Imperial nobility" (438), is an ancient language named **Iotic**, and Kelric makes mention of a language from a planet within the Empire, **Lyshrioli** (the planet is named Lyshriol), whence his name: Kelric is the name of the god of youth and hope. Whether there are any linguistic connections between Skolian, Iotic, and Lyshrioli is unclear.

Teotecan, the modern language of Coba, is just as minimally sketched as Skolian, but more vocabulary is provided, including a few idiomatic expressions (the novel has several appendices, one of which is a glossary). For example, a laser is a *sailing-light device*; a *scowlbug* is both a kind of beetle and slang for "angry person" (441); and a *pog* is an amphibious, mountain-dwelling animal and constituent of the saying *I'll be a pog on a pole* ("I'm amazed" [439]).

However, Teotecan's history and its relation to past languages of Coba are presented in a very fragmentary way, and the hints of other Coban languages remain little more than hints. There is an **Old Script**, a hieroglyphic form of writing used in a previous age, but there are also Teotecan words marked in the glossary as "archaic":

what distinction there is between these categories is uncertain. Furthermore, there is an even older language; Kelric hears one phrase in this language, *Chabiat k'in* (translated literally as "the day is guarded, watched over" [114]), as well as some ceremonial chanting. Presumably this ancient language is **Ucatan**, also called **Tozil**. "Ucatan had been purely hieroglyphic," Asaro relates, "but over the centuries the glyphs had become stylized, breaking into two parts, a Quis shape [one of a number of multisided dice] and an accent" (268). One etymology is briefly traced for Karn, a name of one of the Coban estates (nations or tribes): "Historians believed the name Karn derived from *carn-abi* in Old Script, which in turn probably derived from the even more ancient Ucatan language, the *chabi* glyph, which meant 'to guard, care for, or watch over'" (274–275). The novel does not explain why the Old Script, if it arose from Ucatan, should return to the unaccented hieroglyphic form, nor how modern Teotecan script appears and what differences it has from the previous scripts.

Asaro's series also includes such titles as *Primary Inversion* (1995), *Catch the Lightning* (1996), and *The Quantum Rose* (2000).

Reference: Asaro, Catherine. *The Last Hawk*. New York: TOR Books, 1997.

The Last Starfighter

In this early 1980s science-fiction film, a teenager is recruited to help defend Rylos, a beleaguered galactic civilization, from Xur, a native usurper who is leading an enemy race, the Ko-Dans, against the Rylans. The teen protagonist is enlisted due to his superior abilities in a video game that, in its game play, replicates the ship-to-ship combat required to defeat the Ko-Dan armada.

Upon arrival at the star base where he is to be trained, the hero of this film is greeted by various aliens who speak to him in their native tongue of **Rylan**. Before he is given a pin that functions as a universal translator, there are several exchanges presented in untranslated Rylan. Unfortunately, the only phrase that has been transcribed from this language (in Alan Dean Foster's novelization) is *georg-nat*, which translates as the affirmative "it's yours" (56).

The Rylan written script that appears as signage and on computer consoles throughout the film is Hebrew, which has here been rendered in a more geometric, or linear, form.

References: Foster, Alan Dean. *The Last Starfighter*. New York: Berkley, 1984; *The Last Starfighter*. Directed by Nick Castle. Screenplay by Jonathan Betuel, 1984.

The Left Hand of Darkness

Ursula K. Le Guin's 1969 science-fiction novel takes place on the icy planet Gethen, known simply as "Winter" to the members of the interplanetary Ekumen alliance. *Ekumen* is a "Terran word; in the common tongue it's called the Household" (135). The nature both of "Terran" and of "the common tongue" remain obscure in the novel, and the necessity for such a common tongue is made more puzzling by the fact that the Ekumen have developed telepathic abilities: "mindspeech," as characters from Genthen call it, the "language that has no lies in it" (199).

Seeking to initiate trade and cultural exchange with Gethen, the Ekumen send an envoy, a man from Earth named Genly Ai, who faces the challenge of negotiating with a factious, competitive, and proud people who effectively change sex according to a seasonal pattern. The mad king of the nation of Karhide dismisses Ai's alien language as "Voidish" (37) and shows no interest in the envoy's offer. For him, as for all people of the planet, everything revolves around *shifgrethor* ("prestige, face, place, the pride-relationship, the untranslatable and all-important principle of social authority" [13]), and *kemmer*, an individual's period of estrus. Ai then travels to another rival country, Orgoreyn, and fares even worse there before being smuggled back to Karhide, where he is received differently as a consequence. In the course of these adventures, Ai learns and reveals details of and differences between the languages of the two cultures.

Karhidish has many dialects as well as a lively body of slang, proverbs, and legends. Although it does not have a word for "war" (34), it does contain, by Ai's count, over sixty words for fallen snow and more for types of snowfall, ice, temperature range, wind conditions, and the like. For example, *bessa* denotes fallen snow that is "soft and still unpacked" (210), whereas *neserem* is "fine snow on a moderate gale: a light blizzard" (223). Karhiders generally show little inhibition in discussing sex and kemmer but consider hormonal imbalances and over-favored gender behaviors perversions. Speaking of such a pervert, a Karhider uses "the pronoun that designates a male animal, not the pronoun for a human being in the masculine role of kemmer" (63). A common expression used to close an argument or otherwise save face is *nusuth*, which Ai translates as "no matter" (59).

Genly Ai observes that Karhiders cannot pronounce the "l" in his name and say instead "Genry" (30), but **Orgota** speakers in Orgoreyn have no such trouble. He refers to "the sinuous Orgota language that made Karhidish sound like rocks rattled in a can" (110). Orgota also has its discriminations for types of Winter weather: for instance, "snowing *peditia*" means for a Karhidish speaker "*sove*-snow, a thick, wet fall" (191). Idioms and colloquialisms are hinted at: the word *sarf*, the name of an administrative policing body in Orgoreyn, "means in gutter-Orgota, trash, it's a nickname" (142).

The title of the novel echoes lines from "Tormer's Lay," remembered and translated by a Karhider: "Light is the left hand of darkness / and darkness the right hand of light" (233). The original text of the lay is not given.

Reference: Le Guin, Ursula K. *The Left Hand of Darkness*. New York: Ace Books, 1999.

The Legend of Miaree

Zach Hughes's *The Legend of Miaree* (1974) is a frame science-fiction novel in which a group of students under the direction of a literature professor read, and intermittently discuss, a "legend" left behind by two dead alien civilizations, the Delanians and Artonuee.

The surviving readership, a community of many planets, speak a common language (enforced years previously by "a universal language law" [70]), although variations in dialect, lexicon, and intonation exist on each planet, with strongest variation occurring on the outer "rim" worlds. Because of this relative homogeneity, the unnamed race has lost the discourse of linguistics (more likely philology, but the text claims the former) and is forced to use computers to translate the legend so that the readers of the manuscript suspect that elements of the text have been rendered without the subtlety or nuances that a living translator might have produced.

Part of the legend is also devoted to communication issues as the Artonuee character Miaree is chosen to learn the language of the Delanians in anticipation of their arrival within the Artonuee planet system. The Delanians (who are referred to as men and appear human in every respect) have beamed interstellar messages explaining their culture and providing language instructions throughout the universe, but the Artonuee, a race of humanoid butterflies, are the first "others" the Delanians have encountered. As the Artonuee communicate through a combination of pictorial telepathy and infrequent vocalizations, the Delanians, whose language is completely verbal and textual, do not learn **Artonuee**.

This language of mental pictures and sounds is not fully developed in the course of the novel but, as a matriarchal and pacifist culture, the Artonuee do not possess the concept of "army" and "speak" solely in the feminine gender. As a race that mates with a mind to population control, they also have no concept of love nor terms of affection. As the Artonuee are depicted reading reports on "duppaper," they must also have a written form of their language—likely pictographic rather than alphabetic—but it is not described in the novel.

Reference: Hughes, Zach. *The Legend of Miaree*. New York: Ballantine, 1974.

The Life and Adventures of Peter Wilkins

The hero of Robert Paltock's 1750 novel undergoes a picaresque series of adventures before, lost in an unknown country with little light, he encounters a strange people called, in their language, *Glumms* (men) and *Gawreys* (women). Though human in form, these creatures have natural coverings on their backs that, opened, serve as wings for flight or even as a kind of flotilla. This covering is called a *Graundee*, and Wilkins is told that criminals have their *Graundee* slit to remove their ability to fly and are then referred to as a *Crashee* ("slit": the antonym is *Ingcrashee* [111]).

Wilkins has remarkably little trouble conversing with Youwarkee, the first Gawrey he meets, and even comes to marry her and have children with her. He notes that at first "she spoke part *English*, part her own Tongue, and I the same, as we best understood each other, yet I shall give you [the reader] our Discourse, Word for Word, in plain *English*" (111). After many complex interactions with many other Glumms and Gawreys, Wilkins names their speech "the *Swangeatine* Tongue" (370), after the word *Swangean*, or "flight" (119).

Little is said about **Swangeantine** apart from Wilkins's regular deployment of certain words and names (a glossary of which appears as an appendix). The following are some sample vocabulary: *Abb* (a room without a door), *Barkatt* (husband), *Puly* (an image), *Ragam* (priest), and *Zaps* (lords). The only complete Swangeatine sentence represented in the text is *Ors clam gee*: "here am I" (176).

Wilkins effects considerable changes on the society during his time in *Doorpt Swangeanti* (literally, the Land of Flight): he helps put down a usurper's rebellion, unifies the kingdom under the new name of *Sass Doorpt Swangeanti*, and introduces

Christianity to the Glumms and Gawreys. In accomplishing the second, he helps to abolish *Laskmett* (slavery) and frees the miners of Mount Alkoe, who apparently speak another language, which Wilkins does not know but some Glumms can translate—this language is neither named nor described.

Wilkins's religious revolution requires him to create and disseminate a system of writing, technology previously unknown to these people, and then translate a Latin Bible into the new written *Swangeatine*. He employs the Roman alphabet and replaces Collwarr, the name of the God whose very images were believed to have fatal powers, with the God of the Old and New Testaments. Requiring the manufacture of pens and ink, the subsequent "Increase of Writing" (372) also aids the new free-trading economy Wilkins has helped to start in *Sass Doorpt Swangeanti*.

Reference: Paltock, Robert. *The Life and Adventures of Peter Wilkins.* Edited by Christopher Bentley. London: Oxford University Press, 1973.

The Listeners

James Gunn's 1972 science-fiction novel concerns a SETI program that, after fifty years of searching, receives a message from a race referred to as the Capellans. Rather than trying to communicate in their own language, the Capellans send a message in binary code that is then rendered as a pictographic image. Gunn's novel thus considers the question of a universal language and the issue of interspecies communication.

Having deciphered the Capellan message, earthly scientists send a response that, after ninety years, is rewarded by the aliens sending back the complete **Capellan** language, world history, and literature. Upon receiving this knowledge, however, scientists on Earth also realize that the Capellans have become an extinct race.

Reference: Gunn, James. *The Listeners.* Dallas: BenBella, 2004.

The Lord of the Rings

A professor of Anglo-Saxon language and literature, J.R.R. Tolkien confessed in a 1931 lecture (later published with the title "A Secret Vice") that he enjoyed writing songs and verses in languages he invented. Eventually this habit produced *The Hobbit* (1937), the first of his fictions set in Middle-earth, and then the trilogy *The Lord of the Rings*, composed of *The Fellowship of the Ring* (1954), *The Two Towers* (1954), and *The Return of the King* (1955). These books, along with various other tales and poems (including the twelve volumes comprising *The History of Middle-Earth*), constitute an enduring popular mythology that fans have not only adopted but expanded in films, novels, comic books, Web sites, and role-playing games. This mythology is also notably byzantine: besides the stories of Frodo and Bilbo, Tolkien developed a panoramic history behind the Men, Elves, Dwarves, Hobbits, and Orcs and their languages.

In fact, these histories of different cultures are so elaborately interwoven, it is no easy task to say plainly how many fictional languages there are in Middle-earth. Naturally some are more fleshed out than others, but there are also periods in which speech and orthography may or definitely do change, there are significant but not always clear hints about regional dialects, and several of the languages stem from an earlier form of one of the other languages. Some Tolkien scholars will answer that there are, for example, fourteen complete languages (Ruth S. Noel), while others will hesitate and concede that perhaps two languages are so detailed that one could actually learn and use them, though there are several others less substantially depicted. Much of the information represented below is provided in the last two appendices, E and F, in Tolkien's text.

Westron is "a mannish speech, though enriched and softened under Elvish influence" (1162). It is also known as **Common Speech** (Sôval Phârë) because of its wide usage in the western lands of Middle-earth. Most of the dialogue of The Lord of the Rings is understood to be spoken in Westron, though it is not rendered as such: Tolkien has, as it were, "translated" almost all of the narrative to English. Hobbits (banakil), for example, abandoned their own language, of which very little is known,

	I	II	III	IV
I	1	2	3	4
2	5	6	7	8
3	9	10	11	12
4	13	14	15	16
5	17	18	19	20
6	21	22	23	24
	25	26	27	28
	29	30	31	32
	33	34	35	36

The Tengwar, from *The Lord of the Rings*. The table on the next page defines each symbol. Reprinted by permission of the Tolkien Estate.

The Tengwar, with definitions from Quenya (The numbers correspond with the figure of the Tengwar on the previous page.)

 1. *Tinco* ("metal")
 2. *Parma* ("book")
 3. *Calma* ("lamp")
 4. *Quesse* ("feather")
 5. *Ando* ("gate")
 6. *Umbar* ("fate")
 7. *Anga* ("iron")
 8. *Ungwe* ("spider's web")
 9. *Súle* ("wind") or *Thúle* ("spirit")
10. *Formen* ("North")
11. *Harma* ("treasure") or *Aha* ("rage")
12. *Hwesta* ("breeze")
13. *Anto* ("mouth")
14. *Ampa* ("hook")
15. *Anca* ("jaws")
16. *Unque* ("a hollow")
17. *Númen* ("West")
18. *Malta* ("gold")
19. *Noldo* (a Quenya title of nobility)
20. *Nwalme* ("torment")
21. *Óre* ("heart" or "inner mind")
22. *Vala* ("Angelic Power")
23. *Anna* ("gift")
24. *Vilya* ("air" or "sky")
25. *Rómen* ("East")
26. *Arda* ("region" or "realm")
27. *Lambe* ("tongue")
28. *Alda* ("tree")
29. *Silme* ("starlight")
30. *Silme nuquerna*
31. *Áre* ("sunlight") or *Esse* ("name")
32. *Áre nuquerna*
33. *Hyarmen* ("South")
34. *Hwesta Sindarinwa*
35. *Yanta* ("bridge")
36. *Úre* ("heat")

a full millennium before the events of *The Lords of the Rings* in favor of the Common Speech, an absorptive mix comparable to modern English. Regional dialects and accents differ, but one speaker of Westron generally understands another. Not all tribes of Men use Westron, however: the so-called Wild Men of Drúadan Forest and the people called the Dunendlings speak tongues that are "wholly alien" (1163) to the Common Speech, but Tolkien's text does not contain any examples of these.

The two principal languages of the Elves of the West (and the most developed fictional languages in *The Lord of the Rings*) are **Quenya** (or **High-elven**) and **Sindarin** (or **Grey-elven**). The first is archaic, a sort of ur-tongue not just for Elvish languages but for nearly all of the languages of Middle-earth; the second is retained by its speakers for daily use. Tolkien's fifth Appendix spells out in considerable detail the finer points of pronunciation of these Eldarin languages. *Eldar* simply means Western Elves and, like the general term **Elvish**, serves as a grouping for these languages. The differences between the two languages ought not to be elided, however, and a random example of vocabulary demonstrates both the familial proximities and the practical distances between them: the Quenyan word for "spring," for instance, is *tuilë*, but in Sindarin the season is known as *ethuil*.

Written Elvish uses letters, while runes are used for all manner of inscription. The constituent letters are known as the *Tengwar* of Fëanor, named after the Elf who is thought to have invented it. Because it is phonetic, this alphabet is not limited to speakers of Quenya and Sindarin, but part of the long-standing animosity between Dwarves and Elves registers in the Dwarves' pointed rejection of this alphabet in favor their own style of runes.

THE ANGERTHAS

THE ANGERTHAS

Values			
1 p	16 zh	31 l	46 e
2 b	17 nj—z	32 lh	47 ē
3 f	18 k	33 ng—nd	48 a
4 v	19 g	34 s—h	49 ā
5 hw	20 kh	35 s—'	50 o
6 m	21 gh	36 z—ŋ	51 ō
7 (mh) mb	22 ŋ—n	37 ng*	52 ö
8 t	23 kw	38 nd—nj	53 n*
9 d	24 gw	39 i (y)	54 h—s
10 th	25 khw	40 y*	55 *
11 dh	26 ghw,w	41 hy*	56 *
12 n—r	27 ngw	42 u	57 ps*
13 ch	28 nw	43 ū	58 ts*
14 j	29 r—j	44 w	+h
15 sh	30 rh—zh	45 ü	&

The Angerthas, from *The Lord of the Rings*. Reprinted by permission of the Tolkien Estate.

Cirth is the word for runes, but the runic alphabet is called the *Angerthas*. The *Angerthas Daeron* "was devised to represent the sounds of Sindarin only" (1157), while the *Angerthas Moria* (which appear in the list of values given in the figure below on the right side of dashes), the invention of the Dwarves, "introduced a number of unsystematic changes in value, as well as certain new *cirth*: 37, 40, 41, 53, 55, 56" (1160).

Elvish languages have regional dialects, but these are not represented in any real detail. **Valinorean**, for example, is the name of a dialect of Quenya, once spoken by Elves from the region of Valinor.

It is not true, incidentally, that the Elvish languages are so fully mapped out that one can use them for everyday speech, though they are rich and flexible enough to allow considerable invention in written compositions and translations. Just as *Hamlet* has been dutifully translated into the language of Klingons from *Star Trek*, "The Lord's Prayer" and various songs and hymns have been translated into Quenya and Sindarin.

Dwarvish (*Khuzdul*) is "a tongue of lore rather than a cradle-speech" (1166). Befitting a secretive people given to underground pursuits, the language of the Dwarves is mysterious, and the reader is given only occasional names of places by the character Gimli. The Dwarves keep their language to themselves in the same way they each keep unrevealed their own secret or private names. The battle cry *Baruk Khazâd! Khazâd aimênu!* translates as "Axes of the Dwarves! The Dwarves are upon you!" (1167). Tolkien notes that his translated account of events gives "Northern forms" to Dwarvish names, and it is difficult not to see a Scots or Celtic stereotype behind Gimli's mannered utterances (for instance, "My blood runs chill" [817]) and his people's reputed characteristics, among them stubbornness and lust for wealth. Written Khuzdul employs Elvish runes with modifications, made to include sounds exclusive to Dwarvish speech.

The language of Mordor, and by extension the language of the Dark Lord Sauron, his underlings, and all things and purposes evil, is known as **Black Speech**. The enemies of Sauron are loathe to utter even a word of it. Probably the best example of the language is the inscription on the Ring of Rings (shown on next page), the magical device Sauron forged to become master of Middle-earth and which the heroes of Tolkien's trilogy struggle to destroy: *Ash nazg durbatulûk, ash nazg gimbatul, / ash nazg thrakatulûk agh burzum-ishi krimpatul* ("One Ring to rule them all, One Ring to find them, / One Ring to bring them all and in the darkness bind them" [63]).

The vocabulary of Black Speech as it is presented in *The Lord of the Rings* is largely limited to the names of the servants and means of Sauron. The name Nazgûl, for example, literally means "Ring-wraiths," phantoms who pursue the bearer of the Ring of Rings. Orcs, vicious creatures bred by the Dark Lord to fight for him, no doubt get their name from the word *uruk* (1165). While the first generation of Orcs had no language, Orcs later developed widely varied dialects of **Orkish**, but the disparity between these regional and tribal dialects was so irreconcilable and frustrating that Orcs later assumed Westron for communication, "though in such a fashion as to make it hardly less unlovely than Orkish"; Tolkien dismissively calls this new form of Westron a "jargon" (1165). The failure of Black Speech to unite its speakers is implicitly connected with the failures of Sauron's evil ambitions.

The giant treelike caretakers of forests, the Ents, also have a language and a philosophy of language. "Real names tell you the story they belong to in my language," says the Ent Treebeard, referring to "Old Entish" (486). Tolkien's appendix calls spoken **Entish**—no one has made an attempt to render it in writing—"slow, sonorous, agglomerated, repetitive, indeed long-winded" (1164–1165). The sheer effort of speaking Entish constrains them to speak only what is necessary or worth saying, and in turn reflects their esteem of patience, slowness, and contemplativeness as virtues. One example of Entish vocabulary offered in the novel is "part of the name" for hill: *a-lalla-lalla-rumba-kamanda-lind-or-burúmë* (486). Like so many (if not all) of the languages of Middle-earth, Entish has some roots in Quenya, for the language was formed in order to respond to the communicative Elves in an idiom of their own making.

The languages of *The Lord of the Rings* are not moralist, thematic, or didactic in purpose. (Debates among Tolkien scholars and enthusiasts about the possible allegorical shape the novel has—whether it can be read as a reflection of the Second World

War, in which the rise of Sauron and the "scouring of the Shire" represent the ascendancy of Hitler and the devastation of a once pastoral England—find rather little support in the languages. Although the script of Mordor may have an Arabic look to it, and this fact may play to the idea of enemies from "the East," Black Speech seems nothing like either German or Japanese.) The Baroque level of elaboration and intricacy in their design is for its own

The sinister inscription (in Black Speech, the language of Mordor) on the Ring of Rings in *The Lord of the Rings*. The connection of the evil forces with the "East" in the novel is complemented by the Arabic appearance of this script. Reprinted by permission of the Tolkien Estate.

sake, since Tolkien wanted his Middle-earth to be as complete and self-sustaining a mythology as possible. A very detailed dictionary of etymologies is included in *The Lost Road* (1987), probably the most important of the supplementary volumes on Middle-earth for anyone interested in the languages.

One of the many signs of the ongoing interest in Tolkien's Middle-earth is the number of guides, reference works, and critical studies published each year. Readers interested in the languages outlined above can explore them in greater detail, and even acquire spoken, reading, and writing abilities in them, by consulting works like Ruth S. Noel's *The Languages of Tolkien's Middle-Earth* (1974), which contains "The Tolkien Dictionary"; Verlyn Flieger's *Splintered Light: Logos and Language in Tolkien's World* (1983); and Helge K. Fauskanger's informative Web site, *Ardalambion*, which features many useful links. Also online is Carl F. Hostetter's *The Elvish Linguistic Fellowship*, a site and a society that publishes regular newsletters. With the help of linguistic consultant David Salo, Peter Jackson's recent films of *The Lord of the Rings* managed to piece together workable forms of the languages described here for a valuable amount of spoken dialogue and number of songs.

References: Flieger, Verlyn. *Splintered Light: Logos and Language in Tolkien's World*. Grand Rapids, MI: William B. Eerdmans, 1983; *The Lord of the Rings: The Fellowship of the Ring*. Directed by Peter Jackson. Screenplay by Fran Walsh, Philippa Boyens, and Peter Jackson, 2001; *The Lord of the Rings: The Return of the King*. Directed by Peter Jackson. Screenplay by Fran Walsh, Philippa Boyens, and Peter Jackson, 2003; *The Lord of the Rings: The Two Towers*. Directed by Peter Jackson. Screenplay by Fran Walsh, Philippa Boyens, and Peter Jackson, 2002; Noel, Ruth S. *The Languages of Tolkien's Middle-Earth*. Boston: Houghton Mifflin, 1980; Tolkien, J.R.R. *The Lord of the Rings*. London: Unwin, 1989; Tolkien, J.R.R. *The Lost Road and Other Writings*. Edited by Christopher Tolkien. Boston: Houghton Mifflin, 1987; Tolkien, J.R.R. "A Secret Vice." *The Monsters and the Critics and Other Essays*. Edited by Christopher Tolkien. London: George Allen and Unwin, 1983. 198–223; Tyler, J.E.A. *The Tolkien Companion*. Edited by S. A. Tyler. New York: St. Martin's Press, 1976; Carl F. Hostetter's *The Elvish Linguistic Fellowship*: http://www.elvish.org; Helge K. Fauskanger's *Ardalambion: Of the tongues of Arda, the invented world of J.R.R. Tolkien*: http://www.uib.no/People/hnohf.

~ M ~

Mad Max: Beyond Thunderdome

The third of the Mad Max movies, *Beyond Thunderdome* (1985), finds its hero mistaken by an unusual band of orphans for their prophesied redeemer, the lost pilot Captain Walker. If their tribal warrior costumes and their dream of flying to "Tomorrow-morrow land" point to the Wild Boys of J. M. Barrie's *Peter Pan*, the children's distinctive Australian-English argot is an homage to the language of Russell Hoban's *Riddley Walker*. Naming themselves "The Waiting Ones," they have built both this language and the cherished mythology around Captain Walker years after a plane crash at the time of the world's nuclear disaster (termed *pokky clips* for "apocalypse"). The primitive and immature sorts of vocabulary and construction used by the children are clearly meant to reflect their age, isolation, and affiliation with crude technologies. *Tell*, for example, is the word for a story, as used in this prefatory speech: "this ain't one body's tell; it's the tell of us all, and you've got to listen it and member, 'cause what you hears today you gotta tell the newborn to-morrow."

Reference: Mad Max: Beyond Thunderdome. Directed by George Miller and George Ogilvie. Screenplay by Terry Hayes and George Miller, 1985.

The Man in the Moon

Called an "essay of fancy" by the translator "E. M." (likely a pseudonym of the author himself [71]), Bishop Francis Godwin's *The Man in the Moon* was probably written between 1615 and 1630. The narrator, Domingo Gonzalez, finds himself taken to the moon by geese he has trained to carry him as they fly; there he encounters a civilization of giants whose language, shared by the entire lunar population, "consisteth not so much of words and letters as of tunes and uncouth sounds that no letters can express" (103). These sounds "are not perfectly to be expressed by our characters" (97), so Gonzalez's transcriptions are to be understood as approximations. The Lunars do in fact have words, but the few there are contain many meanings: the "tune," or way the word is uttered, determines the definition in use. This distinction between word and tune becomes rather more obscure when Gonzalez further remarks that "many words there are consisting of tunes only, so as if [the Lunars] like they will utter their minds by tunes without words" (103). *The Man in the Moon* includes only passing examples of both the Lunars' "word" and "tune" vocabularies. We are told that the shortest in height and life span among them are designated by "a word that signifieth 'bastard-men,' 'counterfeits,' or 'changelings,'" but not what the word is (98). When Gonzalez utters the name "Jesus," he is recognized by the Lunars as a fellow Christian, but their nonresponse to "Maria" (96) and the fact that "'Martin' in their language signifieth 'God'" (99) may suggest that (like Godwin, but unlike Gonzalez) the Lunars are Protestants. Their "ordinary salutation," which literally signifies "glory be to God alone," and a version of "Gonzalez" are rendered (again, approximately, as by a narrator who admits to being "no perfect musician" [103]) as tunes in the figures below, respectively.

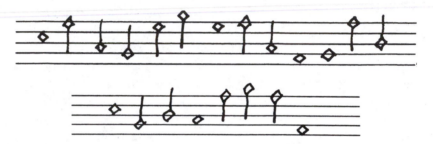

Approximations in musical notation of lunar speech, from *The Man in the Moon*. The first line translates as "Glory be to God alone," and the second reads "Gonzalez."

Interested readers will want to see Cyrano de Bergerac's *The Comical History of the States and Empires of the Moon and the Sun*, in which the voyager encounters Gonzalez on the moon.

Reference: Godwin, Francis. *The Man in the Moon*. Edited by John Anthony Butler. Ottawa: Dovehouse Editions, 1995.

Mardi, and A Voyage Thither

Herman Melville's *Mardi* (1849) is an unusual, Rabelaisian novel of travels through a fantastical, partly allegorized Polynesia: Mardi is the name of a collection of islands. In detailing the peoples and cultures of these islands, Melville is not explicit about the local languages apart from a few names of places and individuals. The novel's heroes remark on "the florid language of Diranda" (445), for example, and the final island's name, "Flozella-a-Nina, or The-Last-Verse-of-the-Song" (642), and they stop to translate occasional inscriptions in "hieroglyphical notices" (515). Most diverting in this regard is the language of the island Maramma, residence of Mardi's supreme pontiff, the Hivohitee. The devotion shown to each Hivohitee extends to banning "the leading sound in his name":

Whence, at every new accession to the archepiscopal throne, it came to pass, that multitudes of words and phrases were either essentially modified, or wholly dropped. Wherefore, the language of Maramma was incessantly fluctuating; and had become so full of jargonings, that the birds in the groves were greatly puzzled; not knowing where lay the virtue of sounds, so incoherent. (334)

Reference: Melville, Herman. *Mardi, and A Voyage Thither.* Evanston, IL: Northwestern University Press, 1998.

"A Martian Odyssey"

Written in 1934, Stanley G. Weinbaum's innovative short story "A Martian Odyssey" tells of a human astronaut's encounter with a variety of strange and very alien Martian creatures. In his recounting of his adventures, the protagonist Dick Jarvis is as freely given to speculation as to colloquial expressions, and his account of the alien he calls Tweel ("as near as I can pronounce it without sputtering . . . something like 'Trrrweerrlll' " [6]) is imprecise in several respects. When Jarvis tries to exchange some rudimentary vocabulary with Tweel, he is frustrated by the apparent changeability of Tweel's definitions: "part of the time he was 'Tweel,' and part of the time he was 'P-p-p-proot,' and part of the time he was sixteen other noises. . . . Nothing was the same for two successive minutes, and if that's a language, I'm an alchemist!" (8). Tweel seems "terrifically amused that the same word [in Jarvis's English] meant the same thing twice in succession," a response that sets Jarvis to wondering whether the Martian's language might be comparable to "the primitive speech of some earth people" like "the Negritos, for instance, who haven't any generic words . . . [and have] no names for general classes" (11). However, Jarvis does not believe that such a comparison is very strong, particularly since Tweel is later able to adapt rather skillfully the expressions Jarvis shows him. For example, referring to another Martian creature the pair encounters, Tweel says, "No one-one-two. No two-two-four" (16). What he means is that the creature he and Jarvis see is not rational, as Jarvis's arithmetical statements (one plus one is two, two plus two is four) are. Apart from these displays of Tweel's linguistic intelligence, his language, culture, and even his species remain a mystery at the story's end.

Reference: Weinbaum, Stanley G. "A Martian Odyssey." *Where Do We Go From Here?* Edited by Isaac Asimov. Garden City, NY: Doubleday, 1971. 1–32.

The Maze Game

The Maze Game (2003) is the first volume of Diana Reed Slattery's Glide Trilogy. Set in a future in which most human beings have been infected with an immortality virus that will quickly repair any level of bodily damage, the novel focuses on a specialized class of uninfected mortals who are as a result celebrities, both reviled and adored. These characters are Dancers, specially trained athletes who perform deadly games of agility, combat, and artful choreography. **Glide**, the immortal Dancemaster Wallenda explains to his students, is a language devised by the servile class of Dancers

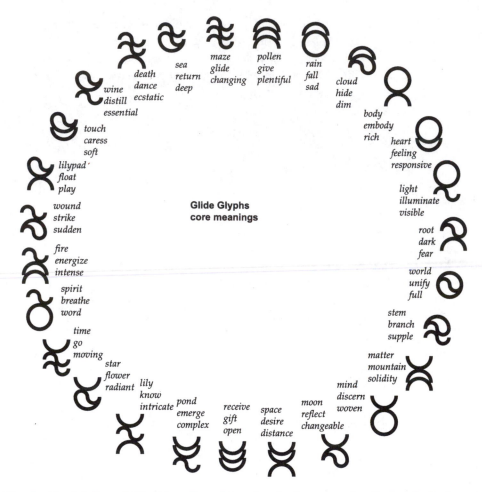

The glyphic alphabet of *The Maze Game*. Note that the "core meanings" of each glyph are as fluid as the differences between the glyphs themselves. Poems written or performed in dance with this language thus invite more than one interpretation. Reprinted by permission of Diana Reed Slattery/Deep Listening Publications.

themselves known as Glides. It "started as a gesture language. A means to sign back and forth using the normal gestures of their work so no one would notice" (45). The Glide language, then, is literally a vernacular (from the Latin *verna*, slave) and a response to oppression.

The visual component of the Glide language is composed of twenty-seven glyphs, as shown in the figure. Mazes generated for a performance are inscribed with the glyphs. In written expressions, the glyphs are typically grouped in threes as both poems and oracles: interpretations involve arranging the glyphs into a pattern. This act of interpretation can mean configuring the symbols themselves into shapes evocative of their explicit and implicit meanings (note how easily one glyph could be slightly altered to become another) or rearranging their order and proximity, but one can also physically be "speaking the maze" (251) if one can somehow incorporate the meanings of the signs beneath one's feet with each move or landing on the dangerous maze surface. Glide poetics is thus a course of study that makes demands on a student's athletic abilities as well as his or her creative and adaptive thinking.

References: Slattery, Diana Reed. *The Maze Game*. Kingston, NY: Deep Listening Publications, 2003; Diana Reed Slattery's Web site *The Glide Project* provides a multimedia complement to her novel, *The Maze Game*: http://www.academy.rpi.edu/glide/main.htm.

Memoirs of a Spacewoman

A pioneering feminist science-fiction title by the prolific Scottish novelist and activist Naomi Mitchison (1897–1999), *Memoirs of a Spacewoman* provides few artificial lexicons or grammatical systems but explores many philosophical problems regarding communication between species and races, both terrestrial and alien.

The 1962 novel is set in the far future, where humans explore vast reaches of space beyond Earth, and features a protagonist who is a communications expert, trained in both linguistics and other, particularly empathetic, means of contact. Yet, while she is able to communicate empathically, to a greater or lesser degree, with all animal species on Earth, as Mary encounters various extraterrestrial races and fauna, numerous difficulties arise.

For example, an early challenge is how to communicate with starfishlike creatures whose entire cognitive, cultural, philosophical, and linguistic discourses are not based on binary structures (as humans' are) but on multiple perspectives and choices existing with equal value, as well as spiral, rather than digital and linear, movement and ordering systems.

The most extensive examination of language form, however, involves communication with allied Martian explorers. Although vocal discourse is infrequently used, **Martian** is primarily a tactile language, capable of great complexity and subtlety through simple bodily pressure and friction, most commonly expressed on (and with) sensitive parts of the body, such as the sexual organs. As Martians are bisexual hermaphrodites, there is little confusion between communication and mating, but while conversing with a wounded Martian under stressful circumstances, Mary becomes pregnant, resulting in the first human-Martian hybrid.

Memoirs of a Spacewoman is a short novel structured in a series of episodes, with each chapter exploring a set problem. Despite its brevity, the novel effectively problematizes the ease of communication commonly depicted in science fiction to examine the pitfalls of communication with genuinely alien life-forms.

Reference: Mitchison, Naomi. *Memoirs of a Spacewoman*. London: Victor Gollancz, 1962.

The Memorandum

Usually pronounced "petty-dip" by the actors who perform Václav Havel's 1966 play *Vyrozumení* (translated as *The Memorandum*), **Ptydepe** is a very complex language designed for use within a bureaucratic office. In sharp contradistinction to natural languages, Ptydepe is a "scientifically" structured language that seeks to propagate "high redundancy" (17) in the name of efficiency by distinguishing any given word and its meaning from any other word or meaning: because no two words are the same (not even homonymically), the vocabulary of this language is immense. To exclaim "boo," for example, requires consideration of the specific circumstances in which the speaker wishes to startle another office employee (38–39). If the speaker hides before ambushing a surprised employee, the speaker uses the term *gedynrelom*; if the employee is aware of the ambush beforehand, *osonfterte* is the operative word; and there are several other variants for cases in which the speaker is in full view, the speaker is the employee's superior, and so on. The logical principle that governs word constructions is this: "the more common the meaning [and presumably, "meaning" here means usage], the shorter the word" (17). Thus, the longest word in Ptydepe (the word for "wombat") has 319 letters, while the shortest is *gh*, the word for "whatever"; the one-letter word *f* is "held in reserve in case science should discover a term even more commonly used than the term 'whatever' " (18). Havel's satirical play presents many examples of spoken and written Ptydepe, but comparatively few words and phrases are translated, such as *hutput* ("quite exact" [26]), *zexdohyt* ("point of view" [27]), *hetegyx ujhoby* (" 'bang!' as the symbol of a shot or explosion" [56]), *maluz rog* (" 'bang' as a colloquial expression for sudden surprise" [56]), and *mykl* ("oops" [56]). Its unwieldy vocabulary effectively excludes the chance of any company employee's learning the language, and Ptydepe is eventually abandoned in favor of the equally ridiculous **Chorukor**.

Where Ptydepe attempted to attain "maximum dissimilarity" between word usages, and thus resulted in an exacting vocabulary so large that no one could learn it, Chorukor relies on "a purposeful exploitation and organization" of the similarities between words (81–82). Learning Chorukor is supposed to be easy because words are grouped and their differences are minimized. For example, the days of the week, in order from Monday to Sunday, become *ilopagar, ilopager, ilopagur, ilopagir, ilopageur, ilopagoor,* and *ilopagor* in Chorukor. The fact that the potential for mistakes and ambiguities is extremely high is, according to Lear, the language teacher in the play, of no substantial importance, and the worst that may result from a typist's mistake on an announcement of the day of a meeting is an early meeting.

While it is difficult to say which of the two languages is the more preposterous, the implementation of the second after the fiasco of the first points to the cyclical shape of Havel's satire: bureaucracies are unevolving and changeless, apart from their exaggerated efforts at compensatory complexity.

Reference: Havel, Václav. *The Memorandum.* Translated by Vera Blackwell. New York: Grove Press, 1967.

Men in Black II

A sequel to the 1997 film based on Lowell Cunningham's comic book series, *Men in Black II* involves American secret agents who continue to control or contain the presence of extraterrestrial visitors on Earth. In this installment, when Agent J (played by hip-hop artist and actor Will Smith) encounters a disguised alien of an unnamed species working for the U.S. Postal Service, he is able to converse with the creature in its native tongue. Although no lexical key is provided, Agent J "speaks" to the alien in free abstract vocalization with a percussive emphasis—what members of the hip-hop community refer to as a "human beatbox" technique. The alien, portrayed by fellow-rapper

Biz Markie, replies in kind, illustrating the often overlooked connections between early hip-hop, jazz scat, and avant-garde sound poetry.

Reference: Men in Black II. Directed by Barry Sonnenfeld. Screenplay by Robert Gordon and Barry Fanaro. DVD, special 2-disc edition, 2002.

"Mimsy Were the Borogoves"

Henry Kuttner's story first appeared in the pages of *Astounding Science Fiction* magazine in 1943. A maker of time machines, living elsewhere than Earth and "a good many million years" in the future (1), transports two boxes of his son's childhood toys to Earth, one appearing in late nineteenth-century England, the other in America, presumably circa 1943. The two children who play with the unusual toys they find in the latter box develop perceptions and ideas alien to their parents and a child psychologist whom they consult. Emma, the younger and more impressionable child, communicates with her brother Scott in "unintelligible conversations" and by writing "meaningless scrawls" (23). At one point, the story's narrator gives the reader a glimpse of Scott's thinking, which is filled with unknown words and expressions: "The fat man—listava dangerous, maybe. But the Ghoric direction won't show—evankrus dun hasn't them. Intransdection—bright and shiny. Emma. She's more khopranik-high now than—I still don't see how to—thavarar lixery dust" (22). Strange though Scott's thinking seems, Emma's thoughts, the narrator implies, cannot be understood at all.

Eventually the children figure out how to transport themselves off of Earth, leaving their confused father to consult their notes—a page torn from *Through the Looking-Glass*, with "interlineations and marginal notes, in Emma's meaningless scrawl" (29). The reader discovers that the other box from the future was found by a young girl whose songs and stories, inspired by her "magic toys," were recorded, with some alterations, and later published by her "Uncle Charles" (27). Lewis Carroll (the pseudonym of Charles Lutwidge Dodgson) had, at least in the first verse of the poem "Jabberwocky," accurately rendered practical directions—for those able to read them—for interplanetary travel—thus Kuttner's use of the quoted line as a title for the story.

The father of Scott and Emma can only guess at the abstract quantities of *brillig*, *wabe*, and *gyre* and *gimble*: "If he could follow [the pattern], as the kids had done—but he couldn't. The pattern was senseless. The random factor defeated him. He was conditioned to Euclid" (30). The story begs the questions, what tenable difference exists between language and functional notation (like musical notes of mathematical symbology), between grammar and calculus, between expression and idea?

References: Carroll, Lewis. *Through the Looking-Glass and What Alice Found There. The Complete Works of Lewis Carroll*. London: Penguin, 1988. 121–250; Kuttner, Henry. "Mimsy Were the Borogoves." *The Best of Henry Kuttner*. New York: Doubleday, 1975. 1–30.

Mistress Masham's Repose

Maria, the ten-year-old heroine of T. H. White's 1946 novel, discovers and befriends a colony of Lilliputians, the same diminutive people described in *Gulliver's Travels*. It turns out that Maria's friend the Professor owns a copy (dated 1735) of

Gulliver's description of the Lilliputian empire and a brief vocabulary of the language—a work only mentioned in Swift's text. Maria studies the book in order to communicate with the Lilliputians, though after she initiates discussion with the phrase *Glonog, lumos Kelmin pesso mes?* ("please, will you swear a peace with me?" [32]), she is told that these exiled Lilliputians have English as their second language. Readers do get a peek into Gulliver's book and find that *Quinbus* ("man," from the *Travels*) has a Latin-like female equivalent, *Quinba*. Two other new words appear: *Ranfu-Lo* (the masculine noun for "breeches") and *Redrelsan* (the neuter term for "secretary" [30]). White's book also tells of the style of poetry practiced by Lilliputians who "still wrote the original meters of their native land" (71). This "highly polished form" is brief and precise; poems typically have no more than two words per line, nor more than four lines in all. The rhyme scheme is also compressed and difficult, as the following example shows: "Mo Rog / Glanog, / Quinba, / Hlin varr" ("Give me a kiss, please, Miss. I like your nose" [72]). Nothing in *Mistress Masham's Repose* directly contradicts *Gulliver's Travels* (though some of Swift's inconsistencies are remarked on), and all of White's elaborations on Lilliputian language and culture are predicated on the earlier text.

References: Swift, Jonathan. *Gulliver's Travels and Other Writings*. Edited by Louis A. Landa. Boston: Houghton Mifflin, 1960; White, T. H. *Mistress Masham's Repose*. Toronto: Totem Books, 1979.

"Modulation in All Things"

A stridently patriarchal government turns with embarrassment for help from a female poet in Suzette Haden Elgin's story. Good trade relations are urgently needed with a planet designated X513, but unfortunately the inhabitants ("known as the Serpent People" [354]) speak a language no one has been able to translate, and to make matters worse they seem to be easily offended. In studying the accounts of failed communication efforts, Jacinth, the poet, recalls her childhood amazement at how a single song could be performed in more than one key and thereby deduces that the problem lies in the key of pronunciation: "this is a language that modulates; the analogy with music is exact and precise" (361). Various transpositions of the sixteen phonemes (or "sound segments" [360]) in the language of X513 change the degree of formality of a given utterance. Thus, "the 'word,' for the people of X513, is not a stable unit. It changes constantly, depending upon the social situation, the status of the speakers and the like" (361).

The government of Abba, which rejects thanking a woman for her help, speaks an undescribed language called **Abban** and also makes reference to **Panglish**. (See "We Have Always Spoken Panglish").

Reference: Elgin, Suzette Haden. "Modulation in All Things." *Great Science Fiction: Stories by the World's Great Scientists*. Edited by Isaac Asimov, Martin H. Greenberg, and Charles G. Waugh. New York: Donald I. Fine, 1985. 348–363.

Molvanîa: A Land Untouched by Modern Dentistry

Molvanîa (2004) is a parody of a travel guide, complete with photographs, city maps, and traveler's tips. Its subject is a fictional eastern European country whose citizens enjoy garlic brandy, pornography, and "that typically warm Slavic sense of humour" (20). A brief outline of the **Molvanian** language (also obviously a lampoon of such bagatelles in guidebooks) warns that it is extremely difficult to learn: it has many irregular verbs and four genders for nouns (one is exclusive to names of cheese), "a record number of silent letters," and, in written Molvanian, a commonly used "triple negative" (26). A list of "Useful Phrases" for the tourist to memorize is divided into three categories: "Common Expressions" (including *Zlkavszka* for "hello" and *Dyuszkiya trappokski drovko?* for "does it always rain this much?" [27]); "Less Common Expressions" (including *Ok hyrafrpiki kidriki* for "what beautiful children" [27]), and "Very Rare Expressions" (*Krokystrokiskiaskya* for "see you again soon" [27]). A few other unpronounceable, consonant-heavy Molvanian words and expressions appear in the book, but perhaps the most illustrative example of the book's approach to the unfriendly language of this unfriendly country lies in this claim: "hospitality is a key part of Molvanian culture and there's an old saying '*zva grek inst ur plebum szunj*' ('better that a stranger be across thy door than a friend upon the road thereon'), which, while perhaps losing a little in the translation, pretty much sums up the Molvanian's carefree attitude to life" (20).

Reference: Cilauro, Santo, Tom Gleisner, and Rob Sitch. *Molvanîa: A Land Untouched by Modern Dentistry*. Toronto: Penguin, 2004.

More Dissemblers Besides Women

Thomas Middleton's 1615 comedy has much to do with "strange language" (623): characters often express their bewilderment about others' statements by questioning what language they are speaking, and in one scene characters engage in a nonsensical dialogue to evade paternal censure. Lactantia (the swain who gets his comeuppance at the play's end) defies the father of Aurelia by answering him in gobbledygook (*Loff tro veen, tantumbro, hoff tufftee lucumber shaw* [565]), but her father recognizes this "language" and says he "can speak it too: *Strumpettikin, bold harlottum, queaninisma, whoremongeria!*" (565). This incident serves as a precursor to another of Aurelia's attempts at subterfuge. When she disguises herself as a "Gipsy," she is dismayed to meet a band of real Gipsies who will spot her as a counterfeit, not least because she does not speak their language (which looks as much a sly improvisation as Lactantia's dissimulation). A few phrases are spoken by the Gipsies, without translation (for instance, *Rumbos stragadelion / Alla piskitch in sows-clows* [607]), though there are also a few expressions whose pig-Latin- or pidginlike structure makes their meanings apparent: thus *Stealee bacono* means "steal bacon" (610). Two specific nouns are defined for a clownish pupil and to make a quick joke: "gipsy for the hind quarter of a woman" is *Nosario*, while the word for "nose" is *Arsinio* (612). The pupil catches the knack of speaking **gipsy** when he replies to his gipsy teacher's "*Cheteroon, high gulleroon*" with "*Filcheroon, purse-fulleroon*: I can say somewhat too" (614), to the praise and pleasure of the other gipsies present. Middleton's gipsy language is probably to be understood as another kind of "dissembling" or chicanery.

Reference: Middleton, Thomas. *More Dissemblers Besides Women. The Works of Thomas Middleton*. Vol. 3. London: Edward Lumley, 1840. 551–644.

Mork and Mindy

Mork, a visitor from the distant planet Ork, resides and strikes up a romantic relationship with a human woman, Mindy, while he studies human behavior. In the course of the zany television program's lifetime (1978–1982), viewers were treated to only a few coherent samples of **Orkan** vocabulary, most famous of which are *na-nu, na-nu,* a phrase that serves as both greeting and farewell and apparently requires that the speaker tug his or her earlobes, and the undefined expletive *shazbot*: both expressions briefly enjoyed some currency in popular idiom. Much of Orkan speech was improvised gibberish and mugging on the part of comic actors Robin Williams (Mork) and Jonathan Winters (who played Mork and Mindy's bizarre son, Mearth), usually delivered in a high nasal pitch. Occasionally the comic design depended on literal inversions: just as an Orkan infant has the body of a senior and will grow younger, some of Mork's vocabulary, like *kayo* ("okay"), follows the same "backward" conceit.

Reference: Mork and Mindy. ABC Network, 1978–1982.

～ N ～

The Name of the Rose

Salvatore, the hunchback monk in Umberto Eco's best-selling novel *Il nome della rosa* (1980; translated as *The Name of the Rose*), is said to speak "all languages, and no language. Or, rather, he had invented for himself a language which used the sinews of the languages to which he had been exposed" (47). This makeshift montage tongue combines medieval Latin, English, Provençal, and others, so a typical exclamation from Salvatore runs like this: "Semper lying in wait for me in some angulum to snap at my heels. But Salvatore is not stupidus! Bonum monasterium, and aquí refectorium and pray to dominum nostrum. And the resto is not worth merda" (47). Interestingly, other characters in the novel do not find it as difficult to understand him as he sometimes does them.

The novel also contains a zodiacal alphabet (190), but this is part of a secret code, not an operative language.

Reference: Eco, Umberto. *The Name of the Rose.* Translated by William Weaver. San Diego: Warner Books, 1983.

The Narrative of Arthur Gordon Pym of Nantucket

Edgar Allan Poe's beleaguered hero Arthur Gordon Pym, whose *Narrative* first appeared in print in 1838, encounters and is puzzled by the indigenous people of an island beyond the Antarctic polar circle. Pym's reportage of their language is fractional, and he records only a few terms, like *Anamoo-moo* and *Lama-Lama*, including fewer interpretations. Panicked cries of *Tekeli-li! Tekeli-li!* are the response to the color white, which these curiously black-toothed peoples apparently abhor. *Mattee non we pa pa si*, the longest phrase recorded by Pym, is translated as "there [is] no need of arms when all [are] brothers." Among Poe scholars there has been debate about possible sources for the **Tsalal** language; cases have been made for similarities to Malayo-Polynesian tongues and even to Hebrew, whereby *Tekeli-li!* hearkens to the biblical writing on the wall: "Mene Mene Tekel Upharsin" (see Ridgley's "The Continuing Puzzle of *Arthur Gordon Pym*"). Further complicating our understanding is the open

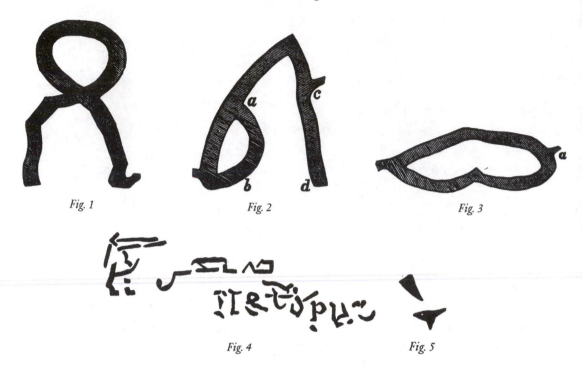

Fig. 1   Fig. 2   Fig. 3

Fig. 4   Fig. 5

Indentures that may be written characters, from *The Narrative of Arthur Gordon Pym of Nantucket.* Poe is notably ambiguous about their import.

question of whether the shapes of chasms and the indentures found in their marl constitute writing in a coherent alphabet. The "Note" that concludes the *Narrative*, written after Pym's death, contends that Pym is wrong to dismiss this possibility and discerns in them Ethiopian (labeled as figures 1, 2, 3, and 5, conjoined) and Arabic verbal roots and a complete Egyptian word (labeled figure 4).

References: Poe, Edgar Allan. *The Narrative of Arthur Gordon Pym of Nantucket.* New York: Modern Library, 2002; Ridgely, J. V. "The Continuing Puzzle of *Arthur Gordon Pym.*" *Poe Newsletter* 3.1 (1970): 5–6.

Native Tongue

Dispossessed of their rights by radical amendments to the Constitution, twenty-third-century American women create a language of resistance in Suzette Haden Elgin's *Native Tongue* trilogy of science-fiction novels (*Native Tongue* [1984], *The Judas Rose* [1987], and *Earthsong* [1994]). Linguists are a class apart—privileged but also despised by the general public—in a society where communication with extraterrestrial beings for trade arrangements is both a priority and a great difficulty. Female linguists, then, are doubly condemned, but under the cover of their private project to design a universal language called **Langlish**, which is tolerated but not taken seriously by the men, they secretly and slowly give shape to **Láadan**. The name of this "woman's language" sounds a little like "Latin, but with a lilt to it" (215). It is primarily an emotionally expressive lexicon, tonal in sound and meant to articulate sensations and experiences ignored or denied expression within patriarchal language(s). There are no articles in Láadan, and adjectives and verbs are the same. Most of the vocabulary has been cultivated by networks of Elgin's readers and by Elgin herself in journal articles and memoranda from the Ozark Center for Language Studies. Examples include *áya* (beautiful), *ramimelh* ("to refrain from asking, with evil intent; especially when it is clear that someone badly wants the other to ask" [303]), *sháadehul* ("growth through transcendence" [304]), and *wohosheni* ("the opposite of alienation; to feel joined to, part of someone or something without reservations or barriers" [304]). An accent above a vowel indicates a high tone. Statements are made with evidence morphemes that attest that the foregoing is either "true because perceived directly" (*wa*) or "true because from a trusted source" (*wáa*). Phrase order is verb or adjective, object, subject: *Bíi eril óoha with wáa*, the woman was weary, literally translates as "statement: was weary woman true (because from a trusted source)" (see Elgin's *Dictionary*).

Extraterrestrial languages in *Native Tongue* are given codified "REM" designations: this moniker is a relic from the bygone era of the computer language BASIC, and in this context merely represents "Alien humanoid language." The native name of **REM41-3-786** (pronounced "remfortyone; three; seven-eighty-six"), for example, sounds to one of Elgin's characters "like 'rxtpt' if it sounded like anything at all, and there was quite a bit more of it" (210). The first number of any given designation (here, 41) refers to a given humanoid species, assigned in the order in which humans have "interfaced" with them. The second number "classifies the language for one of the possible orderings of verb and subject and object" (here, 3 designates a verb-subject-object order), and the last number (here, 786) refers to the numerical order of acquired languages (209); thus REM41-3-786 is the seven-hundred-and-eighty-sixth language acquired by human linguists. Not much more information is available about any of the REM languages, although REM34 is reported to be one of the most difficult.

References: Elgin, Suzette Haden. *First Dictionary and Grammar of Láadan*. Edited by Diane Martin. 2nd ed. Madison, WI: Society for the Study of Fantasy and Science Fiction, 1988; Elgin, Suzette Haden. *Native Tongue*. New York: Feminist Press, 2000; Suzette Haden Elgin's Láadan Web page (with links to her home page) includes occasional vocabulary updates: www.sfwa.org/members/elgin/Laadan.html.

Neutopia

A small group of men happen upon a socialist utopia somewhere beyond an unidentified desert in E. Richardson's 1925 novel. While their system of government, their laws, and their philosophy are thoroughly expounded, the language of Neutopia's people becomes more rather than less of an enigma as the story progresses. At their first encounter with a woman they later come to know as Ooda, the novel's heroes cannot understand her "soft musical tones," but she establishes communication with "the universal language of sign and gesture" (25). This conceit quickly exceeds its plausibility, as the narrative represents as spoken sometimes grammatically complex statements, which the reader is compelled to remember are yet but "sign and gesture." One character finally observes that it is "queer how they seem to understand all we say, don't they? Their gestures are very expressive, but I can't understand their words" (47).

Eventually an explanation of sorts is given. The Neutopians do not, as their visitors guess, possess telepathy, exactly. They claim to "read thoughts by sympathy," and in teaching their guests their language, they effectively teach them to "understand the speech of those you are in sympathy with, even when you don't know the meaning of the separate words" (92). What proportions and dimensions this concept of "sympathy" has are not disclosed. It seems safe to suppose that this language of sympathy is meant to reflect the concord and harmony of the society itself (there is no war, poverty, or illness, and all laws and governing bodies are put into power by direct democracy), though judging from one character's experience with another whom he cannot understand at all, the level of linguistic "sympathy" is gauged on an individual-to-individual basis.

What makes this language even more abstract and difficult to comprehend is the fact that the citizens of Neutopia use writing and have books. Perhaps the reader ought to conclude that books themselves can give and/or receive sympathy, an interpretation that may be supported by the transparently prescriptive thrust of Richardson's book, which ends with an exhortation for social betterment: "The spirit of man is reaching out now to communicate directly with other spirits" (304).

Not surprisingly, *Neutopia* contains no samples of this unusual language.

Reference: Richardson, E. *Neutopia*. London: Simpkin, Marshall, Hamilton, Kent & Co., 1925.

"New Arcadia"

L. Sprague de Camp's "New Arcadia," a satire on utopian societies and aggression, was first published in 1956. Dialogue between a man from Earth and aliens called Cimbrians is made in an "interplanetary pidgin" called **Intermundos**, "based mainly on terran tongues" (339). The narrator explains that the language was "designed to be speakable by different species; hence it is phonetically simple, with only seven consonants and three vowels. It allows for variation in pronunciation: thus the s may stand for any voiceless fricative like f and h; n may be any nasal, and so on" (339). Unfortunately, Intermundos has a "rigid word order" and is "good only for bare statements," which are by necessity longer than they would be "in any natural language" (339). The story includes just one example of spoken Intermundos: *Ula las Sinvlianu! Na aki sal ain knaavu vun saaisu vun vuus?* means "Cimbrians! Where's your chief?" (339).

Reference: Sprague de Camp, L. "New Arcadia." *A Gun for Dinosaur and Other Imaginative Tales*. Garden City, NY: Doubleday, 1963. 315–359.

Nineteen Eighty-Four

Not so much a new language as the diminishment of the English lexicon, **Newspeak** best exemplifies George Orwell's theories regarding language, thought, and ideology. In his novel *Nineteen Eighty-Four* (1949), the totalitarian government of Ingsoc is in the process of implementing Newspeak as a means of limiting dissent by making "all other modes of thought impossible" (312). Newspeak is thus both a dystopian language, in that it is used to control independent thought and curtail individual freedom, and an extreme example of linguistic determinism (Sapir–Whorf) in which language use completely delineates and circumscribes perception and cognition.

In the novel, Newspeak has not completely subsumed the society of 1984 as illustrated by the fact that some Ingsoc party members, such as the novel's protagonist Winston Smith, are in the process of learning the new language, while the "proles" of Oceania (the British Isles) continue to utilize **Oldspeak** (standard English). Readers are given many examples of Newspeak throughout the text, but the language is most clearly explained in "The Principles of Newspeak," an appendix that follows the main narrative.

In explaining Newspeak, the unnamed author of the appendix divides the language into three vocabularies. Vocabulary A is the system of reducing language, and its lexicon consists of words that are used in concrete, denotative ways. It strives to create a system of signification in which each signifier has only a single signified; there are no connotative or multiple meanings to a set signifier. Moreover, this aspect of Newspeak also works to reduce the English lexicon to minimal root words that can then be modified by using simple prefixes to incorporate several, but ultimately limited, meanings. Thus, from the root "good" can be derived *ungood* (bad), *plusgood* (very good), and *doubleplusgood* (excellent). It therefore eliminates three individual words (bad, excellent, very), demonstrating Newspeak's goal of becoming a more reductive language in each year of use.

Other qualities of Vocabulary A words include the idea that "any word in the language . . . [can] be used either as verb, noun, adjective or adverb" (314). That is, the word "thought" is replaced by "think" for all cases, and further, all grammar is regularized to the extent that the past tense of think is *thinked* and the plural of man is *mans*.

The Vocabulary B of Newspeak involves the use of invented and compound words as "a verbal shorthand, often packing whole ranges of ideas into a few syllables" (316). Some examples of this technique given by Orwell include *goodthink* (orthodoxy), *thoughtcrime* (heretical thought), *doublethink* (contradictory thought), and *joycamp* (forced-labor camp). The purpose here is to obscure negative elements through euphemism but also, by joining two words into a single phrase, to eliminate the qualities that each of these words has individually. That is, *Minitrue* (the Ministry of Truth) becomes a unique signifier that prevents users from asking or thinking about the various qualities that make up "truth" or the connotations of a "ministry."

One goal of Vocabulary B words, beyond the aforementioned desire to eliminate unorthodox thinking patterns, is to create a citizenship that communicates in what Orwell calls **Duckspeak**. Compared to the gabbling of a duck in sound, Duckspeak implies orthodox speech generated without thought. Thus, the purpose of Newspeak is to create Duckspeakers—citizens who speak ideologically correct phrases without being conscious of doing so.

The least developed aspect of Newspeak is Vocabulary C, which consists of scientific and technical language. While no examples of these Newspeak words are given, the author makes clear that these words are not used by the general population, and that even scientists use only those words that relate directly to their field and have little knowledge of Vocabulary C words used in other scientific discourses.

Although articulated most clearly in *Nineteen Eighty-Four*, much of the reasoning behind Orwell's use of Newspeak can be found in an earlier essay, "Politics and the

English Language" (1946), where he implies that language can be used as a means of "concealing or preventing thought" and as a "pretext for advocating a kind of political quietism" (11). After all, "since you don't know what Fascism is, how can you struggle against Fascism?" (11).

Most commentators on the novel connect *Nineteen Eighty-Four* to this essay, yet at least one critic has read the appendix on Newspeak as pure satire. Citing Orwell's admiration for Jonathan Swift, and comparing some aspects of the Newspeak enterprise to that of the Academy of Lagado in *Gulliver's Travels, Roger Fowler argues that Orwell's invention of Newspeak is parody and not a warning against linguistic intervention by totalitarian powers.

Nevertheless, the popularity of Orwell's novel has meant that such Newspeak phrases as *doublethink* and *thoughtcrime* have entered common parlance. Indeed, rare is the editorial page or letters column that does not contain at least one reference to Orwellian situations, or that does not point out how advertising, political speech, or business jargon does not exemplify some aspect of Newspeak.

References: Fowler, Roger. *The Language of George Orwell.* Houndmills, United Kingdom: Macmillan, 1995; Orwell, George. *Nineteen Eighty-Four.* London: Penguin, 1989; Orwell, George. "Politics and the English Language." *Shooting an Elephant and Other Essays.* London: Harcourt, 1950. 1–11.

"No Jokes on Mars"

James Blish's short story "No Jokes on Mars" concerns a reporter's discovery of the exploitation of a Martian species called dune cats. Pomanders, a "hibernation organ" (148) for these cats, which are kept in marsupial-like pouches, are fetish commodities on Earth. When a cat in the story is cornered, it tries to buy its life with a shard ("They always do," notes one onlooker [149]). These shards are brick fragments made by "the long-extinct Canal Masons of Mars" (145) and inscribed with a language that has never been deciphered. The planet is said to be "littered" with such shards, and they are without value. Besides the bald assertion that the Martian language here has "no connection to Earthly languages" (149), the story gives no other details about this lost tongue.

Reference: Blish, James. "No Jokes on Mars." *Anywhen.* New York: Doubleday, 1970. 143–153.

Noise

A linguist from Earth visits the oceanic planet of Kainui in Hal Clement's 2003 novel and winds up effectively apprenticing as a merchant sailor. Kainui was first settled by Polynesian colonists, and its inhabitants speak a mixture of Polynesian languages (Samoan, Tahitian, Maori, etc.), though at least some also use a complex gestural language simply called **Finger**, the advantages of which have to do with the noisy waters and storms the sailors regularly face. The only tangible and clear sample of Finger is an "encouraging circle-and-three-finger gesture" (35), which even before he is instructed in the language the protagonist can readily interpret. Although some of the dialogue that is implicitly translated from Finger suggests a considerable vocabulary (there is a sign for a plural "they," for example, so Finger involves more than mere pointing) and room for idiom, there is also "a fairly broad spectrum" of meaning for certain gestures: one sign meaning "perfect" might also be taken for "good" or "fine" (96).

Reference: Clement, Hal. *Noise.* New York: Tor, 2003.

"Not So Certain"

At the center of David I. Masson's 1968 story is a highly technical discussion of the language of seemingly unhelpful aliens called "the Shm'qh, or Sshm-qh, or Sshmeqh (which sounds like 'shmukh', only breathier)" (46). This difficulty in pronunciation, which literally opens the story, signals the problem of translation that effects the troubles that humans have in dealing with the Shm'qh. Although a basic sort of linguistic understanding is already in operation at the beginning of the story, and the aliens are judged "friendly and surprisingly unalarmed by the human invaders" (47), the Shm'qh appear to mock human labors and, invariably, flatly turn down requests to collect samples of "native ornaments, utensils, and cultivated plants" (49) to take to Earth.

The basics of **Shm'qh** grammar are thought to be understood. To ask "Can we return this way?" one says *Tsh'ny lh'ly wh'ng 'zhny' bv'w w'gh'pf 'w* (literally: "Pass shown reverse open eh? self-and-others relevance" [47–48]), and when a man falls seriously ill the aliens are asked "will he live": *ny'p'lw gh'qhty bv'w 'pf'lh 'w* (literally: "activity continuation eh? the-other relevance" [48]). Yet both the question and the answer (the negative *shny'wh*) are misconstrued. Before presenting his solution to the problem, Anson, the "linguistician" in the story, gives a lengthy analysis of the phonemic structure of the language. The apparent monotony of Shm'qh speech is the result of "suprasegmental phonemes" (52), which function in lieu of pitch variation. They have at least thirty-six distinguishable consonants (including "two *b*'s, no *f* or *v* by itself at all, two *w*-sounds, two *wh*-like sounds . . . and two labial laterals" [55]), and their writing is pictographic. (All of these facts relate to the regional variation of the language, Anson makes clear, and not necessarily to Shm'qh from other parts of the planet.) Using slowed-down recordings of Shm'qh utterances, Anson demonstrates that ignorance of the subtleties of meaning in Shm'qh phonology is at the root of the confusion. There is not one simple negative, *shny'wh* or *shnyewh*, but several compound variations with barely discernible differences, differences that Anson illustrates with a "sound-spectrograph" (58). The Shm'qh "no" etymologically means "indeed not so," but the negative variable answer given to requests concerning sample collecting literally means "indeed not so certain," which seems to be an "equivalent of our word 'Perhaps'" (60).

Thus, the misunderstanding boils down to this: when the humans thought they were asking whether the sick man would live and whether they had permission to collect samples, the Shm'qh believed they were being asked whether the sick man *could* live through his disease and whether the humans "could, physically, succeed in getting their specimens safely . . . to Earth" (62). The Shm'qh reply is not an absolute no in either case but a withholding of judgment: "perhaps" or "not so certain."

Talking with the Shm'qh is unusually described as "rather like conversing with moths in moth language: no vowels to speak of—except that now and again a surprising clatter of vowelage broke out" (46–47), an analogy that leaves the reader wondering about **moth language** (though it is not mentioned again in the story).

Reference: Masson, David I. "Not So Certain." *The Caltraps of Time.* London: Faber and Faber, 1968. 46–62.

Nova

Set in the thirty-second century, Samuel R. Delany's 1968 novel utilizes motifs from Melville as well as the Grail myth to tell the tale of a star sailor and his crew as they attempt to secure a vast amount of important fuel (Illyrion) by flying through a star going nova. If successful, this will insure that the outer space colonies (the Pleiades) will become fully independent of the Draco empire (Earth, the solar system, and those nearby planetary groupings it has been able to annex).

While the culture of the known universe is rather homogeneous (everyone watches multisensory psychoramas; the novel is extinct), the inhabitants of the Pleiades attempt to achieve some independence by speaking in their own dialect. Unfortunately, the **Pleiades dialect** consists of nothing more than standard English with the syntactical inversion of the verb always coming last in a sentence: for example, "You a kid I talked about remember? This him is. Hey, Mouse, you a half a foot taller even aren't! How many years, seven, eight, it is? And you still the syrynx have?" (145). As is apparent here, the effect of this dialect is more often comical than intriguing, and reaches such low points as when a character requests a hit of the drug "bliss" and is told, "out yourself knock" (196).

Reference: Delany, Samuel R. *Nova.* New York: Vintage, 2002.

"The Old King's Answers"

A survey team travels to Loric Four to assess that planet's suitability for colonization in Colin Kapp's 1973 short story. They discover that the creatures who live there—whom they simply designate "bears"—not only have a complex system of communication based on highly affective pheromones, but can write, too, after a fashion. Two humans watch a bear cover most of an upright crystal "with a scratch or a tap or a firm pad pressure" (165) and then, later, see another bear approach the crystal and read it "as though it were a poster" (166). This represents more than just domain marking: they "write" with a range of scents "in an amazing spectrum of complexity" that other bears can read olfactorily (166). This discovery, that the "indigenous population publishes its own newspapers" (166–167), becomes one of the factors in the conclusion not to colonize the planet.

Reference: Kapp, Colin. "The Old King's Answers." *Galaxy* (Sept. 1973): 148–175.

"Omnilingual"

The title of H. Beam Piper's 1957 story is a little misleading, since it is not exactly about speaking all languages but has as its central conceit the notion of a universal language among scientific cultures. Some time in the 1990s ("it had been only sixty-odd years since the Orson Welles invasion scare" [387]), a team of archaeologists are digging through the ruins of an ancient Martian city. Among them is Martha Dane, who is keen to interpret the various books they have unearthed, but who receives considerable discouragement from the others, who tell her that "there is no Rosetta Stone, not anywhere on Mars" (350). This opinion is ultimately proven wrong when Martha finds a periodic table of the elements in a university-like building and is able to deduce from it a number system as well as a calendar. A magazine that she had been studying bears the title *Mastharnorvod Tadavas Sornhulva*—evidently the Martians use roman letters—which she can finally translate as "Of-Metal Matter-Knowledge Quarterly" (393–394), a metallurgy journal. Other Martian words revealed in the story include *Darfhulva* (history), *Sarfaldsorn* (Hydrogen), *Sarfalddavas* (Helium), *Trav* (first month of the year), and *masthar* (year).

Reference: Piper, H. Beam. "Omnilingual." *Where Do We Go from Here?* Edited by Isaac Asimov. Garden City, NY: Doubleday, 1971. 347–397.

"Once a greech"

The crew of a spaceship, the S. S. Herringbone, discover intelligent life on a moon called Flimbot in Evelyn E. Smith's 1957 story. However, they misunderstand the Flimbotzik life cycle and culture. A bumbling officer named Harkaway quickly learns **Flimbotzi**, which he calls "not a difficult language" (264), and begins writing a book on (what he believes is) the Flimbotzik theology. It turns out that words like *mpoola* and *mpoo* do not, as Harkaway thinks, signify spiritual reincarnation and social status, respectively; rather, they are terms for the cycle of metamorphosis the species undergoes, a kind of high-speed evolution. Harkaway brings a small, caterpillar-like creature known as a *greech* on the journey back to Earth, mistaking it for a pet animal. It eventually cocoons itself and reemerges as a large kind of butterfly (a *zkoort*), which in turn becomes an unknown blue animal (a *chu-wugg*), then a boa constrictor (a *thor'glitch*), then a humanoid Flimbotnik. Finally, the alien becomes the very consciousness of the spaceship, a transformation that explains how the Flimbotzik, who had seemed technologically primitive, managed space travel.

Harkaway tosses around a number of Flimbotzi words and phrases in the first half of the story, but given his pivotal misreading of the culture, it is difficult to know how much credit to give his usage and translations. For example, Harkaway reports that the *Flimflim* ("the king, you know" [264]) has magnanimously said that "everything on Flimbot" was Harkaway's: "*Thlu'pt shig-nliv, snusnigg bnignliv* were his very words" (267). Exactly what these words do say—and with what irony—the reader does not learn. By the time the greech has become humanoid, it has learned to speak **Terran** (eponym of the narrative English) perfectly.

Reference: Smith, Evelyn E. "Once a greech." *The World That Couldn't Be and 8 Other Novelets from Galaxy.* Edited by H. L. Gold. Garden City, NY: Doubleday, 1959. 258–288.

One Million Years B.C.

The 1966 remake of the 1940 film about prehistoric life on Earth enjoys notoriety for two of its features—Raquel Welch in a furry bikini and lively dinosaur battles created by special effects wizard Ray Harryhausen—but it does also include traces of a language, albeit an incredibly crude one. Exiled from his own tribe, the hero Tumak discovers another, blonder tribe who enjoy both a friendlier communal ethos and more developed skills (weaving, spear making, cave painting). Loana (Welch) is of this tribe, and she teaches Tumak the word for spear, *oodala*, and in the course of the film utters a few other words whose meanings are at least guessable, such as *akita* ("help") and *ootana* ("go," or perhaps "away"). This handful of terms, complemented by pointing, waving, and like gestures, is the full extent of the primitive language of Loana's people, and it suffers in comparison with the carefully designed language of *Quest for Fire.*

Reference: One Million Years B.C. Directed by Don Chaffey. Screenplay by Michael Carreras; adapted by Mickell Novak, George Baker, and Joseph Frickert, 1967.

Out of the Silent Planet

Since its protagonist is a philologist, one might well expect C. S. Lewis's 1938 novel to be dominated by linguistic discussions and abounding in alien languages. However, while there are three artificial languages mentioned in the course of the text, only one is considered in detail and, in fact, languages in this novel appear to serve more metaphorical than linguistic purpose.

Out of the Silent Planet is the first extraterrestrial adventure of Cambridge professor Elwin Ransom, whose further exploits are recounted in **Perelandra* (1943) and *That Hideous Strength* (1945), which complete Lewis's "Cosmic Trilogy." Kidnapped by the megalomaniacal physicist Weston (who reappears in *Perelandra*) and taken to Malacandra (known as Mars by earthly inhabitants) to become what Weston believes will be a human sacrifice to the "monstrous" *sorns*, Ransom escapes and encounters the creatures of Mars on his own terms. Having befriended and obtained recognition from the powers of the planet (the angelic *eldila*, and their ruler, the Oyarsa), Ransom returns to Earth to tell his story to Lewis, who acts as Ransom's amanuensis.

Ransom's first encounter is with the otterlike race known as the *hrossa*. As a philologist, Ransom immediately recognizes this creature's vocalizing as speech and, quite humorously, his initial pleasure at the thought of learning this language is that it might lead to a series of new academic publications: "*An Introduction to the Malacandrian Language—The Lunar Verb—A Concise Martian-English Dictionary* . . . the titles flitted through his mind. And what might one not discover from the speech of a non-human race?" (62). Of the three races on Malacandra, the *hrossa* are the bardic warrior figures, and hence have the most poetic and widest lexicon, yet fewer than a dozen words are given by Lewis. Most begin with a pronounced "h," such as *handramit* (lowlands), *harandra* (highlands), *hnau* (sentient being), or *hnakra* (a predatory sea serpent, which suggests Lewis Carroll's "Snark"). Some rudimentary conjunction and grammatical rules are also assessed by Ransom, where pluralization is indicated by the addition of an "a" (*hross* singular, *hrossa* plural) and where the source of the planet's name, Malacandra, causes the following linguistic speculation on the part of Ransom: "*Handra* was earth the element; *Malacandra* the 'earth' or planet as a whole. Soon he would find out what *Malac* meant. In the meantime 'H disappears after C' he noted, and made his first step in Malacandrian phonetics" (65). Elsewhere, words appear to function as in Old English, where new nouns are created by verbal juxtaposition (e.g., *punt* is "to kill"; thus, a *hnakrapunt* is a *hnakra* slayer). Ransom soon becomes fluent in this new language.

As in the Narnia chronicles, or in Tolkien's **The Lord of the Rings*, racial essentialism is at work, even with alien species. The two other races of Malacandra each excel at certain activities that the others do not practice at all. The *sorns*, the gigantic and ectomorphic humanoids, are scientists, whereas the froglike *pfifltriggi* are artisans and craftsmen. While Ransom encounters representatives from each of these races, they converse in *hrossa*, which appears to be the lingua franca of Malacandra. As a *pfifltriggi* explains, "Once we all had different speeches and we still have at home. But everyone has learned the speech of the *hrossa*. . . . They are our great speakers and singers. They have more words and better. No one learns the speech of my people, for what we have to say is said in stone and sun's blood [gold] and stars' milk [diamonds] and all can see them" (133).

Readers of *Perelandra* will learn that this is not exactly the case, but this example does point to a linguistic conception at work in Lewis's writing—that of language determining consciousness (perhaps formulated as word view=worldview). For example, as the *hrossa* live in a state of harmony and peace, they have no word for "evil"; it can only translate as "bent." Similarly, when Weston tries to explain his ideas of imperialism, or even discourses like law, to the Oyarsa, Ransom can translate only in roundabout ways. As Malacandrians accept death and do not attempt to extend life, explaining "medicine" requires Ransom to say, "there is a thing happens in our world when the body of a living creature feels pains and becomes weak, and . . . we sometimes know how to stop it" (158).

Similarly, proper names on Malacandra seem mimetic and appear to express the racial characteristics of the speakers. According to the *pfifltriggi*, "the *sorns* have big-sounding names like Augray and Arkal and Belmo and Falmay. The *hrossa* have furry names like Hnoh and Hnihi and Hyoi and Hlithnahi. . . . My people have names like Kalakaperi and Parakataru and Tafalakeruf" (133).

Unfortunately, this is the closest readers get to speculating about the sound or structure of the language of the *sorns* and *pfifltriggi*, and linguistic issues appear to become more local color than actual subjects of examination by the novel's conclusion. However, to be fair to Ransom, he does blame this absence on Lewis's editorial choices, objecting to "the ruthless way in which you have cut down all the philological part [and] as it now stands, we are giving our readers a mere caricature of the Malacandrian language" (180).

Reference: Lewis, C. S. *Out of the Silent Planet*. London: Pan, 1976.

P

Pale Fire

In Vladimir Nabokov's playful novel *Pale Fire* (1962), one Dr. Charles Kinbote is (if only in his own mind) a refugee from "a distant northern land" called Zembla (315). In zealously prefacing, annotating, and indexing his deceased American neighbor's poem, *Pale Fire*, the mad Kinbote manages to overwrite the text with his own personality and autobiography, often making howling errors of linguistic and cultural translation in the process. King Alfin the Vague, a past monarch and "wretched linguist," is said to have "only a few phrases of French and Danish" and when speaking to his subjects flavored his words "for topical sense with a little Latin" (102). Add Nabokov's own native Russian and this hodgepodge is a handy recipe for **Zemblan**. The samples of vocabulary dropped in the course of Kinbote's preposterous notes are representative of his capricious, digressive manner. Most are nouns—for example, *vebodar* (upland pastures), *drungen* ("bramble-choked footpaths" [245]), *rusker sirsusker* ("Russian seersucker suit" [273]), and *raghdirst* ("thirst for revenge" [85])—but there are some sample quotations from a dubious Zemblan version of Shakespeare's *Timon of Athens* (titled *Timon Afrisken*). Because he is adept at malapropisms and translational blunders in several languages (witness "blanc-mangé" [142] and "doubleganger" [143]), not to mention completely delusional, Kinbote's own linguistic competence is highly suspect. The word *alfear* is improbably translated by Kinbote as "uncontrollable fear caused by elves" (143), and the adage *belwif ivurkumpf wid snew ebanumf* expands to "a beautiful woman should be like a compass rose of ivory with four parts of ebony" (206). Since the reality of Zembla remains an open question, Zemblan may be the lexicon of madness.

Reference: Nabokov, Vladimir. *Pale Fire*. New York: Vintage, 1989.

"The Pathways of Desire"

Three anthropologists from Earth studying the inhabitants of Yirdo, a moon of the planet Uper, make an unsettling discovery in Ursula K. Le Guin's short story "The Pathways of Desire" (1979). The Ndif, as these people are called, are more or less evenly divided between the Young (most notably featuring "sexually available, eager, and adept" females [237]) and the Old, and there is a conspicuous difference between their language as well as their customs. **Old Ndif**, a character named Ramchandra observes, is "much fuller" (242) than **Young Ndif**: it has greater vocabulary. In contemplating the reason for this difference, Ramchandra notes a bizarre similarity between Young Ndif and English. "People cannot hear their native language," Ramchandra remarks to his colleague Tamara when he reveals the connection (244). Tamara introduces the problematic word *Askiös*: "Please, you're welcome, sorry, wait a minute, never mind, hello, goodbye, yes, no, and maybe, all seemed to fall within the connotations of askiös" (240). Ramchandra points out that *Askiös* sounds rather like "excuse," and one may hear the slightly awkward English phrase "Excuse please I have to go by this path" in the Ndif phrase for the same purpose: "Askiös-bhis iyava oe isbhassa" (244). Young Ndif, it turns out, "is based at least sixty percent upon the structure and vocabulary of Modern English" (245).

The implications of this revelation ultimately make it seem of relatively minor importance. When the possible solutions of telepathy among the Ndif or prior visitation are discarded, the story's protagonists are faced with the fantastic aspect of the Ndif lifestyle and an interview with the elders about God—known as *Bik-Kop-Man*—and the origin of the world. Ramchandra points out that the manner in which all females among the Ndif have names ending with the letter "a," while none of the males' names do, obeys "a cosmic constant established by H. Rider Haggard" (246). That is, Young Ndif is an unsophisticated artificial language, not unlike those found in pulp science fiction (for an example of Haggard's languages, see *When the World Shook*), and Old Ndif is "authentic" but not a precursor; rather, it is "based upon Young Ndif, has grown out of it, or over it. Like ivy on a telephone pole" (265).

Le Guin's story is a meditation on "the ethnology of dreams" (271). The Ndif are very likely the creation of a distant dreamer, someone possibly named Bill Kopman (see the name for God again, above), an English-speaking, story-loving boy who "knows nothing but his own immense desire" (276).

Reference: Le Guin, Ursula K. "The Pathways of Desire." *The Compass Rose*. New York: Harper-Collins, 2005. 235–279.

Patria

See *Dicamus et Labyrinthos*.

Perelandra

Perelandra (1943), also published as *Voyage to Venus*, is the second book of C. S. Lewis's "Cosmic Trilogy," which also includes *Out of the Silent Planet* (1938) and *That Hideous Strength* (1945). This novel is an expansion of the adventures of philologist Elwin Ransom and clarifies some of the linguistic problems raised by Ransom's experiences on Mars (referred to as Malacandra in the series).

Whereas *Out of the Silent Planet* suggests to readers that there are at least three different languages other than English spoken in our planetary system, *Perelandra* postulates that there is one language common to the entire solar system (**Old Solar**), which is the ur-language of all sentient creatures of all terrestrial bodies, and that the other languages that have developed are bastardizations of this original pure discourse. The language that Ransom learns from the *hrossa* (now identified as *Hressa-Hlab*) in *Out of the Silent Planet* is now revealed to be Old Solar, or *Hlab-Eribol-ef-Cordi* in that tongue.

In this novel, readers are also informed that the language of the *sorns*, from the previous book, is known as *Surnibur*, yet few new words are added to our knowledge of Old Solar beyond *hru* (blood) and *albedo* (the cloudy outer atmosphere of Perelandra). Ransom does, however, suspect that the reason he has been selected by the angelic guardians of the planets (the *eldila*) to be their envoy between planets is due to his proficiency in languages.

Perelandra, or Venus, is constructed by Lewis as a prelapsarian paradise, in which there are only two humanoid inhabitants, the Queen and King, who are analogues of Earth's Adam and Eve and who also face devilish temptation through the influence of a demonically possessed earthling—the scientist Weston, who is also encountered in *Out of the Silent Planet*. It is Ransom's task to prevent the "fall" of Perelandra's Eve, and throughout the text he converses with the new Eve in Old Solar. As Ransom succeeds in his mission, it is unlikely that a unique Perelandrian language will develop—indeed, the loss of Old Solar on other planets is one indication that the inhabitants of that body are a fallen race (Thulcandra, the name of Earth in the trilogy, translates as "the silent planet," unable to converse with the other celestial bodies). By the novel's conclusion, it seems that even Old Solar may not be necessary for a sufficiently pure race, as the characters then appear to converse more by telepathy or emotional rapport than they do by verbal language.

As in *Out of the Silent Planet*, the linguistic difference of Old Solar is made apparent through the device of speakers not having the ability to understand concepts for which they have no verbal equivalents. For example, the Perelandrians cannot speak of "knowledge" or "ignorance," only of "growing older," or of "acting young." Similarly, having no concept of war, they cannot understand the word for peace. In fact, it is subsequently revealed that the whole purpose of Maleldil (the Christian God) in sending Ransom and Weston to Perelandra is to teach the inhabitants of this planet the concept of evil by the example of their actions. After defeating Weston and escaping from an *Inferno*-esque subterranean cave system, Ransom carves a memorial to his fallen foe in Old Solar. The fact that Lewis mentions that the letters used are Roman suggests that there may be a different script for Old Solar; whether the fact that readers are left with no examples of this is due Ransom's ignorance of this script, or because Lewis chose not to invent it, is left to speculation.

Reference: Lewis, C. S. *Perelandra*. London: Pan, 1983.

The Player of Games

This 1988 science-fiction novel is the second in Iain M. Banks's "Culture" series, focusing on the highly advanced humanoid society known as the Culture. A completely rhizomatic organization, the Culture has no hierarchy, no central home world, and no established laws. Rather, it is decentralized and constantly in motion, made up of trillions of beings from nine humanoid races (as well as artificial intelligence [AI] machines who have equal rights and privileges to humans), and is an anarchist-socialist utopia. The people of the Culture are enlightened epicureans, and through thousands of years of genetic altering can switch genders without surgery, are disease free, and are able to internally generate any narcotic they wish through drug glands.

The language of the Culture, **Marain**, like the society itself, has been engineered by hyperintelligent AI machines to reflect the philosophical beliefs of the system: "Marain was a synthetic language, designed to be phonetically and philosophically as expressive as the pan-human speech apparatus and the pan-human brain would allow" (247); and, aesthetically, it exhibits a "carefully balanced interpretative structure [with] subtle shifts of cadence, tone and rhythm" (247). As might be expected, Marain is a gender-free language, with one personal pronoun to cover "females, males, in-betweens, neuters, children, drones, Minds, [and] other sentient machines" (99).

No examples of words in Marain are given, but a writing system has been described by Banks in his article "A Few Notes on Marain." Rather than a restricted alphabet, the Marain script is an open system where new sounds (phonemes) can be transcribed as new races are encountered and where none of the old languages of the original nine Culture races dominate. In this system, each phoneme (as well as diacritical marks) is rendered in nine-bit binary code; this code is then arranged in a 3×3 grid, with the "on" bits forming the basis for a linear script that then represents the sound. An example of some common Marain "letters" are shown in the figure.

In *The Player of Games*, the Culture encounters, and attempts to accommodate, a diametrically opposed society, the sadistic and militaristic Empire of Azad. The language of the Empire, **Eächic,** is also used to demonstrate the moral fallibility of the

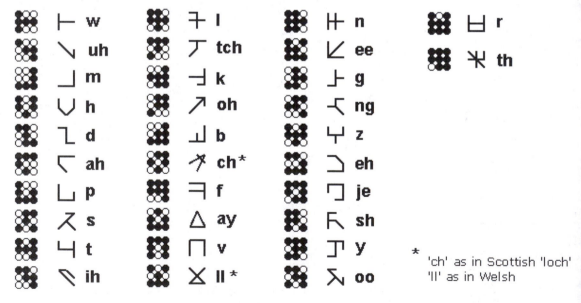

The Marain writing system, devised by Iain M. Banks, is an open form of inscription where new phonemes may be transcribed as they are discovered. Each phoneme is rendered in nine-bit binary code; this code is then arranged in a 3×3 grid, with the "on" bits forming the basis for a linear script that then represents the sound.

Empire (here, as in Marain, Banks seems to support Sapir–Whorf). Eächic is described as harsh, simplistic, gendered (there are three sexes in the Empire—male, female, and apex, with the apex being the dominant gender), and phonetically crude (members of the Empire are rarely able to pronounce the protagonist's name correctly).

The only word given in Eächic is *azad*, which is the name of the metagame (and megagame) that is played by dominant members of the Empire and which determines material and political advancement for victorious players. *Azad* refers to the game, the society, the advancement system, machines and mechanisms, or "any functioning entity, such as an animal or flower" (76).

References: Banks, Iain M. "A Few Notes on Marain": http://homepages.compuserve.de/Mostral/artikel/marain.html; Banks, Iain M. *The Player of Games*. London: Macmillan, 1988.

Possible Worlds

John Mighton's disturbing play *Possible Worlds* (1988) opens with a police investigation into a corpse with a brain missing. The play is difficult to summarize because it deals with abstruse concepts, such as alternate lives and conditioned realities, and one of the unusual possibilities the detectives are left to consider is that the brain snatching is the work of extraterrestrials, or at least unobserved beings of superior intelligence. As different scenes in the play enact these various possibilities, one scene includes masked beings who begin to bring stone blocks from offstage to pile together, apparently building something unknown. One human character, simply called Guide, explains to another that the language of these builders has only three words: "slab" and "block"—which they can routinely be heard calling for—and "hilarious," with which, Guide explains, they can do nothing (42). Guide offers not one reason for these strange beings with their equally strange three-word language but, in keeping with the spirit of the play, several possibilities:

> Some say they were once an advanced civilization. There was a war. Somehow their memories were selectively destroyed. Only three words survived. Others say they're a very primitive civilization. They learned the first two words by trial and error, and somehow stumbled on the third . . . a tourist perhaps. Others say they're an ordinary civilization but very concise. It would take fifty encyclopædias to translate the meanings of "slab" and "block" into our language. (42)

The language is linked to the play's closing image, a small light blinking in the darkness. The light represents an isolated brain's only communication, a desire that is based on programmed delusion.

Reference: Mighton, John. *Possible Worlds*. Toronto: Playwrights Canada Press, 1988.

Priest-Kings of Gor

The third book chronicling the "counter-earth" adventures of Tarl Cabot, the hero of John Norman's World of Gor "swords and science" series, features—alongside scantily clad slave girls and monstrous enemies to be defeated by sword and strength—two languages. The first, **Gorean**, appears to differ from English only in terms of its signifiers; otherwise, the linguistic structure remains consistent. For example, rather than using "miles" or "minutes," the unit of distance measurement is the *pasang*, while the unit of time is the *ihn*. Few other details of the Gorean language are given, other than the fact that there are twenty-eight characters in the alphabet and that there are archaic and modern usages of the language—the former still spoken by the priestly caste of Gorean society.

The second and more developed language is that of the Priest-Kings, a race of hyper-intelligent insects who control "counter-earth" from a vast and hidden underground nest. The Priest-Kings communicate primarily through the sense of smell. As well as exuding scent patterns for day-to-day communication among themselves, the Priest-Kings also have the equivalent of books in their scented scrolls, patterns of odors permanently affixed to walls and doorways as artwork or signage, and machines "played" by talented Priest-Kings that release refined scents corresponding to our sense of music.

Norman spends several pages describing how scents can correspond to linguistic structures, commenting on the number of phonemes in the Priest-Kings' language and how these relate to morphemic structures, suggesting that Norman (the pseudonym of City University of New York philosophy professor John Lange) has some familiarity with linguistics. Yet the descriptions appear more didactic (and pedantic) than necessary and do little to provide a sense of the linguistic culture of the Priest-Kings. For example, in one section Cabot notes, "I do not know whether there are more morphemes in the language of the Priest-Kings or in English, but both are apparently rich languages, and, of course, the strict morpheme count is not necessarily a reliable index to the complexity of the lexicon, because of combinations of morphemes to form new words. German, for example, tends to rely somewhat more on morpheme combinations than does English or French" (79).

Since the Priest-Kings control numerous human slaves in their nest, they all wear mechanical translation devices that convert scent expressions into auditory signals in order to command humans. As in many science-fiction and fantasy novels, there are certain expressions that are untranslatable between species. For example, as a race of coldly scientific and utilitarian beings, the Priest-Kings have no expression for the word "friendship," which can be rendered only as "nest trust."

Reference: Norman, John. *Priest-Kings of Gor*. New York: Ballantine, 1968.

The Princess Hoppy

Jacques Roubaud, a French mathematician and member of the experimental literary group Oulipo (*Ouvroir de la littérature potentielle*), has written *The Princess Hoppy* both as an *Alice in Wonderland*-style fantasy and as a series of mathematical problems. Each chapter of the novel has a narrative, yet each also features numerous word and logic games that are foregrounded by an appendix containing seventy-nine questions for the reader.

There are several talking animals in Roubaud's tale (including hedgehogs, camels, and snails), and some animals converse in their own languages, which are often reproduced untranslated. For example, **Grasshopper** appears only typographically, as shown in figure 1 (p. 152).

Another silent language in the novel is **Posterior Duck**, which is conveyed by the movement of the rear-webbed feet of ducks assembled in a line. Figure 2 (p. 152) demonstrates the movements required to convey the phrase "cool, dude."

The duck language also has a vocal version, known as **Anterior Duck**, which consists of a series of "quacks" and "quins." For example, in order to convey the expression "me too" the following sounds need to be made:

Quack   Quack   Quack

                         Quin'

Quin,   Quin,

          Quin Quin

Quack   Quack   Quack,   Quack

Quin   Quack

                    Quin

Like Duck, the Dog language also has two dialects; the first, known simply as **Dog**, appears to be primarily English, but with various consonant changes. Sometimes, this is achieved by replacing certain consonants with the letter "t" as in *the trotlet is without toubt tittitult, tut it tertainly has a tolution*, which can be translated as "the problem is without doubt difficult, but it certainly has a solution" (51). At other times, Dog is English with certain letters removed, such as *al ight, I as ony tying to hep*, which suggests "all right I was only trying to help" (40).

Superior Dog also appears to be encrypted English but much more difficult to solve. Superior Dog usually appears as verse:

> *t' cea uc tscl rs*
> *n neo rt aluot*
> *ia ouna s ilel-*
> *-rc oal ei ntoi* (7)

Few have been able to translate Superior Dog, and according to Roubaud, "everyone pretends that Dog is a gross language . . . be that as it may: no one, and I repeat no one, has so far been able to translate [the above verse] yet it is luminous and quasi transparent" (121).

Not to be outdone by mere animals, there is also a language of the sun in *The Princess Hoppy*. Although little detail is given of **Sun**, we are told that "he" speaks by using ultraviolet light for consonants and infrared light for vowels.

Reference: Roubaud, Jacques. *The Princess Hoppy.* Translated by Bernard Hoepffner. Normal, IL: Dalkey Archive, 1993.

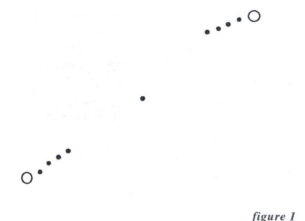

figure 1

A Princess of Mars

Edgar Rice Burroughs's vision of Mars started life in the pages of *All-Story Magazine* in 1912. "Under the Moons of Mars," a six-part serial, which appeared under the pseudonym Norman Bean, was republished as a novel under Burroughs's own name in 1917. *A Princess of Mars* was to be followed by ten subsequent novels about John Carter's boisterous adventures on the red planet, including *The Gods of Mars* (1918); *Thuvia, Maid of Mars* (1920); and *Swords of Mars* (1936). Mars is called Barsoom by its inhabitants, a set of tribes with different skin colors but who all share a common language, **Barsoomian**. The telepathic abilities common to all Barsoomians "accounts largely for the simplicity of their language and the relatively few spoken words exchanged even in long conversations" (38). Some, though not all, tribes and regions have a written language, though these scripts differ among literate tribes (the written language of Helium is "spelled in hieroglyphics which it would be difficult and useless to reproduce" [71]). The novel offers just a handful of Barsoomian words, such as *kaor* (a word of greeting), *sak* (a command to jump), and *o mad* (a man with only one name, one who has not acquired the second name that is won in victory in battle with a chieftain). This minimally described and (conveniently for the hero) quickly learned language is typical of Burroughs's work: see, for example, *Carson of Venus.

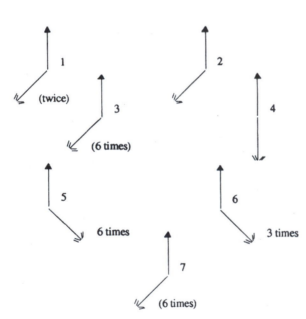

figure 2

The transcription of two of the many languages featured in Jacques Roubaud's *The Princess Hoppy*. The top illustration is a typographical representation of Grasshopper language, while the bottom figure shows Posterior Duck. A silent language of gesture (based on the movement of rear webbed feet), the above motions convey the expression: "cool, dude." Dalkey Archive Press. Reprinted with permission.

Reference: Burroughs, Edgar Rice. *A Princess of Mars*. New York: Ballantine Books, 1969.

Q

Quest for Fire

In order to create believable prehistoric people for his film *Quest for Fire* (1981), director Jean-Jacques Annaud retained the assistance of the novelist Anthony Burgess and the anthropologist Desmond Morris. The latter instructed actors in using a suitably expressive body language, while Burgess broke down various Indo-European roots to construct a plausible kind of ur-language with a working vocabulary. *Atra*, the very first spoken word of the film, means "fire." Burgess explains his working logic:

> I decided, somewhat arbitrarily, to have my fire-seekers call the hot bright magic *atr*. This suggests a taboo if we take it that *atr* could be the ancestor of the Latin *ater/atris*, which means black. The atrium was the open main court of a Roman house, so called because it was blackened by smoke from the hearth. Having chosen *atr*, I had to regard it not as a word but as a root—properly *atr-*. If I see the fire it is *atrom*, if the fire sees me it is *atra*, if I am surrounded by many fires they are *atrois*. Very Indo-European—or shall we say very unChinese, very unMalay. (Burgess 1986, 194)

Rather than one ur-language, there seem to be a few different languages in evidence in the film, or at least there are significant differences in linguistic complexity (including but not limited to dialects) between separate tribes. It is clear, for instance, that the members of the Ulam tribe (the title's seekers of fire) do not understand the speech of a comparatively talkative woman from the Ivaka tribe whom they happen to encounter. There is a definite relation posited in *Quest for Fire* between linguistic sophistication and other technological advancements, for the Ivaka are on the whole more loquacious and have a wider vocabulary than any of the other tribes in the film (the Ulam, the Kzamm, and the Wagabou) and, unlike those other tribes, have tents, throwing spears, and the ability to start fires.

Among the special features included in the DVD edition of the film is a brief summary by Annaud of Burgess's remarkable contribution, with stills of typewritten pages of vocabulary and pronunciation guides. Here is but a short sampling of the glosses the viewer may find there:

jalkan	to make walk or move, hence to bring about
mordoedga	bad luck, misfortune—the root meaning death is attached to the suffix -ga denoting a thing or device or means or instrument
ahaman	peace
mau	to want, wants, want
kas	give, leave to, hand over to

The film is based on a 1911 novel, *La Guerre de Feu* (*Fire War*), by J. H. Rosny, a book that Burgess calls "a fanciful romance" (1986, 197) and which itself does not offer any ur-language.

References: Burgess, Anthony. "Firetalk." *But Do Blondes Prefer Gentlemen?: Homage to Qwert Yuiop and Other Writings.* New York: McGraw-Hill, 1986. 192–198; *Quest for Fire.* Directed by Jean-Jacques Annaud. Screenplay by Gerard Brach, 1981.

R

"The Rats in the Walls"

H. P. Lovecraft's often-anthologized short story, composed in 1923, does not contain a unique language but rather a mixture of several in what might be described as linguistic syncretism.

Disturbed by the sounds and visions of rats moving through his ancient priory, the protagonist of this tale investigates the depths of his recently restored habitation with a group of friends. Dislodging an ancient altar reveals a subterranean chamber leading to a grotto filled with mountains of bones—both human and prehuman—suggesting that this site had been the locus of human sacrifice and cannibalism for millennia. Roman and Celtic buildings and holding pens in the chamber imply that this sacrifice had been ritualistic and continued well into the seventeenth century.

Overcome with horror at this revelation, the narrator succumbs to madness, represented in the story by mental and linguistic devolution, and utters the following phrase: "'Sblood, thou stinkard, I'll learn ye how to gust . . . wolde ye swynke me thilke wys? . . . *Magna Mater! Magna Mater! . . . Atys . . . Dia ad aghaidh 's ad aodann . . . agus bas dunach ort! Dhonas 's dholas ort, agus leat-sa! . . . Ungl . . . ungl . . . rrrlh . . . chchch*" (54). As S. T. Joshi notes, this utterance contains old English, Latin, Gaelic, and primal grunts.

Reference: Lovecraft, H. P. "The Rats in the Walls." *The Annotated H. P. Lovecraft.* Edited by S. T. Joshi. New York: Dell, 1997. 25–55.

"Remarks of the Scholar Graduate"

Presented—as its title suggests—as an alumnus's address to schoolboys, Harry Mathews's story expounds a set of bizarre, convoluted, yet attractive theories about ancient **Bactrian** writing, theories that the narrator says have been much "misrepresented" and shrouded by "the dust clouds of controversy" (41). The Bactrian writings in question are invariably made up of seven horizontal lines, like so:

———————
———————
———————
———————
———————
———————
———————

The unnamed "Scholar Graduate" contends that, contrary to what rival scholars in his field have held, these lines are not identical, because the position of each is in itself a signification of some value. Further, on the basis of "extrapolation from later texts" (44), he claims that each line signifies a consonantal sound, and the spaces between the lines represent vowels:

```
        (a)
———————k (h)
        a
———————l (r)
        e
———————sh (ch, j)
        i
———————t (d, n)
        u
———————s (z)
        o
———————f (v)
        a
———————p (b, m)
        (a)
```

Having reached this understanding, the narrator then "learned"—he does not say how—"that the symbols were to be read from the bottom up" (45), to reveal the only written word in Bactrian: *(a)pafosutishelak(a)*. The narrator interprets this word as the Bactrian name of God and goes on to suggest that "the position of the dashes in a column [where more than one column of seven dashes occur] determined their function, so the positions of the columns in a line determines theirs" (46–47). These theories—which are expanded yet further, to the point that the narrator implies that the Bactrian characters are direct ancestors of the Roman alphabet characters used in modern print—are pseudo-Kabbalistic in manner (determining or calculating the name of God) and colored with a tint of lunacy. The narrator concludes in a rather maniacal way, admitting that a colleague has called him a "chauvinistic liar" (50) in the way that mad scientists archetypically laugh away recognitions of their insanity.

Reference: Mathews, Harry. "Remarks of the Scholar Graduate." *The Human Country: New and Collected Stories.* Normal, IL: Dalkey Archive, 2002. 41–50.

"The Retreat to Mars"

Cecil B. White's short story, which first appeared in the magazine *Amazing Stories* in 1927, takes its inspiration from the observations and arguments of astronomer Percival Lowell (1855–1916), who contended that systems of *canali* visible on the surface of Mars were evidence of intelligent life on the planet. In the story, an astronomer is visited by an archaeologist named Hargraves, who recounts a recent and startling discovery in central Africa. There Hargraves found a large cylinder made of an unknown metal, the sealed entry to which bears "engraved strange characters" (657).

A Martian inscription, in which information is mathematically encoded. Such logic and this phrase itself may or may not be indicative of the Martians' written language.

Hargraves deduced "that the duodecimal system was used by those who had made this thing" (658) and was thus able to figure out how to work the lock mechanism. This system of encryption was devised by Martians, who purposed that the cylinder should be entered only by beings who had developed the intelligence to understand the numerical code. These Martians had come to Earth half a million years ago in hopes of settling, but some unknown environmental quality caused birth defects: each new Earth-born generation of Martians had smaller bodies and displayed lower intelligence than the one before. So the Martians retreated and left behind records of their attempts in three different cylinders.

Hargraves tells of how a "wonderful primer" and a numbered series of data-filled volumes made his study of the Martian language "ridiculously easy" (661). The primer displays three-dimensional pictures (perhaps comparable to holograms), and in describing his lessons Hargraves gives this little detail about the language:

> Take for example the verb "to walk." In one set of pictures a being was shown in the foreground, approaching a hill. The second showed him, bent forward, walking up the hill, while a third showed him at the top. The characters were exactly the same in each case, but over the first was an inverted V; over the second, nothing; and over the third a V. The tenses were all indicated by a symbol above the verb. The degrees of adjectives were similarly indicated, hence it simplified the written language exceedingly. (661)

Of the spoken language, or even whether he knows anything of it, Hargraves reports nothing. It also remains unclear whether the duodecimal numerical script engraved on the outside of the cylinder is representative of the Martians' own number system or script.

Reference: White, Cecil B. "The Retreat to Mars." *The Best of Science Fiction.* Edited by Groff Conklin. New York: Crown Publishers, 1946. 651–667.

Riallaro: The Archipelago of Exiles

Riallaro, first published in 1897, purports to be the account of one Godfrey Sweven (the pseudonym of John Macmillan Brown), who has traveled into and within the mysterious archipelago of the title. Sweven relates how the peoples he encounters are organized by design, categories of lunatics and cranks: these include voluptuaries, journalists, numerologists, diplomats, revolutionaries, and spiritualists, each with their own island and style of social order. While it is not clear whether each island has its own distinct language(s)—in only some few cases is there a tangible suggestion of this—there are several Riallarian languages.

The citizens of Aleofane are devoted to truth above all, but their entire culture and lifestyle are made of contradictions, and their language is flush with subtle and difficult distinctions. **Aleofanian**, which appears to be a kind of lingua franca within the archipelago, is a combination of speech with "overspeech," that is, tone and gesture. The meaning of any word or phrase can depend on, for example, whether a lip is curled, a finger pressed to the brow, or a handkerchief flourished. Even the raising of the eyebrow, Sweven reports, has "a whole grammar and dictionary to itself" (27). Oaths can change to curses, and the same word for "well-bred" may mean "nincompoop" if it is uttered while one is blowing one's nose. The Aleofanians pride themselves on the notion that "it is the highest stage of social development to have a language so ambiguous and difficult that it takes the greatest wits to manage it" (31). Only a handful of Aleofanian words are presented in the novel: for example, *dyoos*, an expletive that is "the popular remains of a prayer that perdition might catch their souls if they did not speak the truth" (36), and *fallallaroo*, the name of a ridiculous gyration performed by women of the highest and most dignified classes to catch the eye of eligible young bachelors.

Aleofanian has a couple of ancestor tongues, **Thribbaty** and **Slapyak**, called "the sacred or rotten tongues" (28). These ancient languages are given little social value apart from rhetorical adornment. Used by speakers who, like the narrator of *Riallaro*, enjoy a "blessed sense of superiority" by being able to confound less-educated people in argument with a choice fragment, Thribbaty and Slapyak are probably best read as components of a satire on the failure of modern society and its education system to teach the classics.

The confusion about whether each island has its own language is demonstrated by mention of an item of linguistic history pertaining to the island of Tirralaria. Everyone there is accounted a king and a priest, and their socialism is founded on a contempt for intellectuals and specialists. A native explains that there were once "two primitive languages" there that had "taken deep root in education" and become "the marks and symbols of culture" (131). Pseudoscholars tried to use spurious knowledge of these languages to defend their elitist position and retain their sway over the culture, but the institutions of art and culture were ultimately abolished by popular vote. Whether these two languages are the same as Thribbaty and Slapyak is hard to know, but they are part of the same satire on the cultural values afforded (for example) Latin and Greek.

Wotnekst, which may be translated as "Godlaw" (but from what language remains a mystery), is an island of compulsive legislators. Not surprisingly, they have passed a law that not only acknowledges the universality and superiority of **Wotnekstian** but affirms that anyone who does not speak Wotnekstian has simply forgotten this primary language and should perforce relearn it immediately.

Mentioned in passing are "the variety of dialects" among the nonstop talkers of Jabberoo (245), "the fulsome conventional language" of the poetasters living on Kloriole (268), and the language of the desperate Figlefians, which "has been forged in unflagging struggle" (298). None of these is described at any further length.

The most vividly depicted language in Riallaro is **Limanoran**. Limanora is the former name of Faddalesa; what has become "the isle of devils" was once "the island of progress" (114). Limanora's language is a construct based on principles complementary to the island's socialist laws and values. In the course of describing it, Sweven includes a paragraph's diatribe against the perniciousness of "uncleansed words": "It is one of the greatest mistakes of European civilization to let words take their own course, the most dangerous source of spiritual epidemics" (390–391). Ambiguities and double meanings are banished by the designers of Limanoran, a language simple and melodious, needing no poets because it is "poetry itself" (393). The "commonest and easiest things and ideas" are represented by "the easiest words" (388), and any one sound has only one possible meaning (e.g., *lul* is "smoke," *lil* is "cloud" [390]). Obviously, the vocabulary needs be vast, and the text gives only a few, apparently representative examples, but the grammar is simple. Common nouns tend to be monosyllabic, whereas verbs ("energy-words") and adjectives ("quality-words," with the same form as adverbs) are generally dissyllabic and formed by means of suffix (for verbs) or prefix (for adjectives and adverbs). The following is an example (388):

kar	dust
karo	to reduce to dust
okar	having the essential qualities of dust

Certain shades of meaning—again, not ambiguity—lie within pronunciation. Tense, for instance, is expressed in how the verbal suffix is sounded (389):

Lo karŏ ti rak	I reduce this rock to dust
Lo karō ti rak	I shall reduce this rock to dust
Lo karōō ti rak	I reduced this rock to dust

Metaphorical meaning is also a tonal matter (390):

kār	dust
kăr	(implications of ephemerality)

The "language sanitation" of Limanora is as utopian an endeavor as the island itself. Sweven's sequel to *Riallaro*, *Limanora, the Island of Progress* (1903), elaborates and expands on the language of the place.

Reference: Sweven, Godfrey. *Riallaro, The Archipelago of Exiles*. 2nd ed. London: Oxford University Press, 1931.

Riddley Walker

In the postapocalyptic "Inland" of Russell Hoban's novel *Riddley Walker* (1980), the title character narrates his adventures in a devolved form of English. Inland's inhabitants are the inheritors of a world devastated by nuclear cataclysm, and their engrossing tribal culture is a heap of broken images, a strange mix of myths of St. Eustace, Orpheus, and Punch and Judy, strung together to suggest an explanation for their irradiated environment. **Riddleyspeak**'s principal distortions of English occur in vocabulary and appear as orthographically transformed terms, phrases, and idioms taken from British speech and culture: in this regard, much of the book is reminiscent of *Finnegans Wake*, and like Joyce, Hoban predicates his narrative and indeed the collective consciousness of his characters on puns. To read *Riddley Walker* is to read slowly and thus both to see an unfamiliar world and to come to awareness only as gradually as the primitive hero does. Only sounding out words like *gready mints* (ingredients), *Pry Mincer* (Prime Minister), *Ardship of Cambry* (Archbishop of Canterbury, but also Hardship), *tryl narrer* (trial and error), *oansome* (alone, lonesome), and *vack your wayt* (evacuate, get going) reveals their sometimes multiple meanings. All names of numbers appear as Arabic numerals: *a hevvy 1* (a heavy, large, or strong one) *every 1* (everyone), *1st, 2nd, 3rd* (first, second, third). Colloquialisms like *arga warga* (very bad, messed up) and *1 Big 1* (the apocalypse, both means and event) are made plain by context and repetition. Riddley also refers to *the old spel*, an earlier standard of writing, when he recounts "The Eusa Story," which is frequently quoted as scripture by characters in Inland. Eusa 19, for example, is the nineteenth verse of the story and begins, "Evere thing was blak & rottin. Ded peapl & pigs eatin them & thay pigs dyd. Dog paks after peapl & peapl after dogs tu eat them the saym. Smoak goin up frum bernin evere wayr" (31; translation: Everything was black and rotten. Dead people and pigs eating them and the pigs died. Packs of dogs hunted people and people hunted dogs to eat them, just the same. Smoke was rising from burning everywhere). The *old spel* is just that much cruder a version of the written language Riddley uses to tell his tale of cruelty, humor, and the narrow route for survival that lies between. An "Expanded Edition" of the novel published by Indiana University Press includes a brief glossary entitled "A Short Guide to Riddleyspeak."

Riddley Walker's use of a phonetic, piecemeal, and ritualized language has won a noticeable amount of homage and emulation in science fiction. See, for example, Jack Womack's *Ambient*, Iain M. Banks's *Feersum Endjinn*, and the film *Mad Max: Beyond Thunderdome*.

References: Hoban, Russell. *Riddley Walker*. London: Picador, 1982; see also Eli Bishop's Web site of *Riddley Walker* annotations: http://www.graphesthesia.com/rw/index.html.

Ringworld

In Larry Niven's "Known Space" series of novels (beginning with *Ringworld* in 1970), while the use of human languages like English, German, and Spanish has declined sharply, a language known as **Interworld** has assumed the status of lingua franca between various space-traveling species. Almost nothing is known about the language's history or structure. The acronym *tanj* ("There Ain't No Justice!" [4])

operates as an all-purpose expletive, functional as noun, verb, adjective, and adverb (examples of usage: "what the tanj?" [3]; "tanj you" [188]; "tanjit!" [140]). *Ringworld* includes reference to "Interworld-Morse" as a means of long-distance communication, but perhaps it should not be inferred that the Interworld alphabet is the same as that of known "real" languages (English, for example).

There are three alien languages in the novel, though none of them is given more than scant description. The two-headed, hypersensitive creatures known as Pierson's puppeteers appear in the "Known Space" series. In *Ringworld*, a puppeteer named Nessus translates the term for "leaders" in his language as "*those-who-lead-from-behind*" (89), and his dual-throated speech is called "orchestral music" (12).

Kzinti, colloquially referred to as "the Hero's tongue," is the language of the large, bellicose, catlike creatures of the planet Kzin (they are known as *Kzin* singular, *Kzinti* plural) and sounds to human ears like "hissing, spitting phrases" (153–154). The Kzinti culture has been developed in subsequent novels by Niven and others (see Dean Ing's *Cathouse*). In his "Notes on the Kzinti Language," Arthur T. Saxtorph offers as a sample of Kzinti script a translation of part of a Kzinti war cry.

Finally, there is the language of the Ringworld itself. It sounds like a "chant, a recital of poetry" (172), and one human character judges "the language of the Ringworld engineers" to be that "of the shaven choir-leading priest" (272). Niven's novel includes just one word from this language, *thrumb*, which seems to refer to the color orange (272–273), and there is open speculation about whether the Ringworld engineers have more than one language, localized variations stemming from some "original" (235).

References: Niven, Larry. *Ringworld*. New York: Ballantine, 1970; Saxtorph, Arthur T. "Notes on the Kzinti Language." *Speculative Grammarian* 147.2 (1993): http://www.specgram.com/CXLVII.2/06 .saxtorph.kzinti.html; see also the Web site *Known Space: The Future Worlds of Larry Niven*: www .larryniven.org.

S

Scoop

In Evelyn Waugh's 1938 satire of the journalism industry, a young gentleman farmer, John Boot, who normally writes a nature column for the London paper *The Beast*, is mistakenly sent to cover an uprising in the fictional African republic of Ishmaelia.

While the novel provides a number of interesting facts regarding **Ishmaelite**, including the existence of tribal patois, a written form, and a societal predilection for the word "Jackson" (the name of the current president), there is almost no vocabulary or grammar for Ishmaelite given.

One exception to this absence is the explanation of the origin of the name of the settlement of Laku, a town that no one has ever visited, yet which appears on many maps of Ishmaelia. According to one British inhabitant of Ishmaelia, when surveyors were mapping the country, they asked a native the name of a hill nearby, to which the Ishmaelite replied *laku*, meaning "I don't know" in that tongue. This area of the nation has been named Laku ever since.

Canadian readers of *Scoop* will recognize this anecdote as a reference to the naming of Canada. When, in 1535, Jacques Cartier inquired about the name of this new country of two Huron youths, they answered *Kanata* referring to the village nearby, rather than the nation as a whole.

Reference: Waugh, Evelyn. *Scoop*. London: Chapman & Hall, 1938.

The Secret Language

Ursula Nordstrom's 1960 book for children is about two young girls at boarding school who bond with a shared "secret language." Martha Sherman teaches Victoria North terms like *ick-en-spick* (which refers to silly or obsequious acts or behavior), *ankendosh* (something or someone "mean or disgusting" [24]), and *leebossa* ("when something is just lovely or when something works out just right. . . . For anything especially nice you can say leeleeleeleebossa" [24]). Calling the three words Victoria and Martha use a "language" is of course an exaggeration, but Nordstrom is hearkening to the idea of a language as both a means of individual expression (one child's way of speaking is unlike every other child's way of speaking) and a basis for community.

Reference: Nordstrom, Ursula. *The Secret Language*. New York: Harper and Row, 1971.

The Secret World of OG

In 1974, popular Canadian historian Pierre Berton tried his hand at children's literature in this illustrated novel. *The Secret World of OG* concerns a group of siblings who journey to a subterranean world under their clubhouse to find their youngest brother who has been kidnapped by a race of green-skinned troll-like creatures known as the Og.

The Ogs have only two words in their language, with the most frequently occurring being *og*. Most sentences are constructed solely of this word, spoken with various emphasis and inflexion, such as "Og! Og . . . og-og-og . . . *og og*" (113).

As the creatures of Og make forays to the surface to steal clothing, toys, and comic books, they soon learn English and begin to converse amongst each other in a dialect derived from genre fiction and Old West stereotypes. When asked why the culture never developed more words than *og*, one Og remarks, "We didn't know we could. . . . Besides you know, it's very much easier to learn things if you only have one word. . . . Spelling was very simple! Grammar was only slightly more difficult. . . . I was *very* bad at grammar. . . . I could never understand that the plural of Og was Og or that the objective of Og was also Og. Nor did I ever understand, I fear, that the first person plural was also Og. As for the subjunctive—I could never master it" (124–126). The other word in the Og lexicon, *glog*, is generally forbidden and to be used only in utmost emergencies. *Glog* means that the Ogs' enemies, the Snake People (who have never been encountered), have attacked or are attacking.

Berton also makes mention of a secret language that some of the children in the novel speak amongst themselves (notably, Patsy and the Terrible Twins), but the only word given is *jalopy,* which does not refer to an automobile; rather, it is used as an adjective to describe annoying or boring circumstances.

A very popular text for Canadian schoolchildren, *The Secret World of OG* has been printed in many editions. The book was also made into an animated television special in 1983 by Hanna-Barbera.

Reference: Berton, Pierre. *The Secret World of OG*. Toronto: McClelland and Stewart, 1974.

The Shadow of the Torturer

At the end of *The Shadow of the Torturer*, the first book in Gene Wolfe's science-fiction tetralogy known as *The Book of the New Sun*, it is revealed that this novel is actually a translation. In an appendix, Wolfe writes that in order to render the future tongue of the society of Urth, a language and culture that has yet to come into existence, he has replaced future concepts and signifiers with arcane English words to give the reader a sense of "foreignness" as well as to indicate creatures, flora, and weaponry that have no twentieth-century equivalents.

The world of Urth appears to be that of Earth in the far future where—owing to either a sustained nuclear winter or else the sun's beginning to extinguish—the world is dying, and society has reverted to a medieval-style civilization of guilds and fortresses where the primary weapon is a sword and transportation is that of horseback.

Yet this latter example gives an indication of what Wolfe is attempting in his reclamation of the *Oxford English Dictionary*. As future horses have been so genetically modified that they are capable of achieving speeds of 100 kilometers per hour and have claws instead of hooves, Wolfe denominates them *destriers*. Similar to this is the use of *monomachy* for "duel" and *oubliette* for "dungeon."

In his essay "Words Weird and Wonderful," Wolfe provides a lexicon of obscure words he has chosen and how he uses them in *The Book of the New Sun*, including such examples as *omophagists, lazarets*, and *ephors* (flesh eaters, hospitals, and judges, respectively).

References: Wolfe, Gene. *The Shadow of the Torturer*. New York: Simon and Schuster, 1980; Wolfe, Gene. "Words Weird and Wonderful." *Castle of Days*. New York: Tor, 1992. 234–251.

"Shall We Have a Little Talk?"

Fred C. Jackson, the protagonist of Robert Sheckley's 1965 story, is a human intent on learning alien languages on different planets so as to buy property and thereby justify that planet's later conquest by Earth. Having "an uncanny intuition for meaning" (177) rather than formal linguistic training, he is proud of his past successes, even among certain "supersonic sons of bitches" whose language required Jackson to "wear special earphones and mike" (174). His modus operandi founders, however, on the planet Na, whose humanoid denizens speak a language called **Hon**. At first Hon seems to Jackson "quite a straightforward affair. It used one term for one concept, and allowed no fusions, juxtapositions, or agglutinations. Concepts were built up by sequences of simple words ('spaceship' was ho-pa-aie-an—boat-flying-outer-sky)" (178). Bored by but confident with such a simple language, Jackson finds dealings with the Naians unusually difficult and cannot manage to purchase the needed property. The necessary legal procedures and paperwork that the Naians insist are simple formalities Jackson finds totally incomprehensible. Asked whether he has "now or at any past time, elikated mushkies forsically" (181), Jackson is at a loss to understand the terms, which appear to contradict his earlier conceptions of simple word formations. The protracted explanations and definitions he obtains merely add to the confusion. The noun *mushkies* has more than one meaning, and the adverb *forsically* describes a mode that might translate as "friendly," but that meaning applies only to conversations and not to the business of *elikating mushkies forsically*, the question about which might be more bluntly rendered, without "fancy talk," as "have you now or at any other time dunfiglers voc in illegal, immoral, or insirtis circumstances, with or without the aid and/or consent of a brachniian?" (182). By the time Jackson works out the meaning of the question, he encounters another difficulty, this time with the request that he "kindly trombramcthulanchierir in the usual manner" (187). Appalled by the sudden appearance of agglutinations, Jackson goes back to his proverbial drawing board (Sheckley's story has the structure of a joke with its repetitions and returns) to study Hon's nuances and puzzling dislocations and "*exceptional* number of exceptions" (190). In his final meeting with the Naians, however, Jackson finds that they now utter only one word—*mun*—in various sequences and with differing emphases.

Just before he abandons the planet Na in frustration, Jackson concludes that Hon evolves just as any organic language does, but at an incomprehensible pace: "By the fact of its change, the language was rendered impervious to codification and control. Through indeterminacy, the Na tongue resisted all attempts to conquer it" (193). The story ends with the remarks of the Naians who watch Jackson's exit: they laugh hysterically, and an alderman comments, "Mun-mun-mun; mun, mun-mun," which is not translated but which the narrator somberly calls "the marvellous and frightening truth of the situation" (194).

Reference: Sheckley, Robert. "Shall We Have a Little Talk?" *Galaxy* (October 1965): 172–194.

The Sirens of Titan

Recurrent in the novels of Kurt Vonnegut are the mechanical citizens of the planet Tralfamadore, whose philosophies of time and influence on earthly affairs are both bizarre and satirically edged. The **Tralfamadorian** language is very briefly described in *The Sirens of Titan* (1959). The name of the planet Tralfamadore itself means both "all of us" and the number 541 (273), and a single dot in Tralfamadorian—the message to Earth around which the plot of Vonnegut's novel merrily revolves—means "Greetings" (306). Stranger and more intriguing are the forms of Tralfamadorian writing used to communicate news from Earth to a native of Tralfamadore stranded on Saturn's moon Titan. Among the many inconspicuous ways in which Tralfamadore has exerted influence on humanity is the use of major architectural structures as text messages. Seen from the stranded Tralfamadorian's incredibly powerful viewer, the ruins now known as Stonehenge once read "Replacement part [for your spaceship] being rushed with all possible speed," while the Great Wall of China reads as "Be patient. We haven't forgotten about you" (276). The other such messages are known to earthlings as Nero's Golden House in Rome, the Kremlin in Moscow, and the Palace of the League of Nations in Geneva.

The stranded Tralfamadorian is said to speak "five thousand languages, fifty of them Earthling languages" (273), but what the remaining 4,949 are the novel does not say.

Reference: Vonnegut, Kurt. *The Sirens of Titan.* New York: Dell, 1998.

"The Slave"

In this 1957 short story, humans are enslaved by an alien race known as the A'rkhov-Yar in order to be used as psychic "fuel" for their interstellar spaceships. The A'rkhov-Yar, being visually blind, perceive by detecting patterns of heat, and many also have telepathic abilities.

Their spoken language, known as **A'rkhov**, is described as "uninflected" and "guttural" and its grammar is:

> merely the word-order of logic: subject, verb, object . . . There were remnants of 'tonality' in it. Apparently it had once been a sung language like Chinese, but had evolved even out of that characteristic.

Phonemes that once had been low-toned were now sounded back in the throat; formerly high-toned phonemes were now forward in the throat. (109)

A number of A'rkhov words and phrases are given in the course of the story, which appear to illustrate the narrator's impression of its grammar and phonology, including *Lakhrut a'g khesor-takh'* ("Lakhrut is the boss of propulsion") and the verb *ga'lt* (to read a mind) which is used to say *Lakhrut ga'lt takh-lyur-Baldwin* ("Lakhrut looks right into underchief Baldwin's head and reads his mind" [110]).

Interestingly, as the A'rkhov-Yar are not visual creatures, the source of their metaphors are often tactile. For example, the expression "if it amuses the fellow to pretend that he can read, I see no obstacle. And if it contributes to the efficiency of your department, we all shine that much brighter" since it uses visual imagery becomes "if it amuses the fellow to pretend that he fingers wisdom, my hands are not grated. And if it smooths your quarry wall, we all hew more easily" in a tactile culture (117). Similarly, A'rkhov, in its written form, is rendered as raised lines on a sheet of plastic, seemingly a form of Braille.

Reference: Kornbluth, C. M. "The Slave." In *A Mile Beyond the Moon.* New York: Doubleday, 1958. 90–123.

"Solus Rex"

Two of Vladimir Nabokov's short stories, "Ultima Thule" and "Solus Rex," are fugitive fragments of a projected novel entitled *Solus Rex*, which the author abandoned during his move to America in 1939–1940. They are set in an imaginary country called Thule, glimpses of whose language may be had in the second story. In interview, Nabokov has acknowledged the similarities between the mountainous kingdom of Thule and that of Zembla in his later novel **Pale Fire*, and has remarked that in each case the native language is "of a phony Scandinavian type" (Nabokov 1973, 91). The longest sample of the tongue of Thule is a quotation from "Uperhulm's ballad": *Solg ud digh vor je sage vel, ud jem gotelm quolm osje musikel* ("Sweet and rich was the wave of the sea and lassies drank it from seashells" [529]). Besides this there are occasional droppings of official names and terms, such as *Peplerhus* ("parliament" [527]), and note of a punning change of a family motto, *sassed ud halsem* ("see and rule") to *sasse ud hazel* ("armchair and filbert brandy" [527]).

References: Nabokov, Vladimir. "Solus Rex." *The Stories of Vladimir Nabokov.* New York: Vintage, 1995. 523–545; Nabokov, Vladimir. *Strong Opinions.* New York: McGraw-Hill, 1973.

The Southern Land, Known

First published in 1676 as *La Terre Australe Connue*, Gabriel de Foigny's book was attributed to James Sadeur, the fictional voyager-narrator, in the same way that authorship of **Gulliver's Travels* would be credited on the title page to Lemuel Gulliver, rather than Jonathan Swift, half a century later. Foigny, a defrocked monk with schooling in several languages, exploits the contemporary novelty and mystery surrounding the idea of an "Australian" continent and presents a distant utopia that is at once in the tradition of such works as Thomas More's *Utopia* and Cyrano de Berg-erac's *Comical History* and notably unique. Sadeur is a hermaphrodite, and thus an outsider in European society, but the Australia he literally stumbles on is populated by hermaphrodites who shun clothing. The **Australian** language, too, is both idealistic and fantastic: it is not an imitation or variation on any of the European languages Foigny knew but a complete invention. The Australians' "admirable uniformity of language" (40), which so impresses Sadeur, is linked to the same quality found in all of their culture and labor.

This "absolute uniformity" manifests itself linguistically in the logical basis of each word: vowels signify the central essence of that which the word names, while conso-nants serve as descriptive modifiers. The five vowels express what the Australians see as the five indissoluble elements: fire (known as *a*), air (*e*), salt (*o*), water (*i*), and earth (*u*). Their thirty-six consonants are more various, and Foigny offers these few defini-tions:

b	clear	*n*	black
c	hot	*p*	gentle
d	unpleasant	*q*	pleasant
f	dry	*s*	white
g	bad	*t*	green
h	low	*x*	cold
l	wet	*z*	high
m	desirable		

i ("the consonant")	red
a-i ("the diphthong")	peaceable

The sun, for example, is called *aab*, and birds are *oef*, "signifying their solid, aerial, and dry qualities" (93). All Australian words are thus necessarily descriptions, made up of groupings of these properties, and presumably the language does without sepa-rate adjectives and adverbs. Foigny writes that "the advantage of this system is that one becomes a philosopher as soon as one learns the first elements of speech. One can-not name anything in that country without at the same time making explicit its na-ture" (93). (This logical structure is reminiscent of contemporary schemes to establish a universal, philosophically satisfying language, such as that propounded by John Wilkins.)

The Australian language has few nouns and no declensions or articles, though verbs can seem abstract and even metaphysical. For example, *af* means "to love" because love is fiery and causes "dryness" (94). Its conjugation is typical and runs as follows:

Present Tense		*Past Tense*	
la	I love	*lga*	I have loved
pa	you (sing.) love	*pga*	you (sing.) have loved
ma	he loves	*mga*	he has loved

lla	we love	*llga*	we have loved
ppa	you (pl.) love	*ppga*	you (pl.) have loved
mma	they love	*mmga*	they have loved

In Australian writing, verbs appear only as dots, distinguished by their position on a vertical scale (the highest is *a*, descending in alphabetical order), while the consonants "consist of strokes surrounding the dots, which have meaning according to the position they occupy" (94). "Clear air" is written *eb !* and "moist earth" is *ul ;*; Foigny writes that "a further eighteen or nineteen consonants" lack any "European equivalent by which they could be explained" (94). In his 1993 edition of Foigny's work, David Fausett notes that he has—unfortunately—elected to omit certain "further baroque signs which Foigny added without explanation or distinct punctuation" (94), but he gives an approximation.

Reference: Foigny, Gabriel de. *The Southern Land, Known.* Translated and edited by David Fausett. Syracuse, NY: Syracuse University Press, 1993.

Space Chantey

R. A. Lafferty's 1968 science-fiction burlesque of Homer's *Odyssey* includes a couple of passing references to alien languages. A species known as Groll's Trolls have a language of which "six basic dialects" (18) are known to the space-traveling heroes, and their chief, Captain Roadstrum, "sometimes used high-Shelta swear words, as did many skymen" (113). The one example of a **high-Shelta** outburst is *Kstganglfoofng!*

Reference: Lafferty, R. A. *Space Chantey.* London: Dennis Dobson, 1976.

Star Trek

As the most successful and extensive science-fiction franchise, the *Star Trek* movies and TV programs span over forty years and encompass hundreds of narratives. For the purposes of this entry, we will focus on the canon of Paramount Pictures programs originally created by Gene Roddenberry, rather than the numerous novelistic treatments, comic books, and other "unofficial" formats. The core corpus thus includes the TV programs *Star Trek* (1964–1969), *Star Trek: The Next Generation* (1987–1994), *Star Trek: Deep Space Nine* (1993–1999), *Star Trek: Voyager* (1995–2001), and *Star Trek: Enterprise* (2001–2005); and the films *Star Trek: The Motion Picture* (1979), *Star Trek II: The Wrath of Khan* (1982), *Star Trek III: The Search for Spock* (1984), *Star Trek IV: The Voyage Home* (1986), *Star Trek V: The Final Frontier* (1989), *Star Trek VI: The Undiscovered Country* (1991), *Star Trek: Generations* (1994), *Star Trek: First Contact* (1996), *Star Trek: Insurrection* (1998), and *Star Trek: Nemesis* (2002). While many alien races are encountered in these programs and films, some with their own languages, here we will focus on the major races of the *Star Trek* universe.

For many, the very concept of alien or artificial languages is synonymous with the Klingon language—or at the very least the most readily called to mind. The Klingon language, **Klingonese**, has been called the world's most successful artificial language, with more speakers than Esperanto, yet this is an urban myth (rough estimates give Esperanto two million speakers to Klingonese's several hundred). Nevertheless, there is a Klingon Language Institute (KLI), replete with a scholarly journal (*HolQeD*) that is recognized by the Modern Language Association, and, like Esperanto, some energies are directed to translating well-known works into Klingon, the most famous example being a Klingon translation of *Hamlet* (2000).

The first examples of Klingonese were developed by James Doohan (the character Scotty on the original series and films), but the language was eventually taken up by linguist Marc Okrand (see also *Atlantis*) with his *Klingon Dictionary* (1992), currently regarded as the best introduction to the language.

There are eighty dialects of Klingonese (or, rendered in its own tongue, *tlhIngan Hol*), but only one dialect at a time is in official usage, based on that of the current Klingon emperor; when a new emperor is crowned, his dialect becomes the officially spoken form. Therefore, Klingons who wish to remain in positions of power learn several dialects in anticipation of such changes.

a	b	ch	D	e	gh	H
I	j	l	m	n	ng	o
p	q	Q	r	S	t	tlh
u	v	w	y	'		
0	1	2	3	4	5	6
7	8	9				

The Klingonese written script, as designed by Lawrence Schoen and Michael Okuda, is based on Tibetan.

One immediately notices that in writing English equivalents for Klingonese there is an unusual use of capitalization; these serve to emphasize distinct and variant sounds. That is, a capital *H* represents a guttural "h" sound (as in Bach), and a capital *Q* represents a coughing sound. Other unique phonetic elements include *thl* (a "til" sound with a hissing "l") and *qh* (a gargled "ar" sound). As expected from the above examples, the overall sound of Klingonese is harsh, guttural, and forceful.

There are numerous grammatical rules of Klingonese, which diligent readers can learn from Okrand's 192-page manual, but in general, sentences follow an object-verb-subject order, and gender is indicated not by sex but by whether the subject has the ability to use language. Some Klingon phrases of interest include *blnep* ("you lie"), *HIjol* ("beam me up"), and *yIbaH* ("fire the torpedoes"). It should also be noted that Klingons have no form of polite greeting or salutation, the closest being *nuqneH*, meaning "what do you want?"

Okrand also indicates that there is a secondary form of Klingonese, **Clipped Klingon**, which is used in times of combat or expediency (compare to **Dune*'s **battle language**). Using one of the above examples, "fire the torpedoes" in proper Klingon would be *yIbaH*, while in Clipped Klingon it would be *baH*.

The written script of the language is known as *pIqaD*, and various versions exist. The one approved by the KLI is attributed to Lawrence Schoen and Michael Okuda (based on Tibetan) and is reproduced here. Schoen has also discussed some problems with Klingon writing in the article "Some Comments on Orthography."

The second major race, present from the very first *Star Trek* series to current manifestations, are the patrician Vulcans. Despite the integral presence of the culturally iconic figure of Spock throughout the original series, little is given of the **Vulcan** language until the cinematic series of *Star Trek* films released during the 1980s. The first two films provide audiences with several scenes in which Vulcan is spoken, which, reflecting the stoic and logical aspects of the Vulcan culture, sounds like a mixture of Latin and German. The Vulcan language also appears to be primarily monosyllabic with an emphasis on vowels—again, perhaps indicative of the Vulcans' laconic nature. For example, the famous *Star Trek* phrase "live long and prosper" is rendered as *dup dor aa'z mub-ster* in Vulcan, and the Vulcan phrase *ish vann-e goomie* translates as "he is so human." The Vulcan written script appears to have evolved over a series of centuries but, with the exception of a more mechanical form used for identifying large vehicles, is generally calligraphic and reads vertically. As is the case in several of the *Star Trek* languages discussed below, many *Star Trek* fans have developed their own versions of Vulcan, a number of which can be found at the Alien Languages of *Star Trek* Web site.

A more militaristic offshoot of the Vulcan race, the Romulans, were first featured on the original series and were created by Paul Schneider. The difference between the Vulcans and Spartans is perhaps analogous to that of the Athenians and Spartans, yet, as their name implies, they borrow more strongly from Latin than Hellenistic sources. Fragments of the **Romulan** language have appeared on *Star Trek: The Next Generation* (*TNG*) and in *Star Trek: Enterprise* (*STE*), including the phrases *jolan true* (both a greeting and farewell) and *veruul* (an expletive), but as of yet, not enough of the Romulan lexicon has been presented to comment extensively on its grammar or morphology. Similarly, a written script has been constructed from a brief appearance on a *TNG* episode. The science-fiction author Diane Duane has developed an unofficial Romulan history and language in a series of *Star Trek* novels, but this lexicon and grammar has yet to appear in the *Star Trek* films or TV programs.

The similarly militarisitic Cardassians, even more aggressive than the earlier depiction of the Klingons, perhaps approach fascism in their social and cultural infrastructure (evidenced by their reverence for the state and the *familias*). This race was introduced on *TNG* and further

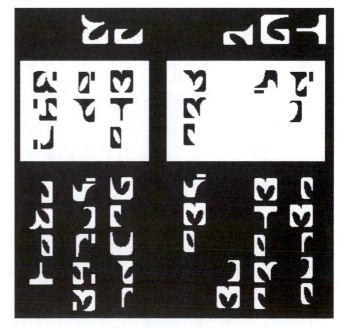

The Romulan script, constructed from a brief appearance on an episode of *Star Trek: The Next Generation*.

developed in *Star Trek: Deep Space Nine* (*DS9*). Little official information regarding **Cardassian** language exists. The few given Caradassian nouns suggest that the language is largely monosyllabic: *odo* (nothing), *nor* (station), *gul* (commander), and *legate* (governor).

A Cardassian script has been made available by Paramount Pictures, but no information has been provided as to how it is to be read, beyond the fact that it appears alphabetic, punctuated, and can be read schematically, rather like a flowchart.

The theocratic Bajorans, apparently modeled after ancient Jewish culture (particularly during oppression under Egypt), were once occupied by the Cardassians and hence continue to bear some cultural trauma from this event (which also allows parallels to be drawn between contemporary Palestine and Israel). This race was introduced in *TNG* and became major players in *DS9*. Their language, **Bajoran**, is featured in several episodes of *DS9* and is relatively simple and direct compared to many other *Star Trek* languages. Like its cultural analogue, spoken Bajoran has an Arabic color and follows a logical morphology. For example, *ha* (light), connects systematically to such words as *ha'dara* ("house of light") and *ha'mara* ("festival of light"). *Pagh* is the Bajoran word for "soul" and two notable verbs are *kost* ("to be") and *amor* ("to banish").

More intriguing, however, is the Bajoran written language, which is primarily ideogrammatic but is also occasionally read syllabically. Consisting of a limited number of base ideograms, each of these individual glyphs can also be permutated (through rotation and flipping) to generate a set of approximately 200 ideograms. These are then paired to signify larger concepts and ideas. While there are ancient and modern versions of written Bajoran, the primary difference seems to be in spacing rather than in conception, with modern Bajoran visibly breaking ideogrammatic pairs into discrete units.

The mercantile Ferengi, introduced on *TNG* but most developed in *DS9*, speak English in most episodes. Apparently, a **Ferengi** language does exist, as demonstrated by brief glimpses of written script in certain episodes, and Timothy Miller has constructed an unofficial version of this language available online.

One alien language of particular interest, which does not originate from a "major" *Star Trek* race, is the language of the Tamarians introduced on an episode of *TNG*. Referred to by *Star Trek* fans as **Darmok**, although it is properly **Tamari**, the Tamarian language is structured on allusion and metaphor and therefore appears unintelligible to audiences unfamiliar with Tamarian culture and history. Thus, although individual Tamari words would be translated through a "universal translator," the "meaning" would not be obvious. For example, a Tamarian would say *Darmok and Jalad at Tanagra* to mean the concept "cooperation" because it is based on the story of these two mythical-historical figures from Tamarian history who work together to defeat a common enemy. Other phrases in Tamari that translate to individual concepts include *Shaka, when the walls fell* (failure) and *Temba, his arms wide* ("a gift" or the verb "to give").

References: Alien Languages of *Star Trek*: www.pinette.net/chris/startrek; Bajoran Language: www.memory-alpha.org/en/wiki/Bajoran_language; Cardassian Language: www.memory-alpha.org/en/wiki/Cardassian_language; Duane, Diane. Romulan Language: www.pinette.net/chris/startrek/

aefvedh.html; Klingon Language: www.en.wikipedia.org/wiki/Klingon_language; Klingon Language Institute: www.kli.org; Miller, Timothy. Ferengi Lexicon: www.pinette.net/chris/startrek/ferengi1.html; Nicholas, Nick, et al., trans. *The Klingon Hamlet*. New York: Pocket, 2000; Okrand, Marc. *The Klingon Dictionary*. New York: Pocket, 1992; Romulan Language: www.memory-alpha.org/en/wiki/Romulan_language; Schoen, Lawrence. "Some Comments on Orthography." www.kli.org/pdf/orthography.pdf; *Star Trek: The Motion Picture*. Directed by Robert Wise. Screenplay by Howard Livingstone, 1979; *Star Trek II: The Wrath of Khan*. Directed by Nicholas Meyer. Screenplay by J. B. Sowards, 1982; *Star Trek III: The Search for Spock*. Directed by Leonard Nimoy. Screenplay by Harve Bennett, 1984; *Star Trek IV: The Voyage Home*. Directed by Leonard Nimoy. Screenplay by Leonard Nimoy, 1986; *Star Trek V: The Final Frontier*. Directed by William Shatner. Screenplay by William Shatner, 1989; *Star Trek VI: The Undiscovered Country*. Directed by Nicholas Meyer. Screenplay by Leonard Nimoy, 1991; *Star Trek: Generations*. Directed by David Carson. Screenplay by Rick Berman, 1994; *Star Trek: First Contact*. Directed by Jonathan Frakes. Screenplay by Rick Berman, 1996; *Star Trek: Insurrection*. Directed by Jonathan Frakes. Screenplay by Rick Berman, 1998; *Star Trek: Nemesis*. Directed by Stuart Baird. Screenplay by John Logan, 2002; *Star Trek*. Broadcast 1964–1969, NBC; *Star Trek: The Next Generation*. Broadcast 1987–1994, Syndicated; *Star Trek: Deep Space Nine*. Broadcast 1993–1999, Syndicated; *Star Trek: Voyager*. Broadcast 1995–2001. United Paramount Network; *Star Trek: Enterprise*. Broadcast 2001–2005. United Paramount Network; Vulcan Language: www.memory-alpha.org/en/wiki/Vulcan_language; Vulcan Variant Languages: www.pinette.net/chris/startrek/vulcan.html; Vulcan Transcription: www.allofvulcan.netfirms.com/language/language.htm.

Star Wars

In various episodes of the incredibly successful *Star Wars* film series, the protocol droid C-3P0 tends to repeat that he is "fluent in over six million forms of communication." The myriad squeaks, growls, burblings, and whistles made by a fantastic array of strange creatures just in one short scene in a lively tavern on the planet Tatooine in the earliest (1977) film suggest that the figure of "over six million" is not an exaggeration; complicating a census further is the difficulty in distinguishing between those alien sounds that denote a language from those that are merely expressive. Obviously, only a small number of these possible languages is represented in any detail in the films, though the multimedia extensions of George Lucas's space opera (which includes novels, Web sites, comic books, and role-playing and trivia games) have naturally allowed additions and elaborations to all aspects of the *Star Wars* mythos, including alien tongues—readers interested in these extensions should consult such works in conjunction with the present text, which retains the films' languages as its focus.

In the *Star Wars* universe (always vaguely identified as "the galaxy"), the lingua franca is called **Basic** and in the films is represented by English—though it is interesting to observe certain distinctions of accent, dialect, and nuanced usage. With some exceptions, members of the Rebel Alliance tend to have an American accent, whereas the agents of the oppressive Empire tend to have clipped British pronunciations. Perhaps the most famous exception to this linguistic norm is the syntax of Yoda the Jedi Master. Yoda's utterances frequently do not adhere to the subject-verb-object pattern typical of English. Statements like "help you I can" and "always in motion is the future," which have been subject to parody in the most popular media, may suggest that Yoda's spoken Basic is inflected with a language he acquired before it, one with another syntactic pattern; but this is speculative, and the point of the eccentricity seems to be simply to stress the character's gnomic qualities.

The most notorious example of an identifiable Basic dialect is **Gungan**, spoken by the aquatic species of that name, from the planet Naboo. The clownish Gungans, who first appear in *The Phantom Menace* (1999), employ something very like Jamaican patois, albeit a notably reductive, even infantilized sort. (This, combined with the arguable resemblance of Gungans' floppy ears to Rastafarian dreadlocks, has drawn charges of racist caricature.) Typical expressions include *Mesa doen nutten* ("I am not doing anything" or "I didn't do anything"); *Oyi, mooie, mooie* ("Oh, my, my"); and the especially puerile *Ex squeezee me* ("Excuse me").

For the most part the completely alien (i.e., non-English) languages of *Star Wars* are not, first and foremost, linguistic inventions or the result of a development of an original grammar and vocabulary. They are instead primarily the outgrowth of sound effects. The rich and diverse soundscapes and unusual noises of the *Star Wars* films are the work of Ben Burtt, Lucas's sound designer. In an essay included in his *Galactic Phrase Book and Travel Guide* and in his contributions to the running audio commentary available on the DVD editions of the films, Burtt explains the challenges of devising what Lucas called "an organic soundtrack," as well as his innovative solutions. For many alien languages, Burtt tried to find recordings of unique sounds that he could inflect with emotional pitches; for a few others, he borrowed the sound patterns of extant human languages, which he then tweaked and altered. For instance, Burtt explains that the conversational soundtrack for the famous cantina scene in *A New Hope* (Episode IV; 1977), in which an array of strange creatures kibbitz and play music, is composed of recordings of barking dogs, squeaking bats, foreign students speaking this or that African language, and people chatting and laughing after inhaling helium.

Probably the most fully developed of the *Star Wars* languages is **Huttese**. A deep and guttural affair, Huttese is based on Quechua, a language found in Peru and along the Andes—based, that is, in the loosest possible sense: Burtt presented recordings of Quechua to a linguist, Larry Ward, who was able to mimic the sounds of the language so as to improvise a "new" language altogether for such characters as Jabba the Hutt. The true disparity between Huttese and Quechua is best illustrated with a simple comparison of rudimentary vocabulary, such as numerals:

English	Quechuan	Huttese
one	*shuj*	*bo*
two	*ishcai*	*dopa*
three	*quinsa*	*duba*
four	*tahua*	*fwanna*
five	*pichica*	*k'wanna*

Huttese is heard in at least three of the films, and subtitled translations appear in every instance. Characteristic utterances are either threatening or insulting, or both:

Koona t'chuta, Solo? ("Going somewhere, Solo?"); *Coo ya maya stupa* ("You weak-minded fool"); *Bargon wan chee kospah* ("There will be no deal"). A singer entertains Jabba the Hutt with Huttese song in *Return of the Jedi* (1983).

The junk-dealing Jawas speak **Jawaese**, a language with the same kind of origins in Zulu as Huttese has in Quechua, but high-pitched and exclamatory. Burtt recalls that he asked Zulu speakers to tell stories in different emotional registers for his recordings, but one speaker "balked" when asked to speak fearfully: "He told me that a warrior such as himself would not know any fear, so certainly he could not express it. I guess that's why the Jawas, despite their size, became so fearless" (136). Dialogue in Jawaese, unlike that in Huttese, is never accompanied by subtitles, so attempts to map out vocabulary, let alone syntax, are provisional. (And unlike Jabba and other speakers of Huttese, the hooded Jawas have no visible lips to read.) Trilled both by droid-seeking scavengers in *A New Hope* and by excited pod-race-watchers in *The Phantom Menace*, the word *Utinni!* serves as an alert or rallying cry (and perhaps a cheer).

When tall, hair-covered Chewbacca the Wookiee moans, growls, and roars—sounds based on Burtt's recordings of bears—he is speaking **Shyriiwook** (also called **Wookiee-speak**). All of his utterances are made at the back of the throat, the practical necessity of the actor's costume and make-up, which restricted his lip movements. Shyriiwook dialogue is not subtitled in the films, and certain Basic speakers (Han Solo, Yoda) who seem to have no trouble understanding Wookiee pronouncements invariably reply in Basic. Burtt's *Galactic Phrase Book* offers some selected small-talk phrases, like *Wu yaga gah ahyag* ("I would like a drink, please") and *Yaag ruggwah maw huah huah?* ("How do you give your fur that shine?" [68]), but these gags seem distant from the on-screen utterances of Chewbacca.

Residents of the Forest Moon of Endor, the Ewoks are a technologically primitive tribal culture of teddy-bearlike creatures. Ewok speech, called **Ewokese**, is made up of much chirping, cooing, and growling. Burtt calls it "a mixture of mock Tibetan, Kalmuck, and even a bit of North American Lakota" (151). *Goopa* is the common greeting and *Yeha* is "goodbye." *Return of the Jedi* concludes with an Ewok song of celebration, which begins:

> *Yub nub . . . eee chop yub nub.*
> *Ah toe meet toe pee chee keene g'noop dock fling-oh-ah.*
> *Yahwa . . . moe whip yahwa.*
> *Coatee-cha tu yub nub.*
> *Coatee-cha tu yahwa.*

Burtt translates this as "Freedom . . . we got freedom. / And now that we can be free, c'mon, let's celebrate. / Power . . . we got power. / Celebrate the freedom. / Celebrate the power" (see Burtt 2001, 174–175).

Sullustan is the name of the language spoken by Nien Nunb, a rebel pilot, in *Return of the Jedi*. It is probably the most distortion-free "real" language used in the films, and Burtt reports that audiences in Nairobi "were thrilled to hear their own language [Hyah]" (155). For those who do not speak Hyah, most of Nien Nunb's dialogue is unintelligible, with the exception of a line like *Uh muttagay dta ooh*, the meaning of which can be estimated from another character's response: "Well how could they be jamming us if they don't know . . . if we're coming?"

Ugnaught is spoken by the diminutive technicians who operate the carbon-freezing chamber in *The Empire Strikes Back* (1980). According to Burtt, "their cries and mutterings derived from a successful recording session with some baby raccoons frolicking in an empty bathtub" (148).

Named after their home planet, the winged Geonosians first appear in *Attack of the Clones* (2002) speaking a "clicking" language reminiscent of !Kung, spoken by the Kalahari bushmen. All **Geonosian** dialogue in the film is translated in subtitles.

The fierce sounds of the Tusken Raiders (also called Sand People) "were inspired by the odd and often chilling donkey braying the crew heard in Tunisia during the location shooting" (139) of *A New Hope*. However, the contempt with which all other characters hold them—they are referred to as "animals"—effectively precludes the film viewer's knowing for sure whether they have a functional language. Burtt's *Galactic Phrase Book* maintains that there is a **Tusken** language and offers sample phrases (*Orukak* is "Hands up," and *Oru uru kak* is "drop your weapon" [93]), but they are noticeably few.

Disguised as a bounty hunter in *Return of the Jedi*, Princess Leia makes her demands in flat-sounding **Ubese**, which C-3P0 then translates into Basic for Jabba the Hutt and his court (and the film audience).

Besides the principal languages outlined above, the *Star Wars* films and sources within the larger cultural phenomenon identify several more whose presence within the films is minor (some are heard in passing without being named, and some are named but not heard at all). These include **Bocce** (a few phrases of which are in the *Galactic Phrase Book*), **Kubazi**, and **Mandalorian**.

Various kinds of writing are seen—always briefly—in the films, but it is difficult to identify with certainty any particular script, symbols, or alphabet with a given language. Ideograms that are glimpsed on the instrument panel or dashboard of young Anakin Skywalker's pod-racer in *The Phantom Menace* may be evidence of Huttese writing, for example, and the tavern sign and bounty hunter's breastplate in *Attack of the Clones*, though in the same city, are not obviously related in any way. It seems likely, given the priority given to sound design in manufacturing the languages of *Star Wars*, that these visual representations are more fantastical than they are systematized.

References: Burtt, Ben. *Star Wars Galactic Phrase Book and Travel Guide.* New York: Ballantine, 2001; *Star Wars, Episode I: The Phantom Menace.* Directed by George Lucas. Screenplay by George Lucas, 1999; *Star Wars, Episode II: Attack of the Clones.* Directed by George Lucas. Screenplay by George Lucas and Jonathan Hales, 2002; *Star Wars, Episode III: Revenge of the Sith.* Directed by George Lucas. Screenplay by George Lucas, 2005; *Star Wars, Episode IV: A New Hope.* Directed by George Lucas. Screenplay by George Lucas, 1977; *Star Wars, Episode V: The Empire Strikes Back.* Directed by Irvin Kershner. Screenplay by Leigh Brackett and Lawrence Kasdan, 1980; *Star Wars, Episode VI: Return of the Jedi.* Directed by Richard Marquand. Screenplay by Lawrence Kasdan and George Lucas, 1983; Philip Wise et al. TheForce.Net: www.theforce.net; Summer J. Wood's Web site. *The Complete Wermo's Guide to Huttese (and other* Star Wars *languages)*: http://www.geocities.com/wermosguidetohuttese/index.html.

Stargate

Like **Star Trek*, the *Stargate* universe covers several discrete productions under a larger rubric: these include *Stargate*, the 1994 film; *Stargate SG-1*, the television series (1997–2005); and the currently running series, *Stargate: Atlantis* (begun in 2004). All concern a circular alien artifact, the stargate, which allows instantaneous transportation between worlds.

In the initial film, a young Egyptologist translates a previously unknown series of hieroglyphs, which provides instructions on the use of an inactive stargate. This allows transport to the planet Abydos, which contains exact replicas of earthly pyramids and other monuments. It is later discovered that an alien being visited Earth in ancient times and took Egyptian people to mine a life-sustaining mineral on this new planet, using the stargate as a way to maintain a hold on both planets. As a result of an earthly uprising, the stargate was closed and both Egyptian races developed independently.

The people of Abydos speak a version of ancient Egyptian, specially developed for the film by anthropologist Stuart Tyson Smith. The **Abydonian** language represents a speculation about how ancient Egyptian would have been pronounced (there is no record of how the hieroglyphs were rendered phonetically) and how that language would have developed after thousands of years on an alien planet. In the film, many characters converse in Abydonian, with some transcribed phrases including *bon'iqua* ("why?"), *di'bro, das weiafei, doo'wa* ("people, welcome them, the gods have come"), and *na'noweia si'taia* ("you are here to destroy me").

In the *Stargate* television series (*SG-1*), the Abydonian language is revealed to be, in actuality, the language of the Goa'uld, an alien race that controls humanoid races by implanting its members in human hosts and often assuming the role of god figures to those societies. The **Goa'uld** language has been more developed by its creators than Abydonian, including details of its syntax and grammatical structure. Goa'uld follows subject-verb-object order, lacks a third-person pronoun, and has no sense of tense (temporality is conveyed by context rather than by word). A more extensive lexicon has also been created for Goa'uld, including such words as *lo'tar* (slave), *a'roush* (village), and *kree* (attention, as an imperative). The Goa'uld written language is essentially Egyptian hieroglyphs, although a cursive script is also apparently used. Because of the dominance of the Goa'uld, their language is the lingua franca of the *Stargate* universe.

Before becoming parasites on humans, the Goa'uld possessed a race of humanoids on their home planet known as the Unas. The **Unas** language is a rather primitive and monosyllabic language, with no verb tense, only a second-person (plural) pronoun, and minimal syntax. Some phrases include *Unas ko tok onac* ("Unas fight the Goa'uld), *ka keka onac* ("don't attack the Goa'uld), and *kel ko keka* ("why did you attack us?").

A major nonhuman race opposing the Goa'uld are the Asgard, who have also visited Earth in the past, influencing the course of human development. As they are said to have established Norse and German cultures on Earth, the **Asgard** language is Germanic in structure and runic in script.

Older than the Goa'uld, and the actual creators of the stargate transporters, the Ancients (also known as the Alterans), are a benevolent and highly advanced human species that have colonized many planets, including Earth, over the millennia. The **Ancient** language is the earliest form of Latin and sounds to modern ears like medieval Latin. Their written script is glyphic, but no detailed alphabet has been made available.

In their efforts to seek immortality the Ancients inadvertently created the Wraith race (who, similar to the Goa'uld, were parasitic creatures that became humanoid by acquiring Ancient DNA). The Wraiths became the foes of the Ancients, driving them from several planets, and are the main enemy race in the television series *Stargate: Atlantis*. Due to their shared ancestry, the **Wraith** language appears to be a form of Ancient.

References: Stargate. Directed by Roland Emmerich. Screenplay by Dean Devlin and Roland Emmerich, 1994. DVD 2001; *Stargate: Atlantis.* Sci-Fi Channel, 2004–; *Stargate: SG-1.* Showtime/Sci-Fi Channel, 1997–2005; see also the following Web sites: http://en.wikipedia.org/wiki/Unas_language (on the Unas language); http://members.liwest.at/reno/transl_goa.htm; http://en.wikipedia.org/wiki/Goa%27uld_language (on the Goa'uld language).

Stars in My Pocket Like Grains of Sand

Delany's lyrical novel *Stars in My Pocket Like Grains of Sand* (1984) is the first part of a diptych that has never been completed (the sequel's working title was *The Splendor and Misery of Bodies, of Cities*) and is set in a universe of thousands of known inhabited worlds. Humans and aliens have a startling variety of interactions in the book: linguistic, sexual, political, gustatory, and so forth. While Delany delights in the polymorphous perversities of difference (between species, cultures, races, sexes, and so on), *Stars in My Pocket* is not as focused on specific differences of language as some of his other writings (see *Babel-17*, for example). The reader is given to understand that the denizens of such planets as Rhyonon, Nepiy, and Velm speak very different languages (including gestural ones), though none of them is named or significantly described. This lack of detail is partly accounted for by the fact that the novel's actions take place in an "epoch of brilliant translation devices" (93).

Despite this abstractedness, the novel does offer a couple of intriguing conceits concerning linguistic difference. One of these is the means by which the evelm, the (literally) multitongued natives of Velm, communicate: they lick, and a conspicuous idiomatic turn in their speech is the focus on "taste."

The other, just as curious, is the "made-up" language of Vondramach Okk, a tyrannical matriarch who decided that "since nobody ever took the poetry of political leaders seriously, it didn't matter what language she wrote it in" (121). The language of Okk's poetry employs "both a phonetic and an ideographic writing system" and complex letters called "shiftrunes" (123). Shiftrunes represent a structured sequence of changing pronunciation, a writing technique that allows the poet to contrast visual and phonetic relations (Delany's theme of difference sounds again in microcosm here). Okk's works include the epics the *Oneirokritika* and the *Energumenika* and collections of lyrics such as *Lyroks* and *Hermione at Buthrot*. No samples of her poetry appear in the novel.

Reference: Delany, Samuel R. *Stars in My Pocket Like Grains of Sand.* New York: Bantam Books, 1990.

The Stone of the Stars

The first in a planned series of novels called "The Dragon Throne," Alison Baird's 2004 novel is replete with prophecies, witches, evil forces, and adolescent introspection. The world of Mera has a number of named languages for different peoples and regions (**Kaanish**, **Marakite**, **Moharan**, **Shurkanese**, and **Zimbouran**), but, as Baird affirms in an appendix, she has "rendered as English the various languages of the peoples of the world of Mera, with the exception of the ancient 'dead' language of Elensi" (405). The Elei, whose name literally means "children of the gods," are a lost race gifted with psychic powers; **Elensi** is their language. The Elensi vocabulary provided in the novel is entirely made up of names of places, characters, and concepts and their simple compound etymologies (e.g., the name of the heroine Ailia is a compound of the words *ai* and *lia* and means "lode star"). Perhaps the most central of the concepts is called *Elvoron*: "containing spirit and matter. Elei concept similar to yin and yang, and ascribed, as with all their knowledge, to the teachings of the gods" (409). The novel's appendix includes a note on the pronunciation of Elensi words (Elensi is pronounced "el-EN-see").

Reference: Baird, Alison. *The Stone of the Stars.* New York: Aspect, 2004.

"The Stones Have Names"

An allegory about colonialism, Mildred Downey Broxon's story "The Stones Have Names" (comparable to, though less complex than, Ursula K. Le Guin's contemporary novel *The Word for World Is Forest*) is set on the planet Calliur. Inona, the narrator, is the leader of her people, also called Calliur. The Calliur have long been subjects of Terran law and its sometimes indifferent, sometimes openly hostile governors. In the story, Inona greets a new governor who turns out to be unlike the others in that he actively takes an interest in the Calliur, their history, and their culture. This governor, named Hopper O'Rourke, notes that reports of Callius stupidity must be inaccurate, not least because Inona can speak his language, **Standard Terran** (which "isn't *that* easy, especially if you don't know any of the old national tongues" [82]). When he expresses interest in learning **Calliur**, the language, Inona is at first very skeptical—she translates his name as "*Kisa la-no-funa* O'Rourke" ("he who leaps"; *Kisa* may mean "governor" [80–81])—but eventually she begins to teach him. The lessons are presented cursorily, and only a few examples of Calliur vocabulary and a few rules of grammar appear. Certain nouns have different cases for different numbers, rather than simply a singular form and a plural form. *Tial*, "a mass ancestral grave," is *tal* when there are two and *talona* when there are three (87). Other nouns may be cased by whether they are "active" or not: *Nar* is an inactive stone or any number of inactive stones, but *Nari* means precisely "one stone, in water" (88). This notion of multiple cases for quantity and states of being is used to highlight cultural difference: Inona says that the Terrans' "concept of *three* does not exist" (88). The theme of possibly appreciating and respecting difference is played out in these brief discussions of the language.

One of the traditions lost to the Calliur in the course of their subjugation is writing. Inona looks at "the whorls and spirals" of ancestral inscriptions without being sure of her ability to read them (91).

Reference: Broxon, Mildred Downey. "The Stones Have Names." *Fellowship of the Stars: Nine Science Fiction Stories.* Edited by Terry Carr. New York: Simon and Schuster, 1974. 77–96.

"Story of Your Life"

Ted Chiang puts a Borgesian spin on the first contact story in "Story of Your Life" (first published in 1998). Louise Banks, a linguist, is the narrator, and her daughter is the listener: while it does not seem obvious from the beginning, this is the story of the daughter's life or, if you will, the story of her mother's prescience of the story of her daughter's life. The narration alternates between two discursive streams, the relation between which is the key to the story. One is a past-tense account of Louise's having been brought in by the military to work with a physicist on opening communication with visiting aliens. The second is Louise's memories of her daughter's entire life—a daughter not yet born, but who will be dead of an accident at twenty-five. Again, the explanation behind these incongruities lies in the connection between the two subjects of "Story of Your Life."

The aliens, called heptapods for their unusual appearance, have completely different vocal equipment than humans and can produce sounds (such as one "vaguely like that of a wet dog shaking the water out of its fur" [119]) that the human larynx cannot. Consequently, Louise uses recordings in playback to engage the heptapods in crude dialogue, but her progress in learning the language she names **Heptapod A** is very slow. With video equipment she tries instead to see what graphemes she might identify in the written language, **Heptapod B**. Rather than using linear sentences composed of divisible words, the heptapods rotate logograms and can integrate them, not linearly but continuously, into any given statement.

Louise eventually recognizes Heptapod B as a "semasiographic writing system" (136) that includes cursive modulations for verbs and "a grammar in two dimensions" (138). In other words, Heptapod B is a more flexible and effectively entirely different language from Heptapod A and is made up not of "logograms" per se but what Louise terms "semagrams":

> The language had no written punctuation: its syntax was indicated in the way the semagrams were combined, and [because Heptapod B is a self-sufficient mode of expression] there was no need to indicate the cadence of speech. There was certainly no way to slice out subject-predicate pairings neatly to make sentences. A "sentence" seemed to be whatever number of semagrams a heptapod wanted to join together; the only difference between a sentence and a paragraph, or a page, was size. (140)

The real breakthrough comes with the discovery of the heptapods' response to the variational principles of physics (e.g., Fermat's principle of least time, according to which light always chooses the fastest possible path), which they view as elementary, not advanced. While thinking about "what kind of perception made a minimum or maximum readily apparent" to the heptapods (151), Louis observes that the act of writing in Heptapod B involves in every case "a single continuous line," which means that "the heptapod had to know how the entire sentence would be laid out before it could write the very first stroke" (153). Just as a ray of light seems to select the fastest path by which to reach a destination, the heptapods perceive and communicate teleologically rather than causally. Moreover, linguistic acts are performative for the heptapods: language is action, though in a nonsequential consciousness like that of the heptapods, modes of action and creation are without corollary concepts of freedom or will. For the user of Heptapod B, any

> utterance that was spontaneous and communicative in the context of human discourse became a ritual recitation. . . . Like physical events, with their causal and teleological interpretations, every linguistic event had two possible interpretations: as a transmission of information and as the realization of a plan. (172)

The heptapods are aware of the past and the future, of all time at once, and the undisclosed purpose of their visit to Earth may simply be to convey the notion of this kind of consciousness to humans, though this is a weak conjecture at best.

Transformed by her study of Heptapod B, Louise cannot help but "remember" the future with all the sadness that comes with it. She uses the future perfect tense when her narrative turns to tell her daughter the story of her life, and the story ends with her foreseen conception.

Reference: Chiang, Ted. "Story of Your Life." *Stories of Your Life and Others.* New York: Tom Doherty Associates, 2002. 117–178.

A Strange Manuscript Found in a Copper Cylinder

James DeMille's satiric and dystopian novel *A Strange Manuscript Found in a Copper Cylinder* (1888) is widely regarded as the first science-fiction novel to be written in Canada. In it, a shipwrecked British sailor, Adam More, discovers a race known as the Kosekins living in a tropical enclave within the South Pole, where, much like in the novels of Edgar Rice Burroughs, dinosaurs continue to flourish.

The Kosekin civilization functions as a parody of socialism, where each member desires poverty, deprivation, and ill health, and where death is the highest honor. In this inverted society, paupers hold the highest rank, while those who possess wealth are regarded as the lower class.

The racial descriptions of the Kosekin, along with their architectural and sartorial achievements, suggest that they have descended from a Middle Eastern lineage, and many of their words suggest a Semitic basis. For example, in **Kosekin** a rifle is a *sepet-ram* ("rod of thunder"), and the longer phrase *Ap Ram! Mosel anan wocosek! Sopet Mut!* translates as "The Father of Thunder! Ruler of Cloud and Darkness! Judge of Death!" (262).

Some grammatical laws are made manifest in the course of the novel, ranging from gender transformations (*iz* is "man" while *izza* is "woman") to a full description of the alphabet:

> For the Kosekin knew the art of writing. They had an alphabet of their own, which was at once simple and very scientific. There were no vowels, but only consonant sounds, the vowels being supplied in reading, just as if one should write the words *fthr* or *dghtr*, and read them father and daughter. Their letters were as follows: P, K, T, B, G, D, F, Ch, Th, M, L, N, S, H, R. There were also three others, which have no equivalents in English. (172)

As the manuscript of More is discovered by a group of educated Englishmen on a cruise, a frame narrative is established whereby this party comments on the events of More's narrative, debating the geographic and zoological probabilities of his adventures. The linguist of this group determines, through an explanation and application of Grimm's Law (which considers consonant changes in language over time), that the Kosekin are one of the lost tribes of Israel and the Kosekin language is actually a modification of Hebrew. One such example of this descent is the Kosekin term for their reptilian flying steeds, *athaleb*, which suggests a connection to the Hebrew word for "bat," *ataleph*, with the *ph* becoming a *b* through Grimm's system.

> *Reference:* DeMille, James. *A Strange Manuscript Found in a Copper Cylinder.* Ottawa: Carleton University Press, 1986.

Stranger in a Strange Land

Although Robert A. Heinlein's novel *Stranger in a Strange Land* (1961) provides only one word of **Martian** vocabulary, and its exact meaning is never "fully" articulated despite various characters' attempts to translate it, that word has since been adopted into American slang. The *Oxford English Dictionary* (5th edition, shorter) defines *grok* as an intransitive verb ("understand intuitively or by empathy; establish rapport with") and a transitive verb ("empathize or communicate sympathetically [with]. Also, experience enjoyment"). The past tense is *grokked*, and *grokking* is an acceptable gerund. *Grok* is "the most important word in the language" (212): it is a central principle in the fluid, serene culture and consciousness of the Martians, and Valentine Michael Smith (called "Mike") affirms that *grok* means "to drink" (213). Dr. Mahmoud, a linguist close to Smith who constructs a phonetic script, with eighty-one characters, for a Martian dictionary, asserts that *grok*

> means "fear," it means "love," it means "hate"—proper hate, for [in the Martian view] you can not hate anything unless you grok it, understand it so thoroughly that you merge with it and it merges with you. . . . "Grok" means to understand so thoroughly that the observer becomes a part of the observed—to merge, blend, intermarry, lose identity in group experience. (213–214)

Thus, there is a qualification Mike sometimes makes: *to grok in fullness.* Mike coins a few other English expressions that may more or less approximate or reflect Martian syntax and/or idiomatic turns, such as the respectful greeting "I am only an egg"

(33–34). One difficult Martian word is repeatedly rendered as "Thou art God," although Mahmoud contends that "that isn't even close to a translation. It's the universe proclaiming its self-awareness . . . or it's 'peccavimus' with a total absence of contrition . . . or a dozen other things" (341). The same linguist notes that "there isn't any Martian word for 'war.' At least, I don't think there is. Nor for 'weapon' . . . nor 'fighting.' If a word isn't in a language, then its culture never has the referent" (223). The language demands a "sore-throat purity of accent" (194), and a conversation in Martian is described as sounding "like a rhinoceros ramming a steel shed" (192). A human character refers to a telekinetic feat—causing an inanimate object to levitate—as a Martian speaker's whistling to the object, but to what extent and precisely how this sort of skill is linked to competence in the Martian language remain open questions.

Reference: Heinlein, Robert A. *Stranger in a Strange Land*. New York: Ace Books, 1987.

"Sulwen's Planet"

On the alien planet of Jack Vance's story's title, a philologist and a comparative linguist compete rather than cooperate when faced with the puzzles of writings from two different alien cultures. As the story is centrally about this kind of conflict, the languages themselves appear only tangentially.

The first alien species, designated the Wasps, "seem to have produced sound by a scraping of certain bony parts behind a resonating membrane," and the comparative linguist makes the strange remark that the form of their writing "corresponds" to this manner of expression in the same way that human writing corresponds to humans speech. The Wasps' "vibrating, fluctuating sound is transcribed by a vibrating, fluctuating line" (212). For his part, the philologist deciphers a numerical system used by the second alien species, the Sea Cows: "An unbroken black rectangle is zero. A single bar is one. A cross-bar is two" (213), and so on. No further details on either language are established, as both of the squabbling professors are ultimately removed from the project.

Reference: Vance, Jack. "Sulwen's Planet." *The Farthest Reaches*. Edited by Joseph Elder. New York: Trident Press, 1968. 200–217.

The Surprising Travels and Adventures of Baron Munchausen

Baron Munchausen, the legendary adventurer and teller of tall tales from Rudolf Erich Raspe's book (first published in 1785), claims: "in the course of my peregrinations I have acquired precisely nine hundred and ninety-nine leash of languages. Well, I allow there are not so many languages spoken in this vile world; but then, have I not been in the moon?" (98). Munchausen had not previously mentioned, when recounting his visit among the moon's fantastic inhabitants, what kind of language the Lunarians spoke, but when he voyages to central Africa he remarks that the language of the natives "is very nearly the same" as that spoken on the moon (128). The Baron provides a sample of African writing and translates these words first into Roman characters as *Sregnah dna skoohtop* and then into English meaning: "the Scythians are of heavenly origin" (129; though backwards the phrase reads "pothooks and hangers").

This is followed by some totally implausible etymology (e.g., English words like "sire, or sir" are said to be somehow derived from *Sgrenah*, "Scythians" [129]) and the assurance that these same words may be found inscribed "upon a pyramid in the centre of Africa, nearly at the source of the river Niger" (129), which fact the Baron challenges naysayers to verify for themselves.

> *Reference:* Raspe, Rudolf Erich. *The Surprising Travels and Adventures of Baron Munchausen*. London: Printed for R. S. Kirby, 1819.

Sylvie and Bruno

Not nearly as famous as *Alice's Adventures in Wonderland* and *Through the Looking-Glass*, *Sylvie and Bruno* (1889) and *Sylvie and Bruno Concluded* (1893) are Lewis Carroll's later and longest books. In the thirteenth chapter of the first volume, the title characters visit Dogland. The various breeds of canine in Dogland speak **Doggee**, which all Fairies (including Sylvie and Bruno) readily understand and speak, but which the reader may find "a little difficult, just at first" (345). Although Doggee speech "at first" looks like random noises, part imitations of dogs' howls and barks and part variations of "bow wow," the attentive reader can quickly distinguish morphemes and a simple syntax (Carroll's logical mind at work). A sentinel dog growls at the approaching Sylvie and Bruno: "Ooboh, hooh, boohooyah! . . . Woobah yahwah oobooh! Bow wahbah woobooyah? Bow wow?" This utterance is translated as "Humans, I verily believe! A couple of stray Humans! What Dog to you belong to? What do you want?" (345). A later phrase, "Bah wooh wahyah hoobah Oobooh, *hah* bah?" ("She's not such a bad-looking Human, *is* she?" [346]), confirms that *Oobooh* is the Doggee term for "human."

The Dog-King, who is grateful for Bruno's throwing a stick for him to chase, reappears in the fourteenth chapter of *Sylvie and Bruno Concluded*. There a little more is learned of Doggee, including the importance of pronunciation: "Bosh!" is the same word in Doggee, "only, when a *dog* says it, it's a sort of whisper, that's half a *cough* and half a *bark*" (502).

> *References:* Carroll, Lewis. *Sylvie and Bruno. The Complete Works of Lewis Carroll*. London: Penguin, 1988. 251–456; Carroll, Lewis. *Sylvie and Bruno Concluded. The Complete Works of Lewis Carroll*. London: Penguin, 1988. 457–674.

Symzonia

Known primarily for inspiring the setting of Edgar Allan Poe's *Narrative of Arthur Gordon Pym, Symzonia* (1820) is a fairly uneventful early American utopian novel. The text concerns a sailor-entrepreneur who tests his hollow-earth theory by sailing with crew to the south pole where an access point allows his ship to enter the second layer of the earth and consequently dock in the land known as Symzonia. The meek and passive Symzonians initially welcome the protagonist to their nation, but he is later expelled after the Symzonians translate some of his books into their language and realize the violence and brutality of the "external" race.

The Symzonian language is described as being "soft, shrill [and] musical"—"as unintelligible . . . as the notes of a singing bird" (107)—but, as the Symzonians almost immediately become fluent in English and converse with the narrator in his own tongue for the entirety of novel, no Symzonian words or further details of the language are given.

Reference: Seaborn, Adam (pseud. John Cleves Symmes). *Symzonia: A Voyage of Discovery.* Gainesville: Scholars Facsimiles, 1965 (originally published in 1820).

T

Tales from Watership Down

See *Watership Down*.

Tarzan of the Apes

Edgar Rice Burroughs's famous hero, Tarzan, Lord of the Jungle, first appeared in his 1914 novel. His vine-swinging, lion-wrestling career extends from two dozen novels to various incarnations in television, film, and comic books. The premise of the Tarzan myth is simple: a couple of English aristocrats wind up deserted in the jungles of Africa, and when they die their infant child is raised by apes. When Europeans and Americans visit the jungle years later, they are amazed by the "forest god" who rescues them again and again from the dangers of the wilderness and benighted African savages.

Tarzan is now synonymous with a kind of impoverished English, thanks to the famous tagline from the 1932 movie *Tarzan the Ape Man* (not in Burroughs's novel), "Me Tarzan, you Jane." The original novel presents a linguistically more complex (even perverse) character. His first language is the language of the apes, the structure of which is not seriously presented but which the narrative clearly states has "few words" (41). Burroughs remains ensnared in a contradiction as he tries to anthropomorphize the apes, on the one hand, by giving them a vaguely limited but effectively very expressive and flexible language, and, on the other hand, to affirm the exclusively human quality of reason, thereby distinguishing the superlatively noble Tarzan from the beasts. Although the apes are, as Tarzan agrees, "unable to reason" and in particular unable to "plan ahead" (210), their language nevertheless allows Tarzan to advise his tribe with conditional expressions and subordinate clauses: "If you have a chief who is cruel, do not do as the other apes do, and attempt, any one of you, to pit yourself against him alone. But, instead, let two or three or four of you attack him together" (152).

As the speech above may suggest, *Tarzan of the Apes* usually depicts the speech of the apes in translation and offers the curious reader only a handful of generic names for animals and natural phenomena, such as *Manu* the monkey, *Horta* the boar, and

Ara (lightning). In one battle, Tarzan asks his opponent to surrender ("*Ka-goda?*"), and surrender is given with the same expression ("*Ka-goda!*" [94]): this is the most expansive use of the ape language represented in the text, but no particular parts of speech can be inferred from the double usage. Burroughs writes: "So limited was their vocabulary that Tarzan could not even talk with them of the many new truths, and the great fields of thought that his reading had opened up before his longing eyes, or make known ambitions which stirred his soul" (91). Tarzan's own name in the language of the apes means "White-Skin" (34), an epithet whose implausibility (the apes have no word for "man," yet the European boy is distinguished from the African humans even before they appear in the story and by a European measure: "white") highlights the racism of the text. Like the apes, Tarzan lets fly cries of anger, challenge, and victory, but these are not rudiments of language per se. Tarzan also claims to speak "a little of the languages of Tantor, the elephant, and Numa, the lion" (191).

It is also worth noting that Tarzan's education in European languages is also unusual and self-contradictory. Unaware of English speech, young Tarzan teaches himself English writing from books, including a child's primer, which he finds in the hut where his human parents lived and where he was born. When Jane Porter and her traveling companions arrive, Tarzan is unable to speak with them until he is taught French by a French officer whom he rescues from cannibals. Yet although he sees no connection between speech and writing before his French lessons begin, Tarzan is able to write a note in English that begins, "THIS IS THE HOUSE OF TARZAN" (103), which begs the question, how can he know how to spell his name? By comparison, the cliché "Me Tarzan, you Jane" seems a much more reasonable representation of a slow but eager learner.

Tarzan comes across other strange languages in the course of his adventures in Burroughs's other novels. See *Tarzan the Terrible; Tarzan Triumphant.*

References: Burroughs, Edgar Rice. *Tarzan of the Apes.* Mattituck, NY: Amereon House, n.d.; *Tarzan the Ape Man.* Directed by W. S. Van Dyke. Screenplay by Cyril Hume and Ivor Novello, 1932.

Tarzan the Terrible

The title of Edgar Rice Burroughs's 1921 novel, the eighth of the Tarzan series, refers to the epithet given the hero by the inhabitants of Pal-ul-don in their own language: *Tarzan-jad-guru*. These creatures are pithecanthropi, humanlike beings with tails who, though divided into two tribes (races), the hairless white *Ho-don* and the hairy black *Waz-don*, share the same unnamed spoken and written language. Most of the vocabulary examples are nouns and names, but it is understood that hyphenated compounds are a general rule (*Pal-ul-don*, for example, translates syllable for syllable as "land of man"). There seems to be an archaic kind of formality to the utterances of the pithecanthropi, at least as it is rendered in English, but given the melodramatic syntax Burroughs often favors in his narrative (e.g., "Fortunate it was for Tarzan" [71]), it is hard to be sure. The novel includes a glossary that the narrator says represents a reproduction of "Lord Greystoke's [i.e., Tarzan's] notes" (303); while this glossary does not shed any light on such mysteries as the language's grammar, it does trouble to point out the formulaic differences between names of different sexes and races (e.g., male Waz-don names have an even number of syllables, begin with a vowel, and end with a consonant, while "the female of this species have an odd number of syllables in their names which begin always with a consonant and end with a vowel" (303). There is also one footnote in the text that quibbles with the "correct native plural form" of *kor*, "gorge": instead of *kors*, the narrator explains, the plural is properly formed by "doubling the initial letter of the word, as *k'kor*," just as it is "for all words in the Pal-ul-don language" (55). The novel once mentions a proverb in the language—translated, without the original given, as "He who follows the right trail sometimes reaches the wrong destination" (280)—but there are no clear signs of a body of literature.

Reference: Burroughs, Edgar Rice. *Tarzan the Terrible*. New York: Grosset & Dunlap, 1921.

Tarzan Triumphant

In an obscure region of Tarzan's Africa, two primitive, zealous tribes are divided on the question of whether the apostle Paul, whom they have conflated with Christ, was a blond or a brunette. The North Midians, uniformly "golden haired and blue eyed" (245), hold the former view, while their enemies the South Midians, composed of epileptics with "enormous noses and chins so small and receding that in many instances the chin seemed to be lacking entirely" (28), contend the latter. They share a language (**Midian**) unknown to Anglophones, though the translations of speech offered in *Tarzan Triumphant* are distinctly biblical in tone and cadence and include many prayers to Jehovah. Another "ecclesiastical tongue" or "gibberish that was not Midian" is also used exclusively by the Prophet (the leader of the South Midians) and his Apostles, but strangely, they "could not understand it themselves" (77). The Midians apparently have no written language.

Reference: Burroughs, Edgar Rice. *Tarzan Triumphant*. Tarzana, CA: Edgar Rice Burroughs, Inc., 1932.

Through the Looking-Glass

Lewis Carroll (the nom de plume of Charles Lutwidge Dodgson) followed up *Alice's Adventures in Wonderland* (1865) with *Through the Looking-Glass and What Alice Found There* (1872). In the opening chapter, young Alice finds "a Looking-glass book" whose pages can only be read when reflected in a mirror. Therein Alice reads "Jabberwocky," a poem that may be the greatest example of nonsensical verse ever written: it has been repeatedly anthologized and illustrated and has inspired films and other poems (Antonin Artaud once daringly translated it into equally nonsensical French). "Jabberwocky" is written in perfect English syntax but is densely populated with neologisms, from "borogoves" and "vorpal" to "galumphing" and "frabjous"; Alice says that the poem "seems to fill my head with ideas—only I don't know exactly what they are!" (142).

The language of "Jabberwocky" might be simply "jabber" and be excluded from this encyclopedia were it not for the later discussion Alice has about the poem with Humpty Dumpty, who maintains that the poem is not nonsense at all. Humpty Dumpty has an inflexibly nominalist view of language: for him, all names must have (descriptive) meaning. "When *I* use a word," he declares, "it means just what I choose it to mean—neither more nor less" (196). Humpty Dumpty listens to the first stanza of "Jabberwocky" and merely says that it contains "plenty of hard words" (198), which he then glosses for Alice. His definitions are both bizarre and dubious (*toves*, for instance, are "something like badgers—they're something like lizards—and they're something like corkscrews," while *outgribing* "is something between bellowing and whistling, with a kind of sneeze in the middle" [199]), but his analogy of unlikely compounds to portmanteaux has added an *Oxford English Dictionary*–recognized definition to the word "portmanteau" and inspired and influenced a number of poets and writers in the twentieth century, among them James Joyce. For her part, Alice finds the didactic egg a bit much: "of all the unsatisfactory people I *ever* met—" (203).

> *Reference:* Carroll, Lewis. *Through the Looking-Glass and What Alice Found There. The Complete Works of Lewis Carroll.* London: Penguin, 1988. 121–250.

"Time Bum"

C. M. Kornbluth's short story "Time Bum" closely resembles Max Beerbohm's *"Enoch Soames" in its postulation of a completely phonetic English language of the future. Although ultimately revealed as a prank, the hero of this short story discovers what he believes is a newspaper clipping from the far future in the pocket of a suspected "time cop."

Future English is radically phonetic, as attested by an advertisement for chairs, which begins with the question "why be ashamed of your chairs?" rendered "HWAI BI ASHEIM'D 'V EUR TCHAIRZ?" and continues: "No uth'r tcheir haz thi immidjit respons 'v a Rolfast. Sit enihweir—eor Rolfast iz their!" (77).

> *Reference:* Kornbluth, C. M. "Time Bum." In *A Mile Beyond the Moon.* New York: Doubleday, 1958. 73–80.

The Time Machine

By the year A.D. 802,701, according to the hero of H. G. Wells's 1895 novel *The Time Machine*, evolution has yielded two very different descendants of humanity: the Eloi and the Morlocks. The former are gentle, childlike, frugivorous beings, all with "the same soft hairless visage, and the same girlish rotundity of limb" (88). They speak in "soft cooing notes" (83) and "chatter" (86) when trying to teach the Time Traveler their language. He reports on his study of **Eloi**: "Either I missed some subtle point, or their language was excessively simple—almost exclusively composed of concrete substantives and verbs. There seemed to be few, if any, abstract terms, or little use of figurative language. Their sentences were usually simple and of two words, and I failed to convey or understand any but the simplest propositions." Although the Time Traveler does not provide any samples or transcriptions of the language, his singular remark upon the name of a young girl he meets—"her name was Weena, which, though I didn't know what it meant, somehow seemed appropriate enough" (103)— may offer some general hints about the register and sound of the spoken language.

Whether there is a **Morlock** language, in the technical meaning of the word, is more difficult to ascertain: these repulsive subterranean creatures make no comprehensible utterances in the novel apart from a sinister "murmuring laughter" (143) and their "whispering odd sounds to each other" (117). Precisely what the "queer sounds and voices" (135) express is never revealed, but given the Morlocks' evident feats of engineering and their cultivation of the Eloi (on whom they feed), as well as the cunning they display in attempting to trap the Time Traveler, it seems reasonable to assume that these sounds represent a functional language that is entirely alien to a nineteenth-century Englishman.

Reference: Wells, H. G. *The Time Machine: An Invention.* Edited by Nicholas Ruddick. Peterborough, ON: Broadview, 2001.

"Tlön, Uqbar, Orbis Tertius"

Posing as the narrator of his own incredible story about obscure reference works and imaginary places, Jorge Luis Borges discovers a 1,001-page book entitled *A First Encyclopædia of Tlön. Vol. XI. Hlaer to Jangr.* He calls this "a vast and systematic fragment of the entire history of an unknown planet," a history that includes "the murmur of its tongues" (71). The publishing history of this book cannot be presented as a linear narrative for a number of reasons: the eleventh volume contains "allusions to later and earlier volumes," though those other volumes may or may not have existed without the a priori existence of the eleventh; a nineteenth-century millionaire allegedly improved upon the notion of a "secret benevolent society" (78) from the seventeenth century by inventing an entire world rather than just a country, so the subject of the writing expanded after the writing had begun; and, finally, "Borges" remarks that whatever fictional or unreal basis Tlön enjoys "has disintegrated this world" by coming into contact with it (81). The inclusion of the languages of Tlön in this gallery of "fictional languages" signifies an immersion into paradox.

According to the eleventh volume of the *First Encyclopædia*, the citizens of Tlön embraced an "idealistic pantheism" (76) and an epistemology based not on truth but on the fantastic. The language and culture of Tlön "presuppose idealism," and the universe is viewed as "successive, temporal but not spatial" (73). Tlön's systemic rejection of sequential time and logic may be best emblematized by the startling concept known as *hrönir* (the singular form is *hrön*). Borges illustrates this phenomenon, "the duplication of lost objects," in this way: "Two persons are looking for a pencil; the first person finds it, but says nothing; the second finds a second pencil, no less real, but more in keeping with his expectations. These secondary objects are called *hrönir*, and they are, though awkwardly so, slightly longer" (77). By the end of "Tlön, Uqbar, Orbis Tertius," there is consideration of "*hrönnir* derived from the *hrön* of a *hrön*" and, strangest of all, the *ur*, "the thing produced by suggestion, the object brought forth by hope" (78). The past of Tlön, it seems, is ever in the future, and its language is not phenomenologically secondary or simply descriptive, but primary and inventive. A word precedes and may even generate its object.

Borges reports that "there are no nouns in the conjectural *Ursprache* of Tlön, from which its 'present-day' languages and dialects derive: there are impersonal verbs, modified by monosyllabic suffixes (or prefixes) functioning as adverbs. For example, there is no noun that corresponds to our word 'moon,' but there is a verb which in English would be 'to moonate' or 'to enmoon'" (73). The phrase *hlör u fang axaxaxas mlö*, given as an example, would approximate the English phrase "the moon rose above the river," but a more faithful translation would be "upward, behind the onstreaming it mooned" (73). As for "present-day" Tlön, its languages are generally distinguished by geography: whereas the languages of the southern hemisphere retain the central principle of "the conjectural *Ursprache*" (73), in those of the northern hemisphere the verb cedes its primary importance to the monosyllabic adjective, the stringing together of which produces nouns. "One does not say 'moon'; one says 'aerial-bright above dark-round' or 'soft-amberish-celestial' or any other string. In this case, the complex of adjectives corresponds to a real object, but that is purely fortuitous" (73). The poets of Tlön's northern hemisphere may literally be acknowledged as inventors of "ideal objects, called forth and dissolved in an instant, as the poetry requires" (73). It is not surprising to find that "there is no limit" to the number of nouns in the northern hemisphere's languages; indeed, they "possess all the nouns of the Indo-European languages—and many, many more" (73).

Given the unique nature of Tlön, it should be understood that its languages can and will only be expanded and expatiated upon indefinitely.

Reference: Borges, Jorge Luis. "Tlön, Uqbar, Orbis Tertius." *Collected Fictions*. Translated by Andrew Hurley. New York: Viking, 1998. 68–81.

Total Eclipse

The scientists of John Brunner's apocalyptic science-fiction novel *Total Eclipse* (1974) investigate the extinction of an alien race from their home planet, Sigma Draconis III, and discuss various doomsday scenarios that may have led to the Draconians' demise after only 3,000 years of rapid advancement.

Ian Macauley, the protagonist, is a "palaeolinguist," who is enlisted to translate the Draconian language. Macauley discovers that the Draconians "speak" through electromagnetic waves that emanate directly from their bodies, communicating their inner emotions and sense of being. These electromagnetic impulses can also be imprinted directly into crystals as a form of inscription. Brunner seems to suggest that this "language" is a pure, unmediated expression, not involving signifiers, and therefore, Macauley has difficulty "translating" these crystals, as there is no symbolic element for him to examine, merely repeating patterns of impulses.

Disappointingly, when the crystals are translated, they appear to be nothing more than records of the genetic makeup of individual Draconians, which function as a type of currency in their culture, used for bartering for breeding privileges.

Reference: Brunner, John. *Total Eclipse*. New York: Doubleday, 1974.

Transfigurations

Michael Bishop returned to and expanded his award-winning 1973 story "Death and Designation among the Asadi": the result was *Transfigurations* (1979), a more thorough exploration of the culture of the Asadi, residents of BoskVeld, fourth planet of the Denebolan System. The original "Death and Designation" is presented as a composite of notes and sound recordings published as a scholarly monograph, the result of "paleoxenologist" Egan Chaney's field study of the aliens. Chaney is following in the footsteps of a previous ethnologist, Oliver Oliphant Frasier, who named the creatures and claimed that although they have "no speech as we understand this concept . . . at one time they had possessed a 'written language'" (14). These claims, vague as they are, turn out to be only partially correct. Chaney discovers that the Asadi communicate by rapidly changing the color of their eyes in an "infinitely complex" set of alterations, and he judges these changes to be "the Asadi equivalent of human speech" (30). Whether this means of expression does indeed constitute a language in the strictest linguistic sense, or is simply a form of communication, is a point on which Bishop's novel seems undecided. Although Chaney discovers what he calls "eyebooks"—plasticlike cassettes whose sequenced flashes of colored light presumably represent a kind of literature—he later discovers that "most of them are garbage" (294). The Asadi, it turns out, are vestiges of a superior culture (called the Ur'sadi) and have been effectively enslaved by yet another species, the huri: "it resembled a winged lizard, a bat, and a deformed homunculus all at once" (23). The eyebooks, Chaney reveals, are of Ur'sadi design but contain "epithets and fear" (294) and were contemptuously made for the huri.

The huri are even more puzzling than the Asadi. Like bats, they "see" with sonar, but as a collective mind they apparently have some sort of psychic abilities; Chaney says they "told" him about the eyebooks (294), but exactly how they did so is not clearly explained.

Reference: Bishop, Michael. *Transfigurations*. New York: Berkley Books, 1980.

Transit to Scorpio

In the tradition of Edgar Rice Burroughs and John Norman, *Transit to Scorpio* (1972) features an earthly warrior transported to an alien planet by mysterious forces in order to fulfill an unrevealed mission by sword and strength. In this, the first of over fifty novels concerning Dray Prescott's adventures on the planet Kregen, author Alan Burt Akers, after utilizing the standard "translation pill" device to explain the communicative shift, introduces several "untranslatable" words and phrases in **Kregish**, or else as "local colour," in a predominantly English narration.

Some examples given include *lahal*, a greeting (pronounced, as Akers notes, similarly to Welsh: "llahal"); *remberee* (farewell); *bokkertu* (legal paperwork); and *obi* (honor). Only the word *jikai* appears complex and ambiguous, indicating, depending on tone and usage, the verb "to kill," the noun "warrior," or the adjective of an "honorable death." There does not appear to be a systemic derivation of Kregish words, although most appear to be homophonic and suggestive of English phrases—the lexicon above, for example, might suggest, respectively, "hail," "remember me," "book," "obey," and "kill."

There is little indication of the grammatical structure of Kregish, although at one point Akers compares Kregish to Latin and suggests that the language is also similar to Italian in its masculine and feminine usages (e.g., *beng*, a male saint, becomes *benga* when indicating a female subject). Although Prescott is informed that there are numerous languages in use on Kregen, and he encounters several diverse societies and cultures, Kregish appears to be the lingua franca, and no other language is described in detail.

Reference: Akers, Alan Burt. *Transit to Scorpio*. New York: DAW, 1972.

The Travels and Adventures of James Massey

Simon Tyssot de Patot's *Voyages et Avantures de Jaques Massé* was probably first published in 1714, and the book and in each instance its hero's name were very quickly translated into a number of other languages. Though obscure, the book today is considered of interest both as an imaginary voyage and as a dramatized argument about religion and the physical sciences.

Massey is, like the narrator of Swift's **Gulliver's Travels* (published a dozen years later), a ship's surgeon who has repeated bad luck with shipwrecks. In one adventure, he and one other survivor happen upon an unknown country, the kingdom of Butrol. The unnamed language of the place's inhabitants is described briefly but in grammar-textbook detail, and its simplicity reflects the utopian lifestyle of its speakers. The alphabet has twenty letters: most of the English consonants (minus c, j, q, v, w, x, and z) and seven vowels, "the Sixth of which is properly the *Aita* of the *Greeks*, and the Seventh is equivalent to the Dipthongue, *ou*" (76). Nouns and verbs are "deriv'd from one another, like the French, *Chat*, a Boar Cat; *Chate*, a She Cat; *Chatons*, Kittlings; *Chatonner*, to Kitten" (77). Nouns are either of feminine or masculine gender. There are only three indicative tenses ("the *Present*, the *Præterperfect*, indefinite or compound, and the *Future*") and two subjunctive ones ("the *Præterimperfect*, and *Præterpluperfect*"), and, most unlike European languages, the grammatical rules have no exceptions (75–77). The language is thus relatively easily for the heroes to learn. Massey offers a full conjugation of the verb *At*, "to eat" (75–76), part of which (the indicative mood) is reproduced here:

Indicative Mood, Present Tense

Ata,   I eat or We eat.

Até,   Thou eateth, You eat.

Atη,   He eateth, They eat.

Præterperfect Tense

Atài,   I have eaten, We have eaten.

Atéi,   Thou hast eaten, You have eaten.

Atiη,   He has eaten, They have eaten.

Future Tense

Atàio,   I shall or will eat, We will eat.

Atéio,   Thou wilt eat, You will eat.

Atηio,   He will eat, They will eat.

Apart from some odds and ends of vocabulary that appear only occasionally in the course of the narrative (e.g., *Baïol* means "benign" [155]), Tyssot de Patot limits his use of the language to this short lesson in his sixth chapter.

Reference: Tyssot de Patot, Simon. *The Travels and Adventures of James Massey.* Translated by Stephen Whatley. London: John Watts, 1733.

Twenty Thousand Leagues Under the Sea

The crew of the underwater vessel *Nautilus* in Jules Verne's classic science-fiction novel *Twenty Thousand Leagues Under the Sea* (1869–1870) speak a language unknown to Professor Aronnax, the novel's narrator, and his two companions (who together have knowledge of French, English, German, and Latin). Captain Nemo's nationality remains an enigma throughout the book, although when one of his men cries out in an octopus attack, he does so in French, leaving Aronnax to ponder whether the crew is a mixed one, of many nationalities and tongues. Only one pronouncement in this submariner's language is transcribed, though not translated: over the course of a series of morning rituals, Aronnax observes the ship's second officer repeat a sentence to the control panel: *Nautron respoc lorni virch* (73).

Reference: Verne, Jules. *Twenty Thousand Leagues Under the Sea.* Translated by H. Frith. New York: Dutton, 1968.

Two Planets

The Martians in Kurd Lasswitz's novel *Auf zwei Planeten* (1897; translated as *Two Planets*) find themselves poorly understood by the Eskimos (called *Kalalek*, perhaps after their tribe's name) they first encounter because the Eskimo language is "primitive." On the other hand, the **Martian** language "could be learned easily and . . . fortunately could be pronounced with facility by people accustomed to the German tongue," in part because German is "a language of a highly developed people" (61). Apart from this quaintly bigoted sort of equivalence, Lasswitz offers little insight into the workings of the language, though a few key words are repeated. Mars is *Nu*, Martian (the singular and plural nouns as well as the adjective) is *Nume*, and *Numedom* loosely means "dignity," but in a broader sense it refers to Martian ideals of autonomy and freedom. *Ba* is the name for Earth, and *Bati* means both "Earthman" and humanity in general. The rest of the available vocabulary is made up of particular names (e.g., *piks* are a Martian kind of stimulant, comparable to humans' cigarettes). The language represents a unification of dialects, a result of the creation of a single federal state for the planet, and as such is a utopian mode of expression: "it had become a means for the most fruitful and exact expression of thought; everything that was ambiguous and dependent only on feeling had gradually become clearer and simpler" (61).

Reference: Lasswitz, Kurd. *Two Planets.* Translated by Hans H. Rudnick. Carbondale: Southern Illinois University Press, 1971.

~ U ~

Under the Skin

Notions of "human beings" and "animals" get roughly shaken up in Michel Faber's novel *Under the Skin*. Aliens have purchased a farm in the Scottish Highlands and converted it into a (largely underground) secret plant for the processing of *voddissin*, an exorbitantly expensive delicacy prepared and shipped to their home planet. A fillet of *voddissin* is said to cost "about nine, ten thousand liss. . . . If it costs less than nine thousand, you can bet it's been adulterated with something else" (246). The source of *voddissin* (which word may well be intended to sound like "venison") are *vodsels*, the human population of Earth. This last qualifying phrase is most important, as the un-named quadruped aliens consistently refer to themselves as "human" and even think of "human" as an adjective reflecting their own exclusive qualities. In the large eyes of these aliens, "vodsels couldn't do any of the things that really defined a human being. They couldn't siuwil, they couldn't mesnishtil, they had no concept of slan. In their brutishness, they'd never evolved to use hunshur; their communities were so rudimentary that hississins did not exist; nor did these creatures seem to see any need for chail, or even chailsinn" (186). What any of these strange "human"-defining words, like *siuwil* and *hunshur*, actually mean goes untold in the novel. However, the propensity for language is itself implied to be a significant criterion for comparison, since the general population of "humans," which does include some with qualms and concerns about the ethics of *voddissin* production, are unaware that "the vodsels had a language" (186). In a crucial scene, Isserley, the novel's conflicted protagonist, pointedly denies to a curious and troublesome visitor to the plant that such a language exists. When a tongueless, castrated *vodsel* writes the word "MERCY" in the dirt, she dismisses the word as "a scratch mark," even though she knows otherwise: "it was a word she'd rarely encountered in her reading, and never on television. For an instant she racked her brains for a translation, then realized that, by sheer chance, the word was untranslatable into her own tongue; it was a concept that just didn't exist" (183).

Isserley has the special job of procuring the bodies of large-muscled men, who apparently make for the best meat. With painful surgery she has assumed a more-or-less *vodsel* shape, with specially added big breasts, which she strategically displays to each male hitchhiker she picks up in her car while she sizes them up. If a given hiker seems a good prospect (i.e., he is indeed well built and, optimally, will probably not be missed), Isserley injects him with *icpathua*, the extract of a plant of the same name from her home planet. (The leaves of this plant, it turns out, may be chewed as a re-laxant or painkiller.) Although Isserley is recognized as being proficient, "a profes-sional," in her work, she is rarely seen partaking in such carnivorous meals as "shanks of voddissin in serslida sauce" (59) but sticks by and large to a diet of bread covered with something called *mussanta* paste or else *gushu*.

A few of the words of Isserley's sibilant language that appear in the novel have clear meanings (*Ahl*, for example, means "hello"), and fewer still have at least guessable con-notations (*Hasusse*, spoken in hatred, may be an expletive). Since Faber's highly moral satire relies on defamiliarization, it is not surprising to find so many undefined, yet ca-sually given samples of vocabulary: the words are made as altogether foreign to us as "mercy" is to Isserley, who eventually and ironically mispronounces the word "murky" (199).

There is a hint of another fictional language in *Under the Skin*. At one point Isser-ley tries to speak with a sheep, and offers three greetings (all unsuccessful): "Hello," then "Awl" (see above), and finally "Wiin." While we are told that "these three greet-ings . . . exhausted all the languages Isserley knew" (66), whether the third greeting is of a different tongue than the second is not divulged.

Reference: Faber, Michel. *Under the Skin*. San Diego: Harcourt, 2000.

"Understand"

In Ted Chiang's short story, the narrator discovers that a new hormonal treatment he has been undergoing has the phenomenal side effect of enhancing his intelligence and mental abilities. When his powers of study and concentration have become much greater than any other human's, he takes up various ambitious projects, among them the designing of a new language. Having "reached the limits of conventional lan-guages" (69), the narrator discards all extant linguistic ideas to give form to a rational language that "will support a dialect coexpressive with all of mathematics" (70) but without being simply a Leibnizian program of symbolic logic (which logic is, accord-ing to this narrator, itself limited). This language will also encompass "notations for aesthetics and cognition" and allow for expressions of more emotions than those ex-perienced by normal humans (70).

The immediate problem of whether so private an idiolect (presumably no unen-hanced human mind could grasp its principles) is compounded by the narrator's ex-planation that this "gestalt-oriented" language is "beautifully suited for thought, but impractical for writing or speech" (71). That is, the means and technologies of lin-guistic communication are insufficient to the purpose: the human larynx has a "lim-ited bandwidth," and for writing "the only serviceable media would be video or holo, displaying a time-evolving graphic image" (71).

The advent of this "meta-self-descriptive and self-editing" (73) language coincides with the narrator's final injection of his drug. Thus, it is impossible to say unequivo-cally that it is an "artificial" language, since it is coexistent with a natural system, how-ever accelerated in its evolution. The narrator contends that his is the language of total self-awareness and thought, a language in which "modifying a statement causes the entire grammar to be adjusted" (73). As a result of this final development, the narrator is supersensitive to the body language of other people, capable of reading thoughts by observing postures, smelling pheromones, and feeling muscle tension.

The story's climax is a meeting with Greco, another mentally enhanced man. Their conversation is almost entirely in a surprisingly rich, tightly measured "somatic language" (85), which allows for expressions (translated for the reader's benefit) as varied as "What about the beauty visible from enlightenment?" and "I have no reason to wait the time it would take to establish the necessary industries" (86). Yet it is spoken language that serves as the narrator's undoing: Greco utters a verbal command—"Understand"—which triggers a preprogrammed series of memories and associations in the narrator's consciousness, "forming a gestalt that defines [his] dissolution" (92). The pansemiotic connectiveness of the narrator's awareness (inseparable from his gestalt language) destroys him.

Reference: Chiang, Ted. "Understand." *Stories of Your Life and Others.* New York: Tom Doherty Associates, 2002. 45–92.

" 'Undr' "

The Urns are a Northern Christian people briefly described in Jorge Luis Borges's 1975 story, whose narrator recounts reading of them in Lappenberg's *Analecta Germanica* (1894), which author in turn purports to have learned of them in an untitled manuscript by Adam of Bremen, the eleventh-century historian. The Urns speak a language vaguely described as "more or less our own" (456: meaning Icelandic, presumably) and are said to practice the carving of script in stone. One poet among them, Bjorn Thorkelsson, explains that the Urns do not possess names for every thing and event in their experience, but instead "encode" all of these things within their song "in a single word, which is the Word" (457). Yet despite the singular and determinate sound of the phrase, "the Word" turns out to be a creation of the individual poet based on that poet's experience. Thorkelsson offers in his dying song "the word *Undr*, which means *wonder*," and when the next man takes up the harp and sings "a different word," he is told that he has "understood" (459).

Reference: Borges, Jorge Luis. " 'Undr.' " *Collected Fictions.* Translated by Andrew Hurley. New York: Viking, 1998. 455–459.

Unearthly Neighbors

Noted for its use of anthropological theory and perspective, Chad Oliver's *Unearthly Neighbors* (1960) recounts humanity's first encounter with an alien race and the difficulties that arise in attempting communication.

Located in the Sirius system, the Merdosi are a humanoid race living on the planet Walonka. Despite the fact that the Merdosi closely resemble humans and have a spoken language, a number of obstacles arise when earthly explorers try to establish contact. At some point in their evolution the Merdosi rejected tool making as a path of advancement and instead—and unlike humanity—focused on the development of empathy, the attainment of harmony within (rather than control of) one's environment, and the cultivation of dream consciousness (akin to the aboriginal concept of dreamtime). The Merdosi, therefore, have no tools, no written language, and various cultural taboos that the Earth explorers violate, which leads to cultural misunderstanding until the novel's conclusion.

As much of the Merdosi's daily life and communication is conducted in dream and through empathy or telepathy, there is little of the Merdosi spoken language represented in the novel. Beyond the name of the race and some proper names, including that of the planet, the only phrase we are given in **Merdosi** is *merc kuprai*, which translates as "it is a tool" or "it is only a tool" (62–63) with a dismissive inflection.

Reference: Oliver, Chad. *Unearthly Neighbors.* New York: Crown, 1984.

The Uplift War

David Brin's 1987 novel is the third of his trilogy concerning the shape and ramifications of "Uplift," the process by which a sentient species is genetically and culturally prepared by another "patron" species for intergalactic travel and trade relations. Brin has also written another subsequent "Uplift" trilogy as well as an illustrated guide to the series, while designers of role-playing games have borrowed the framework and added their own embellishments. Taken as a representative text, *The Uplift War* contains both the recurrent themes of the series (the political and ethical dimensions of these interactions) and examples of the variety of languages spoken in Brin's Uplift universe.

Among Galactics—species who have space travel capability and are party to the accords that govern their dealings with others—there are (at least twelve) numbered languages called **Standard Galactic Languages** for diplomatic parley, and each can serve as a practical lingua franca. "Standard Galactic Language Number Six" can be abbreviated as "Galactic Six" or even, more colloquially, "GalSix." The Galactic languages "had been carefully designed to maximize information content and eliminate ambiguity" (312). *The Uplift War* includes some scattered examples of some of these languages, though few solid distinctions between the languages are made and none of them is itself more than (at best) cursorily described. An alien vainly trying to communicate in Galactic Six with neo-chimps (uplifted chimpanzees) says, *Natha'kl ghoom'ph? Veraich'sch hooman'vlech!* (47; no translation is given). Strangely, though these languages are said to be standardized, Brin does make mention of dialects, like the "obscure dialect of Galactic Twelve" (47). Readers may consult some of the other "Uplift" books (e.g., *Brightness Reef* [1996]) to collect some other minor distinctions between Galactic Languages.

While the logic and formality of the Galactic languages generally win approval from their users, the same aliens tend to deplore **Anglic** ("the beastly, unsanctioned language of the Earthling creatures" [1]). Anglic appears to be a synthesis of various human languages, including "old-style" English, Chinese, and Japanese (312). Unlike the Galactic languages, Anglic allows for elements like homonyms and ambiguity. A character of the alien genus Tymbrimi is vexed by the extensive use of metaphor in Anglic: "No Galactic language allowed such nonsense" (38).

Trinary is a "hybrid language" used by uplifted dolphins (342). It accommodates poetry, involving association and allegory, rather than technical jargon or even linear statements of fact. The name of the language reflects the haiku-like structure of both Trinary poems and neo-dolphin thinking and pointedly distinguishes it from the simplistic "binary" thinking of earthlings.

The species known as Tymbrimi have a complex dual form of communication. Besides having a spoken language, they can radiate "glyphs," psychic projections that assume an ideogrammic form. These glyphs are visible to other Tymbrimi and, less commonly, members of other species who are very empathically aware. A brief glossary of **Tymbrimi** words (like *syullf-tha*, "joy of a puzzle being solved") and glyphs (like *l'yuth'tsaka*, the "glyph expressing contempt for the universe") prefaces the novel (vi–vii).

Finally, there is the "hand language," which neo-chimps use in the novel to communicate in secret in the presence of enemy listening devices. With this makeshift language taught to infant neo-chimps before they develop speech, a "crude but eloquent gesture" may express, for example, "Grownups listening" (308). The expressive limits of this communication are not known, nor is any specific vocabulary given.

Reference: Brin, David. *The Uplift War*. West Bloomfield, MI: Phantasia Press, 1987.

Utopia

The language in Thomas More's *Utopia* (1516), like everything else in the text and the society itself, is ambiguous and problematic. One is never sure whether More is being satirical or in earnest; layers of irony and puns proliferate, and there is little epistemological ground for a reader to stand on. In the case of the **Utopian** language, there are two versions, **Old Utopian** and **New Utopian** (or **Utopian Vernacular**), which contain words for similar subjects that are completely opposite in their connotations, and in terms of the written form of Utopian, there is debate over the authorship— whether More or his fellow humanist Peter Giles designed the Utopian script and the poem that appear in that language in an appendix to a later edition of *Utopia*.

The narrator of *Utopia*, Raphael Hythloday, makes several conjectures regarding the origin and structure of Utopian. The possibility of Greek and Persian roots of the Utopian language arises when Hythloday comments on the Utopians' ability to learn Greek: "I have a feeling they picked up Greek more easily because it was somewhat related to their own tongue. Though their language resembles Persian in most respects, I suspect them of deriving from Greece because, in the names of cities and in official titles, they retain quite a few vestiges of the Greek tongue" (78). Earlier in the text, Hythloday also considers the sound, morphology, and influence of Utopian in a vague fashion by discussing Utopian education: "they study all the branches of learning in their native tongue, which is not deficient in terminology or unpleasant in sound, and adapts itself as well as any to the expression of thought. That entire area of the world uses just about the same language, though elsewhere it is more corrupt, depending on the district" (66).

Beyond these few facts, little is given of the Utopian language in the initial printing of *Utopia*. There is, however, some aforementioned confusion regarding the earlier and later versions of Utopian speech, which can be derived by considering the annotations of George M. Logan and Robert M. Adams. For example, the leader of a household was known as a *syphogrant* in Old Utopian (suggesting "wise old man" in

THE UTOPIAN ALPHABET

a b c d e f g h i k l m n o p q r s t u x y

A QUATRAIN IN THE UTOPIAN LANGUAGE

Vtopos ha Boccas peula chama.

polta chamaan

Bargol he maglomi baccan

ſoma gymnoſophaon

Agrama gymnoſophon labarem

bacha bodamilomin

Voluala barchin heman la

lauoluola dramme pagloni.

The Utopian alphabet and a quatrain in Utopian script with corresponding Roman letters. The invention of the Utopian alphabet is credited to both Thomas More and Peter Giles and, due to its geometric game of transforming a circle into a square, also suggests mathematical precision and perfection.

Greek), but in New Utopian this person is known as a *phylarch* (resembling the Greek for "plainly devouring"). Similarly, a type of scholar in Utopian society is known as *Barzanes* in Old Utopian (Hebrew suggesting "son of Zeus"), but in New Utopian this same figure is called *Ademos* (Greek for "lacking people"). Marina Leslie argues that this ambiguity is deliberate, foregrounding More's interest in translation and the problems inherent.

Leslie also discusses the Utopian script, reproduced here, as representing More's fascination with geometric games, as well as metaphoric aspects of Utopia itself: its attempts at perfection, its orderliness, and its solving of ancient problems (here represented by making a circle into a square). The Utopian alphabet first appeared with the text of *Utopia* in the 1517 edition, along with a poem that also moves the Utopian language into Roman script, and then into an actual Latin translation. The Utopian language appears in the figure to the left.

> *Utopos ha Boccas peula cham,*
> *polta chamaan*
> *Bargol he maglomi baccan*
> *soma gymnosophaon*
> *Agrama gymnosophon labarem*
> *bacha bodamilomin*
> *Voluala barchin heman la*
> *lauoluola dramme pagloni.*

Logan and Adams have subsequently translated the Latin version of this into English:

> Utopus it was who redrew the map,
> And made me an island instead of a cape:
> Alone among nations resplendent I stand,
> Making virtue as plain as the back of your hand—

Displaying to all without argumentation
    The shape of a true philosophical nation.
Profusely to all of my own store I give;
    What is shown me that's better, I'll gladly receive (123).

Despite Hythloday's speculation that Utopian arises from Greek and Persian, consulting the commentary of G. L. Carroll and J. B. Murray, only one word is clearly Greek (*gymnosophaon*, which refers to the "naked philosophers of India"); other words suggest a Hebrew or Latin origin of Utopian.

Readers also encounter—in a somewhat altered, satirical form—More's Utopian language in Rabelais' **Gargantua and Pantagruel*. According to Jed Rasula and Steve McCaffery, the Utopian script was also "borrowed" by Geofroy Tory for his treatise on letter forms and perfection, *Champ Fleury* (1529).

References: Leslie, Marina. *Renaissance Utopias and the Problem of History*. Ithaca, NY: Cornell University Press, 1998; More, Thomas. *Complete Works*. Vol. 4. Edited by G. L. Carroll and J. B. Murray. New Haven, CT: Yale University Press, 1963; More, Thomas. *Utopia*. Edited by George M. Logan and Robert M. Adams. Cambridge: Cambridge University Press, 1989; Rasula, Jed, and Steve McCaffery. *Imagining Language*. Cambridge, MA: MIT Press, 1998.

V

Venus on the Half-Shell

Philip José Farmer borrowed the pseudonym Kilgore Trout from the name of a recurrent character in the novels of Kurt Vonnegut when he published *Venus on the Half-Shell* (1974), a blend of homage to and parody of Vonnegut's fiction. The novel tells of a banjo player named Simon Wagstaff who voyages through space, visiting one improbable alien culture after another, seeking the answer to existential questions, especially "Why are we created only to suffer and to die?" (34). Besides such Vonnegut novels as *Cat's Cradle and Breakfast of Champions, Venus on the Half-Shell* is probably best compared to the film *Flesh Gordon* (which appeared the same year) for its preference for puerile sex comedy and high camp.

In the course of his extraterrestrial travels, Wagstaff picks up a few languages that are only barely described, but these descriptions (and the assumptions behind them) may themselves be read as parodies of conventional science-fiction narratives. For instance, Wagstaff quickly learns the language of the catlike, oversexed inhabitants of the planet Shaltoon and discovers that although **Shaltoonian** possesses "many terms for various sexual positions," which are "all highly technical," it has no "word for love" (51). Nor does it have words for concepts like philosophy, ontology, epistemology, and cosmology, which, by the logic of the Sapir–Whorf hypothesis so popular in science fiction, explains why the Shaltoonians "thought only of the narrow and the secular, or, to be exact, eating, drinking, and copulating" (58).

Among the named languages in the novel are **zeppelinese** (named after the zeppelin-like aliens who speak it) and **Dokalian** (from the planet Dokal, which has "its own version of a Berlitz school of language" [117]). The latter is the only language of which a sample of vocabulary appears in the novel: *Gwerfya* seems to mean "pencil" (117). Certainly the most unusual language is **Lalorlongian**. The inhabitants of the planet Lalorlong resemble "automobile wheels with balloon tires" (99) and communicate by gesticulating with their fingers ("just like deaf-and-dumb people" [101]) and flashing their lights. Wagstaff and his robot companion together manage to converse with fingers and two flashlights carefully coordinated.

Reference: Trout, Kilgore [Philip José Farmer]. *Venus on the Half-Shell*. New York: Dell, 1975.

VOR

An extremely powerful and seemingly indestructible alien being comes to Earth asking for death in James Blish's novel, *VOR* (1958). The title refers to the name of the creature as determined by its communication: it flashes different colors from a "mouth-like patch" on its head, and these patterns of colors can be translated into words (78). The creature identifies itself with a combination of violet, orange, and red, so the scientists studying him call him VOR. Other "words" include yellow, orange, blue for "book"; and green, yellow, green, yellow for "spaceship." (It is never explained how a being with such a language could understand the concept "book.")

Dialogue between humans and VOR attains little sophistication in the novel, since the human characters only employ primary colors, which, while "sufficient for intelligible conversation," do not "encompass any of the subtleties visible in VOR's own 'speech' " (87). Exactly what these subtleties are, what they portend, and how they may relate to ranges of expressible meanings are among the open questions at the book's conclusion (which also includes the fate of the planet), but a linguist, the most cunning of the novel's characters, remarks that VOR's color-code language is "more difficult than ZuZi—much more difficult than Nahuatlian or Athapascan" (92).

Reference: Blish, James. *VOR.* New York: Avon, 1958.

A Voyage to Cacklogallinia

Published only a year after *Gulliver's Travels*, a text to which it is clearly indebted, Samuel Brunt's *A Voyage to Cacklogallinia* (1727) is an unusual hybrid of adventure story, satire, and science fiction. Its narrator runs ashore the country of the title, a place populated by talking cocks and hens of human height (though these heights are various in range, for Cacklogallinians grow or diminish in size according to their wealth and social status). As the word "gall" centralized within their name may suggest, the Cacklogallinians are a caricature of the French, portrayed as vain, obsequious, and greedy. Owing to their love of pomp and class distinction, they maintain a distinction between the **Cacklogallinian** language and a "Court Language" (38). Probusomo, as the Cacklogallinians call the narrator, learns both languages in eleven months, though after his initial encounter with phrases like *Quaw shoomaw? Starts* ("Who art thou? Stand") and *Ednu sinvi?* ("Whence come you?" [32]), he reports to the reader only the odd title, like *Caja* (judge) and *Bable-Cypherians* (Members of the Great Council).

Two other fantastic species appear in Brunt's *Voyage*: the Magpyes (a metaphor for the Spanish, but of their language Brunt says nothing) and, of more interest here, the Selenites. The Cacklogallinians develop the notion that the moon is laden with gold, so they send Probusomo as an emissary to establish diplomatic relations with the lunar inhabitants. A lush, idyllic moonscape is the home of the Selenites, giants who live in tranquillity and equality. Accordingly their language is foreign but admirable to Probusomo: "the Tone of their Voices, and the Smoothness of their Syllables, were divinely Harmonious" (142). This is the full account of the Selenites' language—luckily for Probusomo there is a Selenite who speaks English—but Brunt may be deferring to the description of the language of the Lunars in Godwin's *The Man in the*

Moon, for a Spanish-speaking Selenite claims to have read about "Dominick Gonzales" (145).

Reference: Brunt, Samuel. *A Voyage to Cacklogallinia.* New York: Garland, 1972.

Voyage to Faremido and *Capillaria*

In 1917, the Hungarian satirist Frigyes Karinthy published *Utazas Faremidoba*, subtitled "Gulliver's Fifth Voyage," and four years later produced a sixth voyage, *Capillaria*. The hero of Swift's **Gulliver's Travels* and his faithful though oft-abandoned wife and children somehow survive into the twentieth century, and both of these adventures are precipitated by Gulliver's volunteering for naval service during the First World War. Miraculous rescues from disaster propel him first into the sky, where he finds the land of Faremido, and then beneath the sea, to the land of Capillaria. Both satires share the framework of Swift's fourth book of *Gulliver's Travels*: Gulliver meets creatures who are intellectually and morally superior to his own people and who ultimately hold him and his attempts to justify the history and mores of his people in low regard.

Inhabiting Faremido are the solasis, giant machines whose language is entirely musical. The names of the country and the machines are themselves musical phrases, *fa-re-mi-do* and *so-la-si*; Gulliver urges his reader "to *sing* these words rather than read them silently or pronounce them aloud; this is the only way they make sense" (17). They call the Earth *Lasomi* and regard human beings as *dosires*, "parasites" (Gulliver is recognized as "a *fami-dosire*, a living or intelligent germ" or a *remisolami-sidore*, "which in rough translation meant an 'imitation-human germ'" [28–30]). They apparently have a written language, since Gulliver refers to "golden signs or letters" as an "alphabet": the letters are a sign identifying the building on which they appear as a *so-la-si-mir-re*, "in a rough translation, *solasi* factory or *solasi* workshop" (20). The musical character of the **Solasi** language embodies the harmony in which they live with an equal, inseparable balance of emotion and reason.

Gulliver's sixth voyage introduces two species living together under the Atlantic, the all-female Oihas and the all-male bullpops. The strange and sometimes disturbing relationship between them serves as a satire on various—particularly social and philosophical—differences between men and women. Gulliver calls Capillaria "the Land of Women" because it is dominated by the hedonistic Oihas, who are "definitely and to a greatly intensified extent *feminine*" (67). He is greatly frustrated in trying to learn the **Oiha** language, which "did not attempt to circumscribe any ideas at all. The words only referred to tangible objects or those that could be experienced through the senses" (71). The language is principally an expression of emotional response: it "consisted entirely of interjections and ejaculations" (71), and shades of meaning exist within inflections. The very name *Oiha*, Gulliver notes, is "an exclamation of joy and ecstasy" (71). So sensually minded are the Oiha that they may experience physical rapture at aesthetic pleasure (Gulliver cites as an example an Oiha's "almost orgiastic reactions" at the red hue of a fine fabric [72]), and their "jubilant, purely ejaculative tongue" is as much a stimulus of the senses as it is a response (76). Gulliver phonetically transcribes sounds, such as *Holay! Hola! Whee-hee!*, as poor samples, but no specific words are given and defined. We do learn that "to understand" and "to be interested" are "identical words in the *Oiha* language" (79), but not what those words are.

Although the beautiful Oihas enchant Gulliver, the "horrid little monsters" known as bullpops repel him (79). These "dwarfed, stunted males" (79) are effectively the domesticated servants and livestock of the Oiha. A raw bullpop is not very good, explains the Queen of the Oihas, but the brains of a boiled bullpop, particularly those of a bullpop fattened on the sodden pages of a sunken copy of Nietzsche's *Thus Spake Zarathustra*, are considered a delicacy. When Gulliver foolishly confesses his love for her, the horrified Queen identifies him as a bullpop in disguise (she calls the men of his world, whose actions and views he describes and tries to explain, *bullpops of the land*), and he is sentenced to labor among them. Thus, he learns about these pathetic creatures, whose lives are dedicated to constructing gigantic towers that they never complete: as soon as the Oihas see that the building is of sufficient size for their living needs, they exterminate the confused bullpops, who make "queer chirping sounds" (87). About the **bullpop** language Gulliver is often imprecise, and it is sometimes difficult to tell whether the terms he uses in describing them are part of their own vocabulary, but the (ridiculous) complexity of their society underscores the fact that they do have their own unique language: indeed, they have a history of heated battles between "para-philologists" about the use of "I" or "we," won by advocates of the first person plural. When an Oiha (whom the bullpops consider natural disasters, when they do not deny their existence altogether) elects to use her lethal perfume against a colony of bullpops in order to claim a home, the destruction is sometimes attributed to the *gonchargo*, "the mystic or theosophic theory that the fate of the towers was directed by some miraculous, super-*bullpop* will or intelligence" (117). Those bullpops who try to fight the Oihas and usually wind up killing one another are called *struborgs* or *strindbergs*, but most violent are the *gallants* who attack the strindbergs. Those who try to prevent the Oiha from placing a roof on the unfinished tower are called *gonts* or *kants*, who yearn for "the higher and rarified regions" (87) and who hate and are in turn hated by the bullpops known as *koets* or *poets* (including "sub-species known as *gotes* or *goethes, vuldes, wildes* and *dannunzios*" [88]). The references here to wriers and philosophers—to August Strindberg (1849–1912), Immanuel Kant (1724–1804), Johann Wolfgang von Goethe (1749–1832), Oscar Wilde (1854–1900), and Gabriele D'Annunzio (1863–1938)—mark divisions between both worldviews and polarized attitudes toward women (e.g., Strindberg and Nietzsche, mentioned above, espoused misogyny, while Goethe and Wilde romanticized it). Whereas the Oiha are sensualists at ease with their environment and each is one among equals, the bullpops are industrious and intellectual but also socially divided: Karinthy's satire takes aim at masculine restlessness, insecurity, and rationalization.

Reference: Karinthy, Frigyes. *Voyage to Faremido* and *Capillaria*. Translated by Paul Tabori. Budapest: Corvina Press, 1965.

The Voyages, Travels, and Wonderful Discoveries of Captain John Holmesby

Published in 1757, this English book of voyages is part adventure story, part social satire in the manner of *Gulliver's Travels* (though Holmesby's text is not nearly as famous as Swift's, and its fictional languages not as richly conceived). Holmesby tells of being abducted in 1739 and taken to the "Southern Ocean," where misadventure lands him on the island of Nimpatan, somewhere (he believes) around South America. There he first encounters a hermit, a man who rejects the greedy and hypocritical ways of city people. At their first meeting, this "old Savage" beckons to Holmesby "to follow him, saying 'Rantsegr lofwollem'" (24). Although Holmesby refrains from pointing it out, the utterance is an anagram for "Stranger follow me." Holmesby learns the old man's language by drawing pictures of things and having his tutor identify them, but this method makes it difficult to learn "the Meaning of Verbs, and the Names of Virtues and Vices, and the like" (33).

Bored by workaday life with the hermit and driven by the possibility of acquiring gold, Holmesby ventures to the city of Nimpataneso. Not only are the people there more worldly than the hermit—excessively so, in fact—but Holmesby observes that "the Language which the Savage had learned me was a Dialect of that spoken by these People" (59). Although Holmesby learns this different form of speech quickly, he does not describe it at all or signal the differences between this dialect and that of the hermit. Judging from the few proper names and titles that appear in the book (e.g., *Giroatskee* is the name of a rich stranger recently arrived, and *Glumki* is "one of the first Titles among the Nobility" [62]), the anagrammatical scheme does not seem to apply to the urban dialect.

Holmesby says nothing in particular about the kind of writing practiced on Nimpatan, though he refers to and quotes from a few of its documents. Upon his return to England, he lends a copy of a legal document (his own sentencing) written on "a Skin of some Beast" (191) to his local curate, who plans "to draw some Arguments from" in composing a dissertation contending "that the *Hebrew* tongue is the Mother-Language of Mankind" (191). This gratuitous mention represents a barely concealed jibe at the desperation of modern scholarship.

Reference: Holmesby, John. *The Voyages, Travels, and Wonderful Discoveries of Captain John Holmesby.* London: Printed for F. Noble, 1757.

W

The Water Babies

This 1863 young adult novel by social reformer and clergyman Charles Kingsley concerns Tom, a young chimney sweep who escapes from his cruel master, Mr. Grimes, and is transformed into a "water baby" by good fairies. Consequently, Tom undertakes a series of adventures and encounters with various marine life, learning the values of cleanliness, discipline, and, most importantly, forgiveness. While there are no examples of artificial languages given in the course of the narrative, many of the character and place names are portmanteaus (Mrs. Doasyouwouldbedoneby, or the land of Doasyoulike), and the narrator also notes that every species of aquatic creature speaks its own language: "all the things under the water talk: only not such a language as ours; but such as horses, and dogs, and cows, and birds talk to each other" (69). We are also informed later in the novel that dolphins have learned to speak only one word, the English equivalent of "hush," and that when water babies converse, they sound to those who have closed minds like water rippling.

Reference: Kingsley, Charles. *The Water Babies*. London: Victor Gollancz, 1961.

Watership Down

The rabbits from the novel *Watership Down* (1972) share a language that has little matter for small talk but much for proverbs and stories, particularly concerning the feats of the legendary trickster and hero El-ahrairah. This rabbit's name, whose "stresses are the same as in the phrase 'Never say die,'" means "The Prince with a Thousand Enemies" (35). *Hrair* is the word for thousand, but it generally denotes any number larger than four, and rabbits must be ever watchful for *U Hrair*, the Thousand, the legion of predators and foes (*elil*) that includes "fox, stoat, weasel, cat, owl, man, etc." (16). **Lapine** is, accordingly, replete with names and expressions for these constant dangers and rabbits' responses to them, such as *homba* (a fox), *hrududu* (a motorized vehicle, such as a tractor), and *tharn* ("in that state of staring, glazed paralysis that comes over terrified or exhausted rabbits," but may also be translated as "distraught" [133]). As the fondness for narrative in rabbits is strong, their language accommodates colloquial transfers and poetic combinations: *embleer*, for instance, is "the word for the smell of a fox," but it may be used as an adjective in a phrase like "I'll swim the *embleer* river as many times as you like," to mean "stinking" (46). Rabbits' names are often traits, compounds like *Hyzenthlay* (" 'Shine-Dew-Fur'—Fur shining like dew" [243]) or affectionate idioms like *Hrairoo* ("Little thousand," because the rabbit so named was the little one or runt in a litter of many; the name can be translated as "Fiver" [17]). Besides containing common terms for quotidian activities like *silflay* ("go above ground to feed" [90]), Lapine affords its users room for creative expression, such as verse: *Hoi, hoi u embleer Hrair,* / *M'saion ulé hraka vair* ("Hoi, hoi, the stinking Thousand, / We meet them even when we stop to pass our droppings" [53]) has rhythm, rhyme, and ribaldry. As the name El-ahrairah immediately suggests, the sound of Lapine is akin to Arabic, a language Adams had occasion to study during his military service in the Middle East. Although within individual rabbit tribes and warrens there is potential for mannerisms, a single religious hegemony (according to which, despite the constancy of the Thousand, the god of all, Frith, is ultimately beneficent) and this language appear to be universal among rabbits.

Hedgerow is the name of "a very simple, limited *lingua franca* of the hedgerow and woodland" (153) employed in the course of the novel by mice, cats, birds, and rabbits. No transcriptions but only translations are given, but these suggest that its grammar and syntax are rudimentary (no articles appear in the translation). From the Lapine-speaking rabbit point of view, "hedgerow talk" is a patois: the accents and syntactic patterns of other species, like the "strange and guttural" speech of a seagull who can ask "Vat for you do?" (What can I do for you?), are retained (190). Simple rhymes and elaborate instructions seem to mark the expressive limits of the language.

Adams's follow-up volume, *Tales from Watership Down* (1996), includes more adventures of El-ahrairah as well as a Lapine glossary.

References: Adams, Richard. *Tales from Watership Down*. London: Random House, 1996; Adams, Richard. *Watership Down*. London: Penguin, 2001.

"We Have Always Spoken Panglish"

Published online at *SciFiction* in 2004, Suzette Haden Elgin's story is narrated by Alyssa Miche, a linguist from Earth assigned to study the language of the Yegerrians. They speak **Beydini**, a rhyming language (not otherwise described). Miche is drawn instead to the Sheffans, the residents of the planet Estrada-Blair. The Sheffans are a people firmly and physically divided into two classes, the wealthy Hisheffans and the poor Losheffans. Traveling through the Losheffan slums, Miche is confused and then frustrated to find that each Sheffan she talks to answers her questions about the native language with the phrase of the title: "We have always spoken Panglish."

Panglish is "an artificial synthesis of the many different Englishes that spread over Earth in the twentieth and twenty-first centuries"; it has "been accepted as the international and interplanetary auxiliary language in the 2350s" and is taught to all schoolchildren "everywhere in the known universe." Panglish itself is naturally mutable in practice, and there are localized idioms. Sheffan Panglish, for example, has an expression, "beyond the wall," meaning "expensive and highly valued," while Yegerrian Panglish is filled with flowery phrases.

As Miche probes deeper into the question, she enlists the help of a young Losheffan boy who vaguely recalls a different version of the story opener "once upon a time," which goes: "In the longest of long ago times, when the people could still talk." The boy leads Miche to the female elders, who ultimately, grudgingly admit that there once was a Sheffan language, passed on from mother to daughter, but it was specifically a **Losheffan** tongue, and they refused and, at the story's end, continue to refuse to surrender it to outsiders or the greedy Hisheffans. The death of the language, thus sealed, is a point of pride.

"We Have Always Spoken Panglish" is about language death, but it is also about the ethical dilemmas faced by ethnolinguists and anthropologists. Well-paid Miche's employers are called USCOL—the United States Corps of Linguists—a designation not only nation specific but also conspicuously martial sounding. At one point in the story, Miche rhetorically asks, "just gathering knowledge for the sake of knowledge, what could be more pure?" The female elders' rejection of this so-called purity serves as a pointed answer.

Reference: Elgin, Suzette Haden. "We Have Always Spoken Panglish." *SciFiction*: http://www.scifi.com/scifiction/originals/originals_archive/elgin/elgin1.html.

West of Eden

In *West of Eden*, Harry Harrison's alternate history novel, dinosaurs did not become extinct; rather, they evolved into sentient humanoids and became the dominant intelligent race on the planet. Although primarily based in Africa, as these dinosaur descendants, known as the Yilanè migrate to North America, they encounter, and come into conflict with, humans, referred to in this text as the Tanu. Harrison's novel thus recounts the wars that erupt between these two races as each group struggles for survival.

Both societies speak sophisticated languages, developed by the Tolkien scholar and St. Louis University professor T. A. Shippey. **Marbak**, the language of the Tanu, resembles and appears to follow the grammatical structures of European languages. The example given in an appendix of the novel is the word *hannas*, which translates as "man" and conjugates as follows (p. 501):

	Singular	Plural
Nominative	*hannas*	*hannasan*
Accusative	*hannas*	*hannasan*
Genitive	*hannasa*	*hannasanna*
Dative	*hannasi*	*hannasanni*
Locative	*hannasi*	*hannasanni*
Instrumental	*hannasom*	*hannasom*

The author also notes that Marbak is one variation of a lost ur-language known as **Eastern Coastal**, from which several other dialects have descended, including **Wedaman**, **Levrewasan**, and **Lebnaroi**. Their singular words for "man" are *hennas*, *hnas*, and *neses*, respectively.

The **Yilanè** language is much more alien and complex, incorporating sound, movement, and color as part of the signifying process. Language acquisition is also tied to social class among the Yilanè, with only those individuals who learn the language being allowed to join city structures and only those who master the subtleties of the language rising to the highest ranks of power. Those who possess only the rudiments of Yilanè are known as *fargi* and function as the proletarian class.

The sound of Yilanè follows standard phonetics with a lexicon based primarily on vowels, rather than consonants, as well as a series of phatic sounds, such as lip smacking and throat clicking. This is combined with changes of skin color to indicate mood, and then thousands of stylized movements, resulting in a language with over 125 billion "words." In addition to this complexity, the Yilanè language uses not single nouns, but adjective–noun clusters. For example, instead of "chair," the Yilanè say "small wood to sit on" (493). As movement and color are combined with speech in ways that are often involuntary, Yilanè lack the ability to lie; they remain silent when they wish to withhold information as they are unable to dissimulate without giving themselves away by their gestures.

Harrison and Shippey provide one example of the extreme difficulty of translating between English and Yilanè by using the following poem as the base text (491–493):

> *To leave father's love and enter the embrace*
> *of the sea is the first pain of life—the first*
> *joy is the comrades who join you there.*

A translation of only the sounds of Yilanè (with the apostrophe on the second line indicating a glottal stop) would be as follows:

> *Enge hantèhei, agatè embokèka iirubushei kaksheisè,*
> *hèawahei; hèvai'ihei, kaksheintè, enpeleiuu asahen enge.*

When combined with gesture and the sense of adjective clusters, the poem would translate additionally as the following, with words in parenthesis indicating a gesture:

(Bask)	Love
(Lie)	Maleness. Friend. Senses of Touch/Smell/Feel
(Push)	Departure. Self
(Fall)	Pressure. Stickiness. Cessation
(Fall)	Entry. Weightlessness. Cold
(Swim)	Salt. Cold. Motion
(Cower)	Numeral 1. Pain. Senses of Touch/Smell/Feel
(Star)	Numeral 1. Joy. Senses of Touch/Smell/Feel
(Swim)	Salt. Cold. Hunt
(Stretch)	Vision. Discovery. Increase
(Swim)	Beach. Male/Female
(Reach)	Love

Two variations of Yilanè exist, a children's language, which is only of gesture and color because immature Yilanè live aquatically where sound is diffuse, and graylight language, which is only of sound and gesture, spoken where the visual conditions do not allow clear access to changes of color, such as at dusk or dawn.

Owing to the multifaceted and gestural nature of the Yilanè language, no written form of Yilanè developed, and inscription occurs only through recording devices known as *ugunkshaa*, which are actually biological creatures who have been genetically manipulated to possess a liquid crystal display on which images are retained.

West of Eden is the first part of a trilogy of novels that also includes *Winter in Eden* (1986) and *Return to Eden* (1988).

Reference: Harrison, Harry. *West of Eden*. New York: Bantam, 1984.

When the World Shook

The heroes of H. Rider Haggard's 1919 novel shipwreck on an unknown island in the South Seas, where they discover a tribe of people known as the Orofenans, named for the worship of their god, Oro. The novel's narrator and his companions, who have studied Polynesian languages, are quickly able to communicate in the **Orofenan** tongue, vaguely described as "copious, musical, and expressive in its idioms" (96).

After a contretemps with these people, the heroes explore the island's caves and volcano, wherein they discover Oro and his daughter in suspended animation. Revived from a slumber of a quarter of a million years, they speak a slightly different language; the narrator supposes that it is an archaic form of Orofenan. Oro's daughter explains that her people enjoyed a primarily oral culture: "the only form of writing that was used was a highly concentrated shorthand which saved labour" (253). At one point in the novel, Oro works out some written calculations in "cabalistic signs" (335), but the text provides no samples of these languages' vocabularies.

Reference: Haggard, H. Rider. *When the World Shook*. New York: Arno Press, 1975.

The White Bone

A sort of apocalyptic *Watership Down*, Barbara Gowdy's *The White Bone* is an animal quest narrative featuring families of elephants who seek the mythical "white bone," which will provide direction to a haven safe from poachers and ivory hunters.

The elephants in the novel communicate in various ways; one method is through the use of "infrasonic rumbles." As Gowdy writes:

> Infrasonic rumbles, or "grounders," are long-distance body messages. To reach a specific individual the sender rumbles at that individual's unique body frequency. The rumble originates in the belly rather than in the throat and goes down the feet and legs into the ground where it radiates until it enters the feet and legs of the receiver, provided that he or she is within transmission radius. (46)

Gowdy's elephants also converse by means of verbalization and gestures, and while this language is rendered in the novel in standard English, the elephants also have many unique words—often for nouns and based on metaphor and metonymy. For example, a *roar fly* is a helicopter, a *flow-stick* is a snake, a *grunt* is a warthog, and humans are *hindleggers*. The author does not provide a grammar for the elephant language but does indicate that there are various tenses and forms of address, such as the "formal timbre," which is "characterized by exaggerated enunciation" (5).

Each family is led by a matriarch and usually includes a visionary elephant and a telepathic or "mind talker" elephant. The mind talker is able to read the thoughts of other elephants but is also able to communicate with other animals species. Again, while these languages are written in English in the novel, each animal group has its own tonal and grammatical flavor of speech. For example, birds, such as the oxpecker, speak mostly in ejaculations—"That! It! What! Look! Where!" (173)—while the libidinous and warrior mongooses speak of their battles and sexual conquests in repetitive forms: "sing, sing, sing the song, song about, the song about the hot, the hot, hot, hot fight, fight, fight" (272).

Reference: Gowdy, Barbara. *The White Bone.* Toronto: HarperCollins, 1998.

The Wind on the Moon

Dinah and Dorinda Palfrey, the young heroines of Eric Linklater's 1944 children's book, have two major adventures and encounter a fictional language in the course of each. When the sisters are magically transformed into kangaroos, they are captured and put in a zoo, where they discover that they can speak the language of animals—"and they had learnt it without any trouble to themselves" (70). Thus, they are able to converse with a variety of animals and make close friends with a puma and a falcon. When they escape the zoo and manage to return to human form, the girls find that they "can still talk like animals" (161). Just two pronouncements in the speech of animals are given in English: *Kea yark urbaneesh eeern gnarrh uh* ("How funny that sounds!" comments Dinah [161]) and *gnirk arkee ur bagreer zy rook, shim salee, gnaaar pupu, ror myaah nyiih kling. Shrings kraugh?* (Dinah tells the puma that they intend to free her from the zoo [162]). There does not appear to be a method to the design of the language, and Linklater probably aimed for appropriately funny sounds.

Such is not the case for **Bombast**, the language of the country of Bombardy, to which Dinah and Dorinda travel to free their father from its tyrant's dungeons. The sisters have as a traveling companion their music and dancing teacher, Mr. Corvo, who is originally from Bombardy and speaks the language. Bombast is an anagrammatical blend of English, French, and German words. For example, *Ruhry, mai, reeth tse chum a refai* can be translated as "Hurry, friend, there is much to do" (295) by identifying each of the constituent words and languages:

Ruhry	=	hurry (English)
mai	=	ami (French: "friend")
reeth	=	there (English)
tse	=	est (French: "is")
chum	=	much (English)
a refai	=	à faire (French: "to do")

Count Hulagu Bloot, the leader of Bombardy and villain of the story, speaks entirely in Bombast, and some of his speeches are slightly tougher puzzles.

While Bombardy is an obvious parody of Nazi Germany and fascist states in general, Bombast effectively serves as an educational sort of game for young readers. The first expression in Bombast to appear in the story is immediately translated by Mr. Corvo, but thereafter the proximity between Bombast original and English translation gradually lessens; the reader is thereby gently encouraged to try to translate the Bombast on his or her own.

Reference: Linklater, Eric. *The Wind on the Moon: A Story for Children.* London: Macmillan, 1964.

The Winds of Time

Explorers from the planet Lortas crash on Earth in Chad Oliver's 1957 novel *The Winds of Time.* They encounter early human civilization and decide to use a special drug to hibernate for centuries, in the hopes that they will reawaken in an era in which humans have achieved the technology for space travel (and thus will permit the chance to return to Lortas). Although the aliens are able to learn English "with incredible rapidity," they do not teach their own language to the human they retain as guide and translator. One of the aliens "used recording symbols," which may be "phonetic marks" (38), but that speculation is the sum of information Oliver provides on their language. The novel does, however, suggest that the "natives" or prehistoric tribe the aliens meet have a language: one "said a word," and the undefined word *Nanhaades* is "called" and repeated by one "raising his spear to the throwing position" (108). Oliver implies one other similarly sketchy point of interest: the natives "had come across groups of men before who spoke tongues different from their own" (112).

Reference: Oliver, Chad. *The Winds of Time.* New York: Doubleday, 1957.

The Word for World Is Forest

The natives of the planet Athshe struggle against slavery, exploitation, and abuse at the hands of human colonizers in Ursula K. Le Guin's short 1972 novel, the title of which expresses both the language-based holistic philosophy of the Athsheans and the general flavor of the book.

The **Athshean** language is central to the book's theme, but it is only very generally described. In fact, the "Athshean language" as it is referred to in the novel seems to represent a grouping of individual languages: in the Forty Lands of the planet, "there were more languages than lands, and each with a different dialect for every town that spoke it" (45). There is also an "Old Tongue" spoken by males when Dreaming (a state of consciousness probably modeled on the dreamtime of Australian aboriginal people) in the local Men's Lodge. How this language technically differs from the other forms of Athshean speech is not explained, but we are told that this "Lodge-tongue" has little regional variation and that it "was rarely learned by women or by men who remained hunters, fishers, weavers, builders, those who dreamed only small dreams outside the Lodge" (45). Most Athshean writing is in the Lodge-tongue.

Selver, the principal Athshean character, is called a *sha'ab,* the only Athshean word in the text: "*Sha'ab* meant god, or numinous entity, or powerful being" (121). It also means "translator," a significant notion here since the insurrectionists are said to have learned the concept of murder from their oppressors. Selver is said to have "brought a new word into the language of his people. He had done a new deed. The word, the deed, murder" (122). Given the plurality of the Athsheans and the Athshean language outlined above, it is hard to determine how broadly the phrase "the language of his people" may be understood.

Before the violence began, Selver helped compose a bilingual dictionary in his language and that of the "yumens" (183) with an anthropologist from Terra (Earth). This dictionary reappears at the end of the novel as a hopeful symbol of cooperation and communication.

Reference: Le Guin, Ursula K. *The Word for World Is Forest.* New York: Berkley, 1972.

"Writing of the Rat"

In James Blish's 1956 story, human beings find themselves in a tense relationship with another species that has proliferated throughout the galaxy in giant numbers. "Squat, grey-furred, sharp-toothed" but also "well over six feet tall" and "frighteningly strong" (57), these "rats" are highly intelligent beings who consider themselves to be the custodians "of cultures, of entire ecologies" (70). They are researching and assessing the threat posed by a race of insatiable slavers, from which humans are descendants. To facilitate their ends, they have "evolved" an unnamed synthetic language, "which is adaptable to any culture and carries the implicit assumptions of none" (71). An emissary who makes the unheard-of gesture of giving his name, Hrestce (the word means "compromise"), explains that it was humans' "poetry, to some extent, that deterred us from wiping you all out at once"; Hrestce's own people, he notes, have begun using the synthetic language for "creative work" (71–72). The rats have various civilizations on different planets, and their written languages vary, each one "usually irreconcilable with all the others—pictograms, phonetic systems, ideograms, hieratic shorthands, inflectional systems, tone-modulated systems, positional systems—the works" (62). The spoken language is common, though complex, because it is derived from "vast knowledge of information theory" (62).

Most of the vocabulary given in the story comes from a scene in which a captured rat is tortured. The prisoner divulges where he is from, but when asked for more details says *R-daee 'blk* ("I just told you"). The same response is reiterated as *Stfir etminbu rakolna*, "in the pejorative form—the one they use for draft animals and children" (58–59). *Ocro hli antsoutinys, fuso tizen et tobëe* is "a complex message" that explains or warns or perhaps even apologizes for the coming torture (59). The reply to the peaceful translator is *Seace tce ctisbe* ("The phrase was formal; it might mean 'thank you,' but then again it might mean half a hundred equally common expressions, including 'hello,' 'goodbye,' and 'time for lunch'" [60]), but that to the martinet conducting the interrogation is *Sehe et broe in icen*, the "worst insult": the phrase literally translates as "you couldn't run a maze with your shoes off" (59).

In a prefatory note to "Writing of the Rats," Blish writes that "someone with a taste for cryptanalysis might like to puzzle out the 'synthetic language' used by Hrestce (whose name is a part of the code)." He offers one clue: "It came 100 percent off a theater marquee in Brooklyn, and it is not a foreign language—just English with some letters missing" (57).

Reference: Blish, James. "Writing of the Rat." *Anywhen.* New York: Doubleday, 1970. 57–74.

Selected Bibliography

Besides those books cited in the endnotes of the Preface and of course the various sources cited at the end of each entry, readers may find the following works of interest.

Albani, Paolo, and Berlinghiero Buonarroti. *Aga Magéra Difúra: Dizionario delle Lingue Immaginarie.* Bologna: Zanichelli, 1994. The present volume's older Italian cousin, *Aga Magéra Difúra* surveys all kinds of artificial languages, not just those of fiction. The unusual title is itself a quotation from a fictional language, taken from Tommaso Landolfi's story "Dialogue of the Greater Systems."

Boulton, Marjorie. *Zamenhof: Creator of Esperanto.* London: Routledge and Kegan Paul, 1960. A book with conspicuously hagiographic tendencies, it offers an earnest explication of the milieu in and noble intentions with which the Esperantist movement was founded.

Cornelius, Paul. *Languages in Seventeenth- and Late Eighteenth-Century Imaginary Voyages.* Geneva: Droz, 1965.

Dalby, Andrew. *Dictionary of Languages.* New York: Columbia University Press, 1998. From Abkhaz to Zulu, this large reference helpfully surveys over 400 "real-world" languages.

Eco, Umberto. *The Search for the Perfect Language.* Translated by James Fentress. Oxford: Blackwell, 1995. An accessible yet comprehensive study of the religious and philosophical underpinnings of many European invented languages. Although Eco's interest is focused on those linguistic creators who have practical, rather than aesthetic, goals for their languages, readers will find numerous points of comparison between Eco's readings of Kabbalism, Kircher, and Bruno and many of the languages indexed in this volume.

Large, Andrew. *The Artificial Language Movement.* Oxford: Basil Blackwell, 1985. An admirable survey of the various efforts to construct an "international" language, including Esperanto, Ido, and Novial.

Meyers, Walter E. *Aliens and Linguists: Language Study and Science Fiction.* Athens: University of Georgia Press, 1980. A very edifying survey, from a linguist's perspective, of the trends and patterns of issues of language in science fiction.

Pinker, Steven. *The Language Instinct: How the Mind Creates Language.* New York: HarperCollins, 1994. Written in a clear and forthright prose, this popular book offers accessible explications of linguistics as a science and some provocative contemplations on the limits of difference as well as of similitude between individual human minds.

Rasula, Jed, and Steve McCaffery, eds. *Imagining Language*. Cambridge, MA: MIT Press, 1998. A treasury in the fullest sense of the word, this book offers a remarkably diverse sampling of experimental and poetic approaches to language theories.

Yaguello, Marina. *Lunatic Lovers of Language: Imaginary Languages and Their Inventors*. Translated by Catherine Slater. London: Athlone Press, 1991. Adopting and adapting Raymond Queneau's (proposed, unpublished but ultimately incorporated into his 1938 novel *Children of Clay*) study of "literary lunatics," Yaguello produces an invaluable, thoughtful primer on artificial languages in literature.

General Subject Index

Index of Named Languages

About the Authors

TIM CONLEY is Assistant Professor of English and Comparative Literature at Brock University. He is the author of *Joyces Mistakes: Problems of Intention, Irony, and Interpretation* (2003), and of a collection of short fiction, *Whatever Happens* (2006). His essays have appeared in such journals as *Comparative Literature*, *James Joyce Quarterly*, *Papers on Language and Literature*, and *Studies in the Novel*.

STEPHEN CAIN is Assistant Professor of English at York University. He has published on such topics as experimental poetry and music, the politics of publishing, and poetics. His work has appeared in *Studies of Canadian Literature*, *Open Letter*, and other journals. His three books of poetry include *American Standard/Canada Dry* (2005), *Torontology* (2001), and *dyslexicon* (1999).